THE GOSPEL ACCORDING TO MARK

By
G. CAMPBELL MORGAN, D. D

NEW YORK   CHICAGO
Fleming H. Revell Company
LONDON   AND   EDINBURGH

New York: 158 Fifth Avenue
Chicago: 851 Cass Street
London: 21 Paternoster Square
Edinburgh: 99 George Street

Foreword

THIS volume is a broad survey of the earliest of the Gospel narratives from the viewpoint of pulpit exposition. It consists of thirty sermons, preached to my old congregation at Westminster Chapel, London, on consecutive Sunday mornings. In each case a text was selected, and made the center of an exposition of a longer paragraph.

These sermons were stenographically reported, and are now issued in this form, with no revision beyond the simplest elimination of repetitions and asides, which, while giving force to the extempore utterance, would render the reading tiresome.

The Gospel according to Mark has its own peculiar charm, much of which is created by the bluntness and brevity of the writing of a man, evidently untrained in literary methods; and also by its chronological continuity. There is a freshness and a vigour about it, which grips and holds the reader.

In reading it we are able swiftly, but with keen and alert interest, to move with Jesus of Nazareth through the wonderful crowded years of His more public ministry.

In the very spirit of the Book, moving rapidly, but with captured heart, these sermons were prepared, and preached, and I now send them forth in this form, praying that they may help some hurrying men and women in these rushing days to go in the company of Jesus,—Who ever moved with haste, but always with poise and peace,—along the highway.

G. C. M.

Glendale, California.

[3]

Contents

CONTENTS

The Gospel According to Mark

I

"The Beginning of the Gospel."—MARK 1:1.

Mark 1:1-3.

THE Gospel according to Mark is the briefest of the four. In all likelihood it was the earliest written. It was written probably before the death of Paul, but not later than the destruction of Jerusalem. Irenæus definitely said that it was written after the deaths of Paul and Peter, but more recent investigation would place it earlier, that is before 63 A. D.

Patristic testimony agrees that it was influenced by Peter, that indeed it is the record of the facts concerning Jesus as they were told by Peter in his preaching, and recorded by his friend, Mark. This view is strengthened by modern scholarship.

Mark gives us practically no material other than that which is recorded by Matthew. The difference between the Gospels is that of method, rather than that of matter. The method of Mark is characterized by directness and brevity (almost amounting to bluntness), accompanied by certain circumstantial touches which give us a most vivid sense of the Lord, in many details of look, gesture, and habits of speech.

The history of the writer of this Gospel as it may be traced in the New Testament, is a most interesting one. His Jewish name was John, Mark being his Latin surname. His mother, as Luke informs us in the book of Acts (12:12) was a woman of wealth, living in Jerusalem, evidently a personal friend of Peter, and hostess of the Christian disciples in the early days after Pentecost. By a reference, in the first letter of Peter, we may surmise that Mark was spiritually a son of Peter (5: 13), that he was brought to a knowledge of the Lord Christ savingly under the ministry of the great apostle. He was also a cousin of Barnabas. The first appearance of Mark in New Testament history is found in the story of the journey of Paul and Barnabas from Jerusalem to Antioch, upon which journey he accompanied them. He then went with them on the first missionary journey, suddenly leaving them at Perga. Why he left them, we do not know. It is an interesting fact that almost all expositors assume that he was afraid of the campaign, and went home, but there is no shadow of evidence that fear was the reason for his return. Certainly later on, discussion and separation occurred between Paul and Barnabas upon this very subject, for when starting upon another journey, Barnabas desired to take Mark with him, and Paul objected, because Mark had " gone back." That may be the reason why it is supposed that Mark turned back from fear. But, though Paul refused to take him, Barnabas desired to do so; and it is quite as possible that Barnabas was right, as Paul. So we may give Mark the benefit of the doubt. It is certain that he went with Barnabas to Cyprus, and subsequently was with Paul in Rome, a "fellow labourer," and a comfort. From a reference in Peter's first letter we gather that he accompanied that apostle to Babylon; and the last glimpse of him is that in Paul's last letter to Timothy, wherein he charged him to bring Mark with him again to Rome.

The general concensus of opinion leads to the conclusion that the narrative was written by Mark in Rome, and was intended primarily for Gentiles. It is interesting to remember that there are no references to the Jewish law in this Gospel; that there are only two quotations from the ancient Scriptures, one of which is in this brief introduction; and that he constantly explains peculiarly Jewish terms and customs, which it would not be at all necessary to do to Jewish people. That however is a purely incidental matter, and in no way affects the presentation of the Lord which the narrative makes.

Bernard in his Bampton Lectures in 1864, entitled "The Progress of Doctrine in the New Testament," than which a more valuable series of Lectures was never delivered upon that great subject, said of this Gospel something which so perfectly describes it, that I will quote the paragraph:

"It is the Gospel of action, rapid, vigorous, vivid. Entering at once on the Lord's official and public career, it bears us on from one mighty deed to another with a peculiar swiftness of movement, and yet with the life of picturesque detail. Power over the visible and invisible worlds, especially as shown in the casting out of devils, is the prominent characteristic of the picture. St. Peter's saying to Cornelius has been well noticed as a fit motto for this Gospel. 'God anointed Jesus of Nazareth with the Holy Ghost and with power, who went about doing good and healing all those who were oppressed of the devil.'"

Thus while Matthew presents us with the picture of the Messiah as King in all the royalty of His Person, the dignity of His office, and the grace of His mission; Mark gives us the picture of the Messiah as Servant, divested of all official dignity, save that of consecration to His work.

Our first meditation is concerned with the brief paragraph contained in the first three verses of chapter one.

With regard to the study of this Gospel I propose a perfectly free method; that is, I shall break through the trammels of chapters, verses, paragraphs, and punctuations as found in our versions.

This paragraph is the key to the whole Gospel, and therefore we must pause with it. It is complete within itself. The narrative proper of Mark begins with the fourth verse, with the words, " John came." The story begins with the appearing of John. I should say after careful reading, that probably the last thing Mark wrote was the opening paragraph. After he had finished his story, that vivid, wonderful story in which we become almost breathless sometimes as we follow our Lord on the swiftness of the path of His earthly mission, Mark went back to write a title or preface, and in this preface we find the key of all that is to follow:

" The beginning of the Gospel of Jesus Christ the Son of God, even as it is written in Isaiah the prophet.
Behold, I send My messenger before Thy face
Who shall prepare Thy way.
The voice of one crying in the wilderness,
Make ye ready the way of the Lord,
Make His paths straight."

Mark first declared that he had written a " beginning of the Gospel of Jesus Christ the Son of God as it is written in Isaiah the prophet." He then immediately wrote an exclamatory quotation, not from Isaiah, but from the last of the Hebrew prophets, Malachi.

" Behold, I send My messenger before Thy face who shall prepare Thy way." Having done so, he quoted from the prophecy of Isaiah at the point in the prophecy where the Gospel began: " The voice of one crying in the wilderness, Make ye ready the way of the Lord, Make His paths straight."

Let us turn back to Malachi, in order to see the setting of the exclamatory quotation: " Behold, I send My messenger, and he shall prepare the way before Me." In the prophecy the words run on thus: "And the Lord, Whom ye seek, will suddenly come to His temple; and the messenger of the covenant, whom ye desire, behold, he cometh, saith Jehovah of Hosts." In this prophetic word reference was made to two messengers, the Messenger of the covenant, and the messenger who precedes the Messenger of the covenant. Mark only quotes the words concerning the messenger who was to foretell the coming of the Messenger of the covenant.

He then went back to his starting point: "the Gospel of Jesus Christ the Son of God, even as it is written in Isaiah," and quoted from the prologue of the second part of Isaiah:

"The voice of one that crieth. Prepare ye in the wilderness the way of Jehovah, make level in the desert a highway for our God. . . . O thou that tellest the Gospel, *good tidings* to Zion . . . O thou that tellest *good tidings* to Jerusalem" (40 : 3 and 9).

To read Isaiah from the fortieth chapter to the end of the prophecy is to discover the Servant of God; it is an unveiling of the suffering Servant of God; while yet the same Servant of God is seen ultimately in triumph, a triumph won out of travail. This book then gives an account of the beginning of that Gospel, which according to Mark, was written in Isaiah.

We have said that Peter was in all probability the source from whom Mark derived his information. In his first letter (1 : 24, 25) he quoted from Isaiah, and from the same passage:

"All flesh is as grass,
And all the glory thereof as the flower of grass.
The grass withereth, and the flower falleth:
But the word of the Lord abideth forever."

He then went on to say, "And this is the word of the Gospel which was preached unto you."

Here then, we are admitted to the spirit of this Gospel of Mark. It is the Beginning, the starting point of the Gospel of Jesus Christ, the Son of God, as it is written

[11]

in the prophet Isaiah. The paragraph is an inclusive introduction to all that is to follow. The word "Beginning" refers, not to the paragraph, not to the ministry of John, not to the ministry of Jesus. It refers to the Gospel. In this book we have the story of the beginning of the whole Gospel. Here Mark has written the story of how the Gospel which Isaiah predicted became historic. Light is flung upon this matter, by the way in which Luke commenced his second treatise. "The former treatise I made, O Theophilus, concerning all that Jesus *began* both to do and to teach." That former treatise was also the story of a beginning; so that the Gospel according to Luke is also the account of the beginning of the Gospel.

The reference to Isaiah admits us to the spirit of all that is to follow, and so constitutes the key to its spiritual interpretation. What Isaiah predicted, Jesus fulfilled. Isaiah foresaw that the way of comfort was the way of the coming of Jehovah in His suffering and victorious Servant, to deal with sin and bring in righteousness. Here then is the story of how that Gospel became a fact in human history.

It is sufficient therefore now for us to notice, as the completion of this initial study; first, the supreme subject referred to; and secondly, the special theme of the book.

The supreme subject is "the Gospel of Jesus Christ, the Son of God." What does the word "Gospel" mean? In many senses there can be no better translation of the Greek word than that of which we constantly make use, the Evangel. What is an evangel? Dr. Maclear says that in classical Greek the word first meant a reward given to the bearers of good news; that it subsequently came to mean the sacrifice offered in thankfulness for good news; until finally it was used of the good news itself.

This last is the invariable New Testament sense. The

Gospel is in itself a message of salvation, a message of comfort, a message of hope, a message of joy; a message that should always thrill to the tireless music of a psalm, a message that has nothing to do with denunciation. The Gospel is not preached when sin is denounced. The Gospel is good news to sinning men, a message of salvation from sin.

The word does not occur very often in the Gospel itself, but the occurrences illuminate the theme. After this opening paragraph it is almost immediately found twice. Mark tells us that when Jesus began His preaching in Galilee, He began to preach " the *Gospel* of God," the good news from God. Mark alone tells us that when Jesus began to preach, He not only said, " Repent, for the Kingdom of heaven is at hand "; but that He also said, " and believe in the *Gospel*." The word is not found again until after Peter's confession at Cæsarea Philippi, when Mark alone tells us that Jesus called His disciples to deny themselves and take up the Cross for His sake, and for the sake of *the Gospel*. Soon after, in those shadowed days while He was instructing these men, approaching the Cross, He used that same phrase a second time, " for My sake and the *Gospel's*." There is one beautiful incidental use of it, when the disciples, misunderstanding the prodigality of the love of the woman who anointed Jesus with ointment, He said, " Wheresoever the *Gospel* shall be preached . . . that also which this woman hath done shall be spoken of for a memorial of her." Only once more it occurs, in the final chapter, as He appointed His disciples, to " go . . . and preach the *Gospel* to all the cosmos." There is always music in the word, hope in it, comfort in it, gladness in it; it is a veritable song to cheer the heart, and renew the courage; the Gospel, good news.

In this opening word, " the Gospel of Jesus Christ, the Son of God," everything is gathered up. By these words we are at once reminded, as we commence to study this

[13]

book that the centre and circumference of the Gospel is Christ Himself; for whatever may be the harmonies of the varied notes of the infinite music, they are all homed and centred in Him. Not carelessly does this writer name Him at the commencement by the Old Testament word, Jesus. That is the name that places Him upon the level of my comprehension; for in the Man Who bore the name we find the point of contact between ourselves, and the One Whom He supremely came to reveal. Take Him away from me, and remind me merely of the administrative power of God in His universe, and I am lost, for I cannot grasp the unfathomable truth. Take Him away from me, and speak to my soul of God in all the wonder and mystery of His being, and He is utterly incomprehensible to me. A gospel that is a Gospel of God, but is not spelt out into my language and rendered observable by my finite nature, becomes no Gospel to me. Mark commences where God began to fulfil the prophecy of His servants. The charm of this Gospel is that through it we shall be following Jesus, walking with Him, watching His gestures, listening to the very habits of His speech.

In the title "Christ," Mark suggests the way by which God administers that salvation, the proclamation of which is good news. Christ is the Messiah, the anointed One. The name Jesus brings us into the presence of the Galilean peasant. But Messiah, the anointed One, brings us into the presence of One upon Whom the holy chrism rests, the chrism of the Holy Spirit; enduing Him for service; and empowering Him for dying, for it was through the eternal Spirit that He offered Himself.

The ultimate phrase of the great description, "Son of God," suggests the infinitude of His power, reminding us that whereas men lay the hand of flesh imaginatively upon the hand of His flesh, they will yet be conscious of the thrilling power of essential Deity when His hand closes upon theirs; reminding us that men may look into human eyes, capable of human tears, the gleams of human laughter, and the tragedy of human sorrow; and yet see shining through them the light of essential Deity. Jesus, the anointed One, Son of God. It is the Gospel of One, sent, anointed of the Spirit, of the very nature of the Father. What He says is the Gospel. What He does is the Gospel.

Recently I came across some striking words from the pen of Mazzini:

"He came. The soul the most full of love, the most sacredly virtuous, the most deeply inspired by God and the future, that men have yet seen on earth—Jesus. He bent over the corpse of the dead world, and whispered a word of faith. Over the clay that had lost all of man, but the movement and the form, He uttered words until then unknown: Love, Sacrifice, a heavenly origin. And the dead arose, a new life circulated through the clay, which philosophy had tried in vain to reanimate. From that corpse arose the Christian world, the world of liberty and equality. From that clay arose the true Man, the image of God, the precursor of humanity."

The Gospel is the good news of Jesus, the Anointed, Son of God. Alas that men sometimes proclaim it, as though there were no music in it! It is the music of all music; the inspiration of all music that is worthy the name: The Gospel!

That emphasizes the special theme of the book. We shall not look for, neither shall we find, the philosophy of the Gospel. We shall not discover here the explanation of the Divine operation by which the Gospel became possible. The full content of the Gospel, and its final application, are not here, save by implication. This is the beginning. Isaiah predicted the Gospel, and there was no prophecy of the ancient time with which these Hebrews were more familiar than his. Paul proclaimed it, and probably Mark knew that. It is almost certain that this book was written in Rome. Then think of this fact that Paul sent to Rome a letter, constituting the philosophy and explanation of the Gospel. Therein he wrote, "I am not ashamed of the Gospel; for it is the power of God unto salvation to every one that believeth . . . for therein is revealed a righteousness of God from faith unto faith." He then went on to explain the Gospel; and the probability is that Mark had read that letter before he wrote this Gospel. He came to Rome, was there with Paul; and Paul's letter was there before Paul ever reached Rome. So that when Mark had written out Peter's story, he prefaced it with a statement of how the Gospel began, which Isaiah predicted, of which Peter told the story, and which Paul explained in his book. This is how the prediction was fulfilled in history, how the Gospel came to be.

Our purpose in studying this Gospel is to watch the Servant of Jehovah, Jesus Christ the Son of God; to watch Him, rather than the people about Him; to observe Him as He is revealed here in the workings of His mind, and His attitude toward those who came into contact with Him.

Matthew wrote of the King, and of His method for establishing the Kingdom. Luke wrote of the perfect Man, and the universality of His Saviourhood. John wrote of the hidden mystery of His Being. Or again Matthew wrote of the Christ, Luke of Jesus, John of the Son of God. Mark here portrays that One Who is at once Jesus and Messiah and Son of God, as the Servant of God creating the Gospel. As we consider Him we shall know the Gospel.

II

Mark 1:4–13.

THESE are the central words of this first paragraph of
the Gospel of Mark. The subject of the book, as we have
seen, is that of how "the Gospel of Jesus Christ the Son
of God" began. The story is developed along the lines
suggested by that opening description of the Servant of
Jehovah. He is referred to as *Jesus* consistently, through
all the first stages to the confession of Peter at Cæsarea
Philippi, and never as Christ. At Cæsarea Philippi He
was confessed to be *the Christ* by Peter, and subsequently
that title recurs five times. Jesus used it of Himself
(9:41); He used it of the predicted Messiah when
speaking of His relationship to David (12:35); He used
it when warning His disciples against the coming of
false Christs (13:21); the high priest used it when chal-
lenging Him as to who He was (14:61); and finally the
high priests used it when they mocked Him in the hour
of His dying (15:32).

The designation, *Son of God,* was twice made use of
before Cæsarea Philippi, on each occasion by an evil
spirit. Apart from these instances it is never found
until the high priest challenged Him in the words, "Art
Thou the Christ, the Son of the Blessed?" and He replied, "I am." It is found finally in the story of the
crucifixion, when the centurion after the death of Jesus
said, "Truly this man was the Son of God."

We shall best apprehend the early part of the story
as we look at Him as He is presented by the name Jesus,
divesting ourselves of many of those attitudes of mind
which are necessary as we know Him fully as the Christ,
and as the Son of God. In order that we may come to a

[17]

more perfect apprehension of the meaning of that title, of that sacred and mystic designation, we shall attempt to see Him first as these men saw Him, as Jesus of Nazareth.

In this paragraph we have the story of the beginning of the Beginning of the Gospel. In a few sentences, full of life and colour, Mark gives an account of the ministry of John the Baptist, the forerunner of the Messiah, whose coming had been foretold by Malachi, and whose mission had been described by Isaiah. Then, with brevity and haste, but most graphically, he records the stages through which Jesus of Nazareth, the Servant of Jehovah passed to the actual service to which He was appointed.

In a phrase, "From Nazareth of Galilee," he refers to the past; and then records the facts of His baptism, His anointing, and His temptation. This is how "the beginning of the Gospel" began. Jesus came from Nazareth to baptism, anointing, and temptation. These facts had a bearing on His service, and therefore are recorded. Let us consider them in that order, and in that relation.

Jesus came "from Nazareth of Galilee," where He had been the Self-emptied One for a generation, one of the people; undistinguishable from other men by the eyes of those who looked upon Him; undiscovered as to any deep secret of personality, or any profound anointing for service. He had borne one of the most commonplace names of the day, Jesus, which is the Greek form of Joshua. The probability is that there were many named Joshua in Nazareth and Jerusalem, and throughout that district. Nobody distinguished Him from others by the name; no halo was round His brow; there was nothing strange about Him; He was one of the crowd, a man among men.

He came from Nazareth, of which place so devout and sincere and simple a soul as Nathaniel said, "Can any good thing come out of Nazareth?" He came from

Galilee, referred to always with contempt by the Judæans, " Galilee of the Gentiles ! "

Nazareth to Jesus had been the place of growth from boyhood to manhood; the place where He had grown in wisdom as well as in stature; the place where He had grown in grace with God and with men. Nazareth had been to Him moreover the place of ordinary human experiences, where He had faced ordinary human responsibilities in fellowship with God; a fellowship strange and mystic, different from that experienced by other men, but a fellowship which was the birthright of all men. There in Nazareth He had wrought through the working days; and on the recurring Sabbaths, " as His custom was " He had mingled with the worshippers, reading the law, and hearing it expounded, being brought up in the atmosphere of the conscious nearness of Jehovah, the God of His fathers. There, He had passed through busy days, a carpenter, learning the use of tools until He mastered them, making yokes and ploughs, and building houses. He was an ordinary workman, bearing ordinary human responsibilities, and entering into ordinary human experiences.

But Nazareth had been more than all this to Him. It had been the place of quietness, the place of seclusion, the place of meditation. In the statement that He grew in grace with men is revealed the fact that He was undisturbed by hostilities and criticisms. There in the quietness of the years, from boyhood's age of twelve to manhood's age of thirty, He had the opportunity of the thinking that comes to every man who has the high privilege of spending early years in a quiet country town, out of the way of the rush of cities.

From all this " Jesus came "; and He came " in those days," when in Judæa there were strange, religious awakenings under the ministry of John; when that proud, self-centred countryside around Jerusalem was moved to its heart as it had not been for long, by that wonderful ministry; when men were pouring out to listen to the strange ascetic preacher who lashed them with whips, and ploughed up their conscience, and called them to repentance; and when they, repenting, went out from Judæa and Jerusalem to his baptism, confessing their sins. In that hour of spiritual and religious revival the young Carpenter turned His back upon Nazareth and came. So the day of the Gospel dawned.

He came to baptism, anointing, and temptation. In our study of this Gospel we may deal with these stories with the brevity that characterizes the narrative itself.

He came to baptism. In order to understand the meaning of His coming to baptism, the ordinary facts concerning the ministry of John must be remembered. John had been preaching repentance *unto* remission of sins, not repentance *for* remission of sins. There could be no remission of sins apart from the ministry of Jesus. It was repentance *unto* remission of sins. John had exercised a ministry that produced repentance, in order to prepare for a ministry that should issue in remission. That is the reason why Mark is more particular than Matthew at this point to record one aspect of the burden of the preaching of John. He himself declared, "There cometh after me He that is mightier than I, the latchet of Whose shoes I am not worthy to stoop down and unloose." Then he defined his own declaration. "I baptized you with water"—which is the symbol of washing, and accompanies repentance—"but He shall baptize you with the Holy Spirit"—which is not a symbol, but a strength, renewing and regenerating the life, through which remission of sins shall come, and the beginning of a new life with new possibilities. John's ministry was to produce repentance unto remission; and to declare the coming of the One Who should accomplish all that was made necessary by repentance. To that ministry Jesus now came.

He "was baptized." Here we are face to face with

a most amazing fact. If John's baptism was for repentance, and was the outward sign of repenting souls, how are we to understand this baptizing of Jesus? Matthew tells us that when John saw Him coming, he looked at Him and said, "I have need to be baptized of Thee, and comest Thou to me?" It is of supreme importance that we understand that when John said that, he did not know Who Jesus was, he did not know that He was the Messiah. John himself distinctly declared that he did not know the Messiah until he saw the Holy Spirit descending upon Him. John looked into those eyes;—John, than whom a greater never had been born of women as Jesus said, who in many respects was the greatest of the long line of Hebrew prophets; John, the man of clear moral perception, who had been looking fearlessly, as prophets ever do, into the eyes of the crowds that gathered about him;—John looked into the eyes of this One Who came to be baptized, and said: No, this is a baptism of repentance! I am here to baptize men repenting of sins! I need to be baptized of Thee! Comest Thou to me? This was a prophetic recognition and declaration of the sinlessness of Jesus.

Then why was He baptized? He was baptized as a repenting soul. His also was a baptism of repentance. His also was a baptism of the confession of sins. In that hour He repented, He confessed sins. But the repentance was not for Himself, the sins were not His own. In that hour He identified Himself with the multitudes who had been thronging out to baptism, identified Himself with them in the consciousness of sin, in repentance for it, in confession of it. In that hour of baptism we see the most solemn and wonderful sight of the Servant of God, Who had come from the silence and seclusion of Nazareth, taking upon Himself the burden of human sin, counting it as if it were His own sin, doing that to which an apostolic writer ultimately referred by declaring, "He was made sin."

[21]

So "Jesus came," in the hour of widespread concern and change of mind, to identify Himself with sinners that they might be identified with Him, thus, as Matthew tells us that He Himself said, " to fulfil all righteousness." Righteousness is never fulfilled by repentance. Repentance will lead toward it, repentance is the condition for it; but repentance alone can never produce righteousness. He repented, and confessed sins, as symbolizing the fact that He, the Sinless, was identifying Himself with the sinful, in order that,—in an infinite mystery, for ever beyond our understanding,—in that identification, through infinite love and compassion, righteousness should become possible to the sinners whose sins He bore, and whose sorrows He endured. Thus He came to a baptism that indicated the method of His service as that of an identifying of Himself with sinning men; of being numbered with the transgressors, that He might bear the sins of many, as Isaiah had said, when speaking of this Servant of God.

What immediately followed? " Straightway coming up out of the water, He saw the heavens rent asunder, and the Spirit as a dove descending upon Him: and a voice came out of the heavens, Thou art My beloved Son, in Thee I am well pleased." The word " straightway " marks the immediateness of heaven's response to all that was suggested by His baptism. Luke alone declares that when thus the heavens were opened, and the Spirit descended, Jesus was praying. He descended to the waters of baptism, was immersed beneath them, emerged from them, came to the banks, and prayed. Then, " straightway," in that hour, He was endued for that service to which He had now dedicated Himself. His baptism was His act of dedication, the coming of the Spirit was God's act of consecration. Not that here and now Jesus of Nazareth received the Spirit of God for the first time. His whole being was attended by the operation of the Spirit. His very human life was due to the mystic and

[22]

mighty operation of the Spirit, and all the years in Nazareth were years in which He had been filled with the Spirit. Yet this was something new, something separate, something remarkably beautiful for Him and for us, to the end of time. An enduement of the Spirit was given to Him as the Servant of God in a new sense, in a new significance, and with new powers.

This is the only occasion in the whole Bible where the Spirit is referred to as taking this particular form of manifestation. He came as a dove; and so as the symbol of the infinite gentleness and harmlessness of Jesus of Nazareth. There came an hour when in the teaching of Jesus He said to His disciples that they were to be " wise as serpents, and harmless as doves." Here the harmlessness of Jesus was suggested, and that quality of harmlessness as necessary, if the work to which He had dedicated Himself was to be accomplished.

Yet to Him, a Hebrew after the flesh, this symbolic form had more in it than the suggestiveness of harmlessness. It was in itself a suggestion of sacrifice on the lowest level; on the lowest level that is, not as to intrinsic value, but as to the capacity of a worshipper. The poorest, who could bring nothing else, were permitted to bring a dove as their offering for sin. Now, in an infinite beauty harmonizing with the Self-emptying of the Son of God, the Spirit of God took this form of the dove, the symbol of harmlessness and of sacrifice brought to the level of the poorest. In that hour of anointing there came to Him enablement for the service to which He had formally dedicated Himself, thus fulfilling the word of Isaiah, " Behold My Servant, whom I uphold; My Chosen, in whom My soul delighteth; I have put My Spirit upon Him; He will bring forth justice to the Gentiles. He will not cry, nor lift up His voice, nor cause it to be heard in the street."

There came to Him also the Father's ratification, the voice that sounded in His own soul, whether others heard it or not we have no means of knowing. To translate it literally, this is what the voice said: " Thou art the Son of Me; the Beloved. In Thee I am well pleased." By the symbol of His baptism He had manifested His dedication to all the mystery of His suffering and death. Then, said the Voice, " Thou art the Son of Me, My Beloved." There came a day later on in His ministry, when He said, " Therefore doth the Father love Me, because I lay down My life." In that hour of dedication, He had testimony borne to Him by His Father, of the Divine approval of that act of dedication by which He presently would fulfil righteousness in men through and beyond repentance, by giving them remission, regeneration, and renewal.

Again, the Voice said, " In Thee I am well pleased." The words, " My Chosen, in whom My soul delighteth " had been written by Isaiah long before; and Mark declared, This is the story of the beginning of the Gospel of which Isaiah wrote; this is how it came to be.

Here then we see Him, setting His face toward His mission, receiving the enduement enabling Him to fulfil it, and the ratification within His soul of the fact that He was coöperating with God. So He came, not only to identification with sinners, but to all the resources of God, in order that He might accomplish His mission.

Finally He came to temptation. Here again, with that illuminative suggestiveness that characterizes Mark, he used words that arrest us: "And straightway the Spirit driveth Him forth into the wilderness." Both Matthew and Luke indicate the fact that He went into the wilderness under the guidance of the Spirit, but Mark has used a strange word. " The Spirit driveth Him forth "; quite literally, " the Spirit casteth Him forth." It is the very word afterward employed of the casting out of demons by Christ.

We shall come nearer to the spiritual value if we see the physical fact, and get nearer to the profound intention of the writer as we look at the humanness of the story. As we read that " the Spirit driveth Him forth," casteth Him out, there comes before the vision a graphic picture of Jesus of Nazareth hastening, hurrying to the wilderness. No leisured, meditative walk this, but swift, impetuous movement, as of one driven irresistibly forth, so that there could be no halting. The resolve of His soul was revealed in His baptism. The resources at His disposal for the fulfilling of His resolve had been revealed in His anointing. Now He hastened to face the foe; not with a spirit buoyant perchance, but with a spirit filled with foreboding, for this was real temptation, actual temptation. The Spirit after His anointing drove Him to face the forces that ruin and blight and blast and spoil humanity.

Mark here records that which is most remarkable; not that He was in the wilderness for forty days and afterward was tempted, but that He was " forty days tempted of Satan." We have here no account of the specific temptations, but we are not wronging the Gospel story if we assume that the temptations of the forty days were along the lines revealed by Matthew and Luke as they record the story of the final temptations, for in those stories we have an exhaustive picture of every avenue along which evil can approach Mansoul. Temptation today seems very varied, but it may always be classified under one of these headings.

When He began to preach He said, " The Kingdom of God is at hand: repent ye, and believe in the Gospel." The Kingdom of God is at hand. In that declaration was revealed the master passion of His Service. Why did He descend to the waters of baptism? To fulfil righteousness. Righteousness is the establishment of Divine Kingship, the setting up of the Kingdom of God. In order to do that it was necessary that He should deal with existing conditions of location, necessity, and failure. It must be a Kingdom of bread, dealing with man's material necessities; but it must go infinitely beneath that, it must be a Kingdom of fellowship with God, dealing with man's spiritual nature. It must also be a Kingdom of beauty and of glory, which, in its ultimate establishment, shall realize all the highest things of beauty in the Being of God.

Jesus had come to establish that Kingdom, and for forty days He was tempted; tempted by His hunger to wonder whether God cared; tempted in the presence of the tremendous work that had opened out before Him, as to how far He might venture outside the Divine direction, how far He might proceed upon His own initiative; tempted as to whether the Kingdoms of the world, with all their glory and beauty, might not be gained apart from the method symbolized by His baptism.

The one inspiration of such service as that to which He had dedicated Himself, must be threefold; the inspiration of love, of faith, and of hope. For forty days He was tempted to doubt the love, to traffic with the faith, to question the hope; and at the end of forty days these things became most devilish, most concrete, and most terrific. It was real temptation! I know the old controversy of the theologians and the scholars as to the peccability of Christ. But unless He was *tempted,* then He was *not* tempted; unless He felt the lure of the suggestions made, there was no temptation! This lasted for forty days; it was continuous, insistent!

How did it all end? The statement of Mark is wonderfully graphic. He does not say anything about the victories as does Matthew or Luke; but simply says, "And He was with the wild beasts; and the angels ministered unto Him." Many expositors say that the sentence, "He was with the wild beasts" is intended to suggest the terribleness of the situation. I do not so read it. The Greek preposition marks the closest association and unity. "He was *with* the wild beasts"; but they were not wild with Him! He was God's archetypal Man,

realizing the first Divine intention of a perfect and beneficent mastery over the lower creation. The beasts that
were wild with other men gathered about Him in the
wilderness and knew their Master, not as God, but as
man in the perfection and sinlessness of His nature.
" He was with the wild beasts." I never go to the Zoolog-
ical Gardens without wishing I could play with the lions!
In the Kingdom that is to be, the lion shall lie down
with the lamb, and a little child shall lead them. Then all
their ferocity will have vanished. " He was with the
wild beasts." Morally victorious, He was Master of the
creation beneath Him, and angels ran upon His errands,
for such is the real suggestiveness of the word. Thus He
is seen as God's Man, perfect in spite of temptation!

So " Jesus came from Nazareth," where for thirty
years He had lived the self-emptied life; where for thirty
years He had been without the prerogatives of sovereignty which were His in the inherent mystery of His
being; where for thirty years He had been subject to
parents and to human conditions. He came to men, and
found them sinning, and joining them, repented with
them and was baptized. He came to God, and had the
answer of the anointing of His Spirit, and the ratification of His high purpose. He came to Satan, and entered into conflict with him, and mastered him.

How can I better end than by quoting again the words
of Isaiah? " Behold My Servant, whom I uphold; My
Chosen, in whom My soul delighteth; I have put My
Spirit upon Him." So spake Jehovah of Him centuries
before He came. Thus spake Jehovah of Him in the
hour of His coming. " Thou art the Son of Me, My
Beloved; in Thee I am well pleased."

III

" Jesus came into Galilee."—MARK 1 : 14.

Mark 1 : 14–35.

LIKE Matthew and Luke, Mark commenced the record
of the ministry of Jesus at the point where He left
Judæa—John being imprisoned—and in Galilee began a
more public and positive propaganda.

Between the thirteenth and fourteenth verses in the
first chapter of this Gospel we must allow for the passing
of a year, during which our Lord wrought His first
signs, and uttered His first teaching, travelling between
Judæa and Galilee. The signs were wrought in Galilee
and in Jerusalem, but the teaching was chiefly given in
Judæa during that period. This year Dr. Stalker has
fittingly described as " the year of obscurity." The record of it is found only in John.

The first two verses of this paragraph (14, 15) constitute an introduction to the whole period from the arrival in Galilee to the hour of the confession of Peter at
Cæsarea Philippi; an introduction to that period of the
ministry which Mark records in the first eight chapters
of the Gospel; a period in which our Lord probably
never went to Jerusalem, but remained itinerating in
Galilee, making Capernaum the base of His operations.
The rest of the paragraph (verses 16–35) gives some
incidents of the first days of His public ministry.

Let us then survey the paragraph, and observe the
Lord at His work.

The first matter which arrests attention is the time at
which Jesus left Judæa for Galilee. It was the hour in
which John was " delivered up." The great herald of
Jesus had fulfilled his ministry in a certain sense a year

before this time, in pointing to Jesus as the coming One, the latchet of Whose shoes he did not count himself worthy to stoop down and unloose. But he had evidently continued his work of proclaiming the nearness of the Kingdom, and of calling upon men to repent. There came an hour when he was arrested by Herod. His voice therefore was silenced; his public ministry was entirely at an end. At that hour, Jesus moved from Judæa into Galilee, into the district of Herod; not escaping from danger, but moving into the danger zone; not withdrawing Himself from peril because John was arrested, but going into the very region over which the man who had arrested John was reigning. Men may silence the voice of a prophet; but they cannot hinder the Word of God.

The next matter of importance is the declaration that He went into Galilee "preaching the Gospel of God." Observe the change in the Revised Version; not "the Gospel of the Kingdom of God," but "the Gospel of God." This is what we describe as the genitive of the author; "the Gospel of God," the Gospel that came from God, the glad tidings which God had sent to men. That was His message in Galilee. That indeed was the burden of His message throughout the whole of His life; not accusation, nor denunciation, but a proclamation of good news. "Think not that I will accuse you," He said upon one occasion. "There is one that accuseth you, even Moses." "God sent not the Son into the world to judge the world," He said upon another occasion, "but that the world should be saved through Him." He came preaching the good news. It is perfectly true that there were times when He accused men; but follow the method of our Lord, and observe that almost invariably when it was necessary for Him to accuse, He did so by such parabolic teaching, as compelled those who heard to accuse themselves in His presence, to find against themselves a verdict, and to pronounce a sentence. His mission was not that of accusation, nor of denunciation. His mission was that of the proclamation of the good news of God.

Then Mark proceeded to give the content of the Gospel, and the terms of Christ's appeal. "The time is fulfilled, and the Kingdom of God is at hand." That, in brief, is the whole content of the Gospel of God which Jesus came to proclaim. The time is fulfilled; the preparation is complete; the last thing that must necessarily be done before the Gospel can be preached is done. The Kingdom is at hand, brought to men, made nigh, made possible.

Upon the basis of that Gospel He made His constant appeal, which was twofold. First, "Repent ye," literally, think again, change your mind! Deal with the inspirational centres of life, by changing the conceptions. Think over again. There is no suggestion of sorrow in this word. I admit that no man will repent in the way suggested by this word without feeling sorrow sooner or later. There is another word for repentance that does include sorrow, but that was not the word Jesus used here. It was not the word used by John. This word was one that called men to think again, to change their conceptions, out of which all conduct proceeds, which conduct issues in character. Repent! Think again!

Repentance was the message necessary to the establishment of the Kingdom; but there was more in the Gospel, and the final appeal was not to "repent," but to "believe in the Gospel." Not to "believe the Gospel." There are many people who believe the Gospel, but they do not believe in it. It was an appeal not only to accept it as an intellectually accurate statement; but to rest in it, to repose in it. It was a call to let the heart find ease in it.

That was the key-note of His preaching throughout;— good news; the Kingdom of God is at hand; it is made available to men; and the appeal consequent upon good news was ever, repent, think back toward that Kingdom,

readjust life by setting it in true relationship with that
Kingdom; and then rest in this Gospel, that what men
thus choose to become, is made possible to them.

That introductory passage strikes the key-note of all
the music that is to follow in the teaching of Jesus; it
focusses all the glory of the light that is to flash upon
the pathway, and flame through every activity of this
anointed Servant of God, in the days of His flesh.

Before surveying the incidents that are recorded in the
following paragraph, it is well to remember that an incident here occurred on the way to Capernaum which only
Luke records. Jesus went to Nazareth, and into the synagogue with which He had been familiar from boyhood.
There, taking up the roll of the prophet Isaiah, He read
those remarkable Messianic words, " The Spirit of the
Lord is upon Me, because He anointed Me." In the synagogue of His boyhood, among the people most familiar
with Him in the flesh, He spoke words of such grace
that they were filled with wonder; and yet they attempted
to murder Him. Leading Him to the brow of the hill,
they endeavoured to cast Him down headlong. He moved
away from them in mystic, strange, startling power, and
escaped.

On His way into the city of Capernaum, passing by
the seashore, the place of the boats of the fisher-folk,
He called four men to Himself; Simon and Andrew,
James and John. They knew Him; they had met Him
at least a year before, and for some weeks, if not months,
had travelled with Him; until at Samaria He had dismissed them to their own folk, and had gone back alone
to Jerusalem. Now He called them, and said this significant thing to them: " Come ye after Me, and I will
make you to become fishers of men." Thus He came to
Capernaum.

Then Mark recorded, in his own characteristic style,
the story of the first Sabbath at Capernaum (1 : 21–35).
It is an account of what Jesus did in the morning, in the

[31]

afternoon, and in the evening. In the morning He was in the synagogue; in the afternoon He was at home; in the evening He was in the streets outside His home.

In the morning He went to the synagogue. One can imagine that synagogue service in Capernaum, with its liturgy, its reading of the Benedictions, its chantings of hallelujahs; the reading of the portion of the Thorah or Law appointed for the day; and then the reading of the portion of the prophets appointed for the day. Finally Jesus taught. There is no record of what He said, but we have heard the key-note. He was preaching the Gospel. Speaking of the Kingdom of God, He told them that it was nigh, at hand; and appealed to them to believe in that Gospel. That service was suddenly disturbed by a man possessed of an unclean spirit crying out: " What is there to us and to Thee? " "Art Thou come to destroy us? " " I know Thee who Thou art, the Holy One of God." Jesus turned, and said to him, quite literally, " Be muzzled, and come out of him "; and at once the evil spirit came out. The crowds were amazed, and said, " What is this? a new teaching! " His teaching was thus emphasized by His power. So passed the morning, in teaching and healing.

The afternoon was passed at Simon's house, whither He went with Simon and Andrew, James and John. Immediately on arrival they told Him of Simon's wife's mother who was in the grip of a fever. Jesus went to her, and raised her up, and the fever left her. Those who have had a sick one in the home can imagine that afternoon, when the woman who had been in the grip of a burning fever and all had been troubled about her, was once again busy about the house, ministering to them!

The fame of that morning of teaching and healing spread throughout the city, and the multitudes gathered, carrying sick people, round about that door, and bringing demon-possessed men and women to be healed.

[Mark 1 : 14–35]
Jesus went out, and healed many, casting out demons.
The day being ended, He went to rest.

Early in the morning, while it was yet dark, Jesus
rose from rest, with great quietness, not to disturb the
other sleepers; and leaving the house and Capernaum,
climbed one of the wild desert heights outside the city
for prayer.

These are the incidents. Let us now look at Jesus,
carefully observing Him at His work. Four view-points
are suggested. First, taking into account that early incident at Nazareth to which Mark makes no reference,
we see Him facing His work. Journeying on from
Nazareth, we watch His arrival in Capernaum, and observe the calling of His first comrades. Then we see
Him in contact with men. We next see Him in conflict
with demons. Finally we see Him, in the early hours of
the following morning, in communion with God. When
Jesus commenced His ministry, He came to men and
identified Himself with them in the baptism of repentance; came to God, and received the attestation of the
Father, following baptism; came to the under-world of
evil in temptation, and mastered it. So now He is seen
coming again to men as the Servant of God, coming
again into the realm where demons held despotic sway
over human souls and lives, coming again into quiet,
close fellowship with God.

We first observe Him facing His work, when entering
into Capernaum He called the disciples to Him. Nazareth had rejected Him. He had come to His own place,
and His fellow townsmen would have none of Him.
Now work was opening out before Him, and He called
four men. The Servant of God, conscious of His rejection at Nazareth, suffering on account thereof, desired
the fellowship of men in the enterprises of God. To
Simon and Andrew, to James and John, He said, " Come
ye after Me, and I will make you to become fishers of
men." He was the Son of man, the Saviour of men.

[Mark 1:14-35]

The master passion of His heart was that of the establishment of the Kingdom of God, and nothing interfered with that except men. But in order to the establishment of the Kingdom of God, man must not be destroyed. He said of His presence in the world, " I am not come to destroy, but to save." He needed help.

These were the men He called. Simon, a man impulsive and wayward, lacking the principle which masters passion, and makes it strong. Andrew, His first Judæan disciple, James and John, brothers, but so different; the one a poet, a dreamer, attractive; and the other quiet, retiring, unknown. To these He said, " Come ye after Me, and I will make you to become fishers of men."

" *Fishers* of men." He employed this figure because they were all fishermen. To some men He would never say that. He did not say it to all the early disciples. There were others who were farm labourers. Therefore He also said, " The fields are white to harvest." " Thrust in the sickle and reap." He changed His figure according to the men to whom He wished to appeal. The principle underlying His call was that He called men to consecrate to His enterprises the capacity they had. Jesus is thus seen asking for comradeship; indicating the fact that when men are willing, He is able to fit them for the very comradeship in service to which He calls them.

On the Sabbath day, with its wonderful scenes, we observe Jesus dealing with men; teaching and healing. In these days of public ministry He went into synagogues for teaching, as in the earlier years of private life He had gone habitually for worship. The synagogue was the place of the gathering together of those of the Hebrew religion, the Jews who were true to the monotheistic idea, and desired to worship God. The synagogue unified the scattered peoples everywhere, if in no other way, by the very liturgy they employed. Jews in Capernaum, in Nazareth, and in all the cities, who could not reach the

Temple, gathered at the same hour on the Sabbath day, using the same forms of worship.

A study of synagogue worship is a very interesting and profitable one. In passing we may observe that they who thus worshipped were forbidden to turn to the east. These synagogues usually faced the west, not only because, according to Ezekiel's prophecy, there was a danger of idolatry in turning to the east, but also symbolically they were thus taught not to look in worship toward the place from whence religion came, but toward the place to which religion was intended to reach. It was the missionary attitude. Jesus went into these synagogues, and conformed to their habit and worship, as He had done through youth and young manhood in Nazareth. But now He went to teach. Opportunity to do so was undoubtedly offered Him everywhere, in accordance with the custom of the time, for all Rabbis travelling were welcome to teach in the synagogues. He employed the opportunities which the synagogue and its assembled people offered, to preach the Gospel.

That which specially arrests our attention was the effect produced. Here at Capernaum, after the first Sabbath teaching, they were astonished, because He taught them with authority, and not as the scribes. The contrast is a very striking one in that it is unexpected. It is made here, and again later on. It is the contrast between Christ's teaching, and the teaching to which the people had been accustomed. He taught them as having authority, and not as their scribes. Now the scribes were the authoritative teachers. Their position was that of authority to teach the law and interpret it; to explain the Kingdom, to emphasize and insist upon the fact of the rule and reign of God, and to show how that rule was applied. The contrast was not between what they said, and what He said. It was a contrast between the effects produced by what they said, and by what He said. I do not agree with Edersheim when he suggests that the au-

thority of Jesus was that of manner. Not that His
manner lacked dignity. I believe that physically Jesus
was the most beautiful Man Who ever walked this earth.
Marred with sorrow was His face undoubtedly, but far
more perfect in form and feature than the highest dream
of Greek sculptor ever led men to imagine man could be.
His authority was not in His manner, nor in the thing
He said; for He said nothing that had not been said before He came. Everything that He said may be found
in germ in the Old Testament Scriptures.

Then wherein lay this authority? In the thing He said,
as He said it, for He carried to the souls of men conviction that it was true. Stripped of all the things that hid,
and all exposition that destroyed, the truth gripped men.
It was not the authority of the law, it was not the authority of a manner, it was the authority of naked, eternal
truth, uttered through an absolutely perfect Man. That
is the authority of Jesus until this hour, and nothing is
more marked than the continuity of that authority. Take
some passage from His teaching, out of the Manifesto,
or some casual word He spoke, and listen to it, and then
ask this question, Is that true? The only criticism ever
offered of the teaching of Jesus worth any consideration,
is that He gave men counsels of perfection, that His
teachings were impracticable. There is no question as to
their accuracy, or their truth. The hearts of men always respond to the truth. His was, and is, the authority
of eternal, naked truth, from which there can be no
escape. Some of the things He said search and scorch
us. We want to escape, but we know that He is right.
This is one of the supreme proofs of the finality of Jesus.
His authority is authority to the end of time. Only it
must be remembered that the authority diminishes, if
these records be lost. The authority of Christ is not the
authority of what we think of Christ, for to-morrow we
may think differently of Him. It is always the authority
of the actual words so marvellously preserved for us;

and never wholly apart from them is Christ authoritative
to-day.

As we watch Him on that first Sabbath day, this authority arrests us; it is the authority of essential truth,
coming out of eternity, and appealing to essential humanity; however humanity may have become blunted and
dwarfed, it hears and knows the voice, and recognizes
the authority.

Then beyond the teaching, there was healing. This
healing ministry was twofold;—mental healing in His
dispossession of those who were mastered by evil spirits;
and bodily healing in His renewal of all bodily powers.
These miracles of Jesus were not violations of natural
order, but restorations to natural order. That man demon-possessed, was unnatural. Then said Jesus to the
demon, "Be muzzled, and come out." That woman in
a burning fever, was unnatural; "He touched her, and
the fever left her." He did not violate order; but restored it.

Thus the Servant of God is seen moving out upon the
pathway of service; first teaching men, for this is supreme, and touches the spirit life; and then healing mind
and body, restoring natural conditions, in order to the
fulfilment of life.

The last thing in this paragraph is full of beauty. To
take the Greek words as they come: "And very early,
while yet night, having risen up, He went out, and departed into a desert place, and there was praying." That
reveals the deliberate purposefulness of Jesus. The word
"praying" here connotes far more than asking. It suggests the going forward in desire to God, not for God's
gifts only, but for God. It is the word for true worship,
the word that describes the soul moving out toward
God, desiring Him, and all He has to give.

It is impossible to read that statement and observe our
Lord in the early hours of the morning, leaving behind
Him the four men He had chosen as comrades, and the

[37]

people He had healed in the city, to go into the desert place, without asking the nature of His communion with God. This Gospel has been introduced by the declaration that it is " The beginning of the Gospel " according to Isaiah. In the second part of the great prophecy of Isaiah, there is one paragraph which lights up this early morning hour, and Jesus at prayer. It is taken from the description of the Servant of God (50:4-7). "The Lord Jehovah hath given Me the tongue of them that are taught, that I may know how to sustain with words him that is weary: He wakeneth morning by morning, He wakeneth Mine ear to hear as they that are taught. The Lord Jehovah hath opened Mine ear, and I was not rebellious, neither turned away backward. I gave My back to the smiters, and My cheeks to them that plucked off the hair: I hid not My face from shame and spitting. For the Lord Jehovah will help Me; therefore have I not been confounded: therefore have I set My face like a flint, and I know that I shall not be put to shame." That passage suggests the nature of that early morning hour of communion. Let us ponder it carefully.

IV

"To this end came I forth."—Mark 1 : 38.

Mark 1 : 35–2 : 12.

THIS paragraph commences with the story of how the quietness of the morning watch of Jesus was broken in upon by the arrival of Simon and the rest of His disciples. The declaration made by the evangelist is really very striking; it means that they pursued Him, they hunted Him down. The word marks the anxiety and the eagerness of their search, and the almost terror that possessed them, when wakening in the morning, they found that Jesus was not in the house at Capernaum. Having found Him they said to Him, "All are seeking Thee," a declaration revealing the effect produced in Capernaum by that wonderful Sabbath with its teaching, its healing of the demoniac, its healing of Peter's wife's mother, and that most wonderful eventide when they brought to Him all that were sick, and possessed with demons, and with apparent ease He healed the sicknesses, and cast the demons out.

In this paragraph we have an account of our Lord's answer to the statement of His disciples, and the things that immediately followed. He was interrupted in His fellowship, but not disturbed by the interruption. Quietly He said to them, when they told Him that all in Capernaum were waiting for Him, "Let us go elsewhere into the next towns, . . . for to this end came I forth." A great lesson lies within that fact, its ultimate value being that converse with God prepares us for converse with men, and that a true fellowship with God is never selfish; it is willing to be interrupted when men need help. In their eagerness, their intense anxiety lest somehow He had departed, they hunted Him down, pursued Him until they found Him, and then with eagerness they said to Him, "All are seeking Thee." He, with open ear was listening to God, and holding communion with Him in the secret place. With no perturbation of spirit, with no rebuke for these men, looking at them with great love and tenderness He said, Let us go elsewhere into the next towns, that I may preach there also; for to this end came I forth. The word "towns" is a singularly arresting one, occurring nowhere else in the New Testament, translated, "to the next village towns"; and perhaps more happily, "to the next country towns." The reference was to the smaller towns that were not walled around completely, the little centres of population unified by the presence of a synagogue. He told them that He must go to the other country towns. He had come to Capernaum, for Capernaum sat in the shadows of darkness and death; and He had opened His ministry there in the midst of night, but Capernaum must not detain Him. The other country towns needed His help; not the metropolis alone, but those other towns and cities scattered through Galilee; and not the towns only, but the unwalled villages. To this end came He forth.

The Sabbath in Capernaum had prepared the way for this wider ministry, for after the happenings in the synagogue, "the report of Him went out straightway everywhere into all the region of Galilee round about." Mark records the fact of that first itinerary of our Lord in the briefest words: "He went into their synagogues throughout all Galilee, preaching and casting out demons." No details are given. Then he gives two illustrative incidents, that of the cleansing of the leper; that of the forgiving of the sins, and the healing of the palsied man. These two incidents at the end of a general declaration, illuminate all that ministry.

The cleansing of the leper took place at the foot of the mountain after the giving of the Manifesto. Mark was not dealing with the King and the Lawgiver, but

with the great Servant of God Who is Priest and
Saviour; and so he did not record the Manifesto. Between the hour of His disturbance in worship, and the
healing of the leper, there had been journeyings. The
gap may be filled by turning to Matthew, and discovering
from how far and wide an area the people had gathered
to Him, flocked after Him. They had come from Judæa
and Decapolis and from beyond Jordan. The crowds
were flocking after Him everywhere; and there came a
moment when, seeing the multitudes, He went into the
mountain with His disciples, and sat and taught them,
and gave them the Manifesto. Immediately following,
as Matthew records, this leper came to Him. The other
incident occurred when, after a period of absence from
Capernaum, made necessary by the disobedience of the
cleansed leper who published Him, Jesus went back into
the city, and there in the house the palsied man was
brought to Him, and He forgave and healed him.

Again endeavouring to observe the Lord Himself
rather than the people about Him, or the incidents themselves, let us consider the text we have chosen, as revealing the inspiration of His ministry; and in the light of
the context, as revealing the nature and power thereof.
With all the lights and shadows of these two incidents
playing about the Person of the Lord, let us listen to Him
as He said, " To this end came I forth." Let us attempt
to discover the inspiration of Christ's service as it is
marked in the words, " Came I forth "; and secondly, the
nature and power of His service as it is revealed in the
incidents, and appears in the phrase, " To *this end* came
I forth."

The first meaning of the words of Jesus must detain
us. There are two possible interpretations of His declaration, " Came I forth." He either meant, I came forth
from Capernaum, or, I came forth from God. The declaration was either purely local and geographical; or it
was essential and eternal. The first interpretation, al-

though given by many expositors, seems to me impossible and almost grotesque. I am in agreement with Morison when he says that " Such an interpretation . . .
involves a sudden, arbitrary, and almost unpleasant descent to bathos." Besides, it is not true to the simple
story. Jesus did not leave Capernaum to preach, but
to pray. He did not go out in the early morning hour to
seek the crowds, but to be away from them. He had not
gone out in the early morning hour to reach cities, but to
escape a city. He had gone out to have communion with
God.

The second interpretation, which I resolutely adopt, is
that upon this occasion in the simplest words, as the
Servant of God He revealed the fact that He recognized
that His ministry here in the world was dependent upon
the fact that He had come out from God. He had been
in the place of communion with God, His ear had been
wakened by God to listen to the secrets which God had
to speak to Him as His Self-emptied Servant, and now
He said, To this end came I forth.

That interpretation is in harmony with His claims on
other occasions, as chronicled specially by John, and with
the revelation of the Servant of God in this Gospel.
Whereas our Lord is presented by Mark stripped of His
dignities, devoid of the purple, girded as a slave, for
evermore under the compulsion of His service; yet constantly there are gleams of glory flaming forth and reminding us that the Servant of God is also the Son of
God. The key-note of the Gospel struck by the evangelist in that opening word, " The beginning of the Gospel of Jesus Christ, the Son of God," finds its continuity
in the harmonies as they run; for all the things of lowliness are combined with things of might; in the stories we
see Him as the Self-emptied One, and yet as the One in
Whom all the fulness of Deity dwells corporeally; the
Kenosis of the Philippian letter, and the Pleroma of the
Colossian letter are merged in this one Gospel.

We have already seen some of these gleams in the Divine attestation at His baptism; in the awful and agonized cry of the evil spirit in the synagogue, " I know Thee who Thou art, the Holy One of God"; in the wonderful power by which the demon was subdued; and in the power which had wrought so marvellously on that Sabbath evening. In all these there was a power and a dignity and a glory, which did not belong to man alone. Now in the chill dawn of the early morning, to those perturbed disciples He said in effect: I am not going back to Capernaum, though all men seek Me; because there are others waiting for Me. I must go and preach to them, because for that purpose came I forth. Whether they understood Him perfectly or not, the dignity of the assertion shows that He related His journeyings, His teaching, and the things He did by the way, to the eternal Purpose, to the Divine programme, to the Divine mission. " To this end came I forth."

John chronicles how that once in the midst of His critics He said, " I came forth and am come from God"; and again in the seclusion of the upper room He said to His disciples, covering the whole fact of His mission, " I came out from the Father, and am come into the world; again, I leave the world, and go unto the Father." In the light of these statements upon other occasions, we understand the text, " To this end came I forth." The Self-emptied One had come forth from God. God had not left Him, and He had not left God in certain senses, for there came a day when He said, " I am not alone, but I and the Father that sent Me." That was not the language of His Deity, but of His humanity. As a Man, God never left Him through all the years. He had all the privileges of fellowship with God during His human life as a Man that we have, and none other. He lived the life of relationship to God that every man may live. He had come forth from God, He had emptied Himself, He had left behind Him all the riches and glories and the mysteries of His essential and eternal relationship to God. Yet carefully observe Him;—and this illustrates the whole profound and tremendous theme;—again and again He exercised the powers of Deity, which are the powers of sovereign supremacy, *but never on His own behalf, it was always on behalf of others.* He had come forth from God. Therein we discover the strength of His purpose. The strength of His service lay in the complete abandonment of the Servant to the One Who commanded. He moved everywhere, not with the dignity of Deity, but with the dignity of the authority under which He served. He was in the world for a purpose. Jesus was never afraid of loneliness, never afraid of the desert places. He knew full well that naught could harm Him until His mission was accomplished, and His work was done. " Mine hour is not yet come," He said to His enemies. That was not the language of God. God has no " hours." His is the eternal " Now." It was the language of the Servant Who knew God, and Who moved forward with a great sense of the authority of His mission, knowing that He was in the world for a purpose. Very early in the morning He rose up, leaving the other sleepers undisturbed, and went out to prayer in the desert place. He prayed as a Man facing the task before Him, knowing that presently He must give His cheek to those that would pluck off the hair, and His back to the smiter. God communed with Him of the coming passion; and in resolute agreement, He set His face toward the goal. " To that end came I forth." In that sentence is the key-note of His confidence, the secret of His strength, the unveiling of the power that made Him the prevailing Servant of God.

The immediate application follows. He said He was going to preach, to herald the Gospel; to proclaim it, which includes talking and working. He was going to herald the Gospel both by word and work in the nearest towns, Bethsaida, Chorazin, Dalmanutha, Magdala. He was going to a ministry of power and blessing, statistically a failure, spiritually a triumph.

We turn therefore to consider the nature and power of His service as it was revealed in the journey through Galilee, and especially in the two incidents.

The end to which He referred was that of heralding or proclaiming, and that of casting out. This is a most suggestive statement, covering the story of that ministry: "He went into their synagogues throughout all Galilee, *preaching and casting out demons.*" Mark shows what the Servant of God, when passing out of the place of communion with God, did in the presence of men, and in the presence of the underworld of evil. In fellowship with God in prayer He was interrupted but not disturbed. Then He went through all the towns and villages, "preaching and casting out demons." His relation to men is suggested by the word "preaching." His relation to the underworld of evil is suggested by the phrase, "casting out demons." He was proclaiming the Gospel of God, and there were two notes therein; first, the Kingdom of God is a fact; secondly, it is nigh. Its nearness through Himself constituted the special note of good news that He came to proclaim to men. He went everywhere proclaiming this Kingdom and Gospel.

He illustrated both Kingdom and Gospel as He cast out demons. None of the other evangelists draws our attention so constantly to this power of Christ over the underworld of evil as does Mark. The first incident to which Mark drew attention, was that wrought in the synagogue when He cast the demon out. Doubtless He also healed the sick, for Matthew specifically declares that He did. But the thing that impressed Mark, as he looked at the Servant of God, was first of all His relationship to God in prayer; then as He went out to His work, His relationship to men, as He proclaimed the Kingdom and the Gospel of God; and finally His power over the underworld of evil, as He cast out demons.

[45]

To come to the incidents, and to watch the Lord: we observe Him first with the leper. He acted in two realms, those of health and holiness, showing their inter-relationship. First He cleansed the leper; then He sent him to the priest with a definite and specific command that he should take with him the sacrifice or offerings which Moses commanded. In the second incident, that of the palsied man, the same two realms are manifested; first holiness, " Thy sins are forgiven "; secondly health, " Take up thy bed and walk."

Surveying the incidents in their entirety, and observing, not so much the man, nor the crowds about the Lord, but the Lord Himself at His work as the Servant of God, we are brought on both occasions into the presence of health and holiness, and their inter-relationship is marked.

In the first case He healed a leper; and then sent him to the priest for the fulfilment of those ceremonial offerings which had to do with holiness. In the second case He forgave sins, and restored holiness to a soul; and then gave him health in the presence of criticism, thereby showing the inter-relationship between health of soul and health of body. It is Mark alone who tells us that when the leper came to meet Him at the foot of the mountain, after He had uttered the great Manifesto, He was moved with compassion. In our familiarity with some of the New Testament phrases, we are in danger of losing the sense of their value. " He was moved with compassion." Let us try and see what He saw, when He looked at that leper, in order that we may the better understand His compassion. Observe the stage of leprosy that he had reached; that strange, awful stage of cleanness, due to hopeless corruption. The law of the leper is found in Leviticus (13 and 14); and to that law our Lord referred. All the instructions given to the priest were for distinguishing between false and true leprosy, and afterwards for dealing with a man in whose case the awful fact of leprosy was established. He must be segregated in certain stages of the disease; but when at last the disease had become all whiteness, when the man was entirely a leper, then he was clean, so far as contagion was concerned, and need no longer be segregated. He might then mix again amongst men, for while the death sentence was on him, the period of contagion was over. This man was in that condition. Later on in our Lord's ministry ten lepers approached, but they did not come near Him. They stood at a distance and cried out. They were unclean lepers, in the early stages of the disease when they must be segregated. This man was in the midst of a crowd, who undoubtedly loathed him, but who were in no danger from him. He came close to Christ, with all the whiteness of the ultimate corruption upon him; no hope for him, in himself; no value in him to society. Jesus was moved with compassion, and the nature of His compassion was manifested in what followed. There is a very genuine compassion that recoils and shudders and passes on its way. It is compassion, but it is not the compassion of Christ, it is not the compassion of God! "He was moved with compassion"; but there was no contempt for the man; there was no recoil from him. There was a forward step, and the hand was laid upon him, on the whiteness of his complete corruption! Jesus was not breaking law; for the period of contagion was passed. Or even if He were so doing, He was breaking it because He was superior to law, in that within Him purity was not negative merely, but positive. There had come from that mass of corruption a plaintive, pitiful cry, "Lord, if Thou wilt, Thou canst make me clean." Immediately He advanced and touched him, and said, "I will,"—do not question My willingness;—"I will; be thou made clean." His leprosy was instantly cleansed; not healed. The New Testament never speaks of the healing of leprosy, always of cleansing, which is a profounder word.

[47]

He was then sent to the priest, sent back to the representative of that economy which was the Kingdom of God in foreshadowing, in order to obey the law of the leper. The moral and spiritual suggestiveness of that can only be discovered as the law of the leper is considered, in which in the ancient economy, if a man was cleansed of leprosy, there followed ceremonial functions that marked the necessity for sacrifice and cleansing from moral taint. Jesus said, " Go shew thyself to the priest "; thus linking the man's cleansing or health, with his spiritual cleansing or holiness. Thus without argument or statement of philosophy, Christ revealed in a flash the fact that in all His ministry He recognized the union between material suffering and limitation, and spiritual disability and corruption.

Exactly the same things are found in the second of the pictures. The Revisers say, " They uncovered the roof." Such a rendering is entirely misleading. The force of the word is that they broke up the roof of the house, tearing up the fabric, in order to lower the man down on his pallet into the presence of Jesus.

Again most carefully observe what He did. He looked into the man's eyes, and said, " Son, thy sins are forgiven." This was a word of absolution, a word of God. The Scribes were quite right when they said: "Who can forgive sins but One, even God?" They were wrong when they said: "Why doth this Man thus speak? He blasphemeth." They did not know Him. He claimed that the authority which was that of God alone, was vested in Him as the Son of Man. At that point the title " Son of Man" emerges in this Gospel. That title linked Him to other men, yet marked His relationship to God as the Self-emptied One Who laid aside the powers and attributes of Divine Sonship, and limited Himself within humanity as a perfect vehicle for the doing of the work of God. When they questioned Him, He proceeded to that which was the material result of holiness; the res-

[48]

toration to health of the bodily powers. That was the
demonstration of the fact of holiness, and so also that
the authority to forgive sins was logically vested in, and
made possible through, the Son of man. " To this end
came I forth."

In all this is seen the value of the Kenosis, or Self-
emptying of the Son of God as the condition for the redeeming activity of the fulness or Pleroma of Deity that
operated through Him. He came forth emptying Himself, and now became the instrument through which
power was proclaimed, and operated, on behalf of the
Kingdom and the Gospel.

So far as we are permitted to speak or think of Him
as the Pattern of our service—for there are limitations in
any such consideration—we may summarize the value of
this paragraph by saying that it reveals the relation between prayer and power. He was praying in the early
morning, and all the consequent influence followed upon
that prayer. Prayer is listening for God, hearing what
God has to say, consenting to what God does say, asking
of God power to obey. To neglect these things is to be
powerless when we meet the lepers, and the palsied men
of the world. God, through the self-emptied, always
pours out His fulness for the blessing of others; and
prayer is the exercise finally of self-emptying that prepares the soul, that makes us channels through which
the power of God may proceed to the accomplishment
of His purposes in the world.

"And the Pharisees went out, and straightway with the Herodians took counsel against Him, how they might destroy Him."—MARK 3:6.

Mark 2: 13–3: 6.

THIS is a singularly sad text. It is the record of the climax of a hostile movement manifest throughout the paragraph of our reading.

In our consideration of the early morning communion of Jesus with His Father after the first Sabbath in Capernaum, we turned to the prophecy of Isaiah, and saw the picture there presented of the Servant of God, wakened by His Lord to hear the secrets of His will. In that picture we saw also, the Servant of God resolutely giving His back to the smiters, and His cheek to them that plucked off the hair, going forward with courage to face all opposition in order to accomplish the will of His God. The suggestiveness of that picture of Isaiah is illustrated in the paragraph. Jesus, passing down from the place of solitude, went throughout all Galilee, followed by great multitudes of people. Mark briefly records that fact; and gives two illustrative incidents, those of the leper and the palsied man.

That ministry was exercised in the face of constant opposition. This was first manifested in the reasoning of the scribes when He pronounced the sins of the palsied forgiven. Now, following the chronological sequence, Mark records four incidents specially revealing the growth and the nature of that opposition.

Each of these incidents has values beyond those now to occupy our attention. Each conveys messages of truth concerning the Lord Himself in His dealings with men.

We propose now to observe that opposition which found its climax, as the text declares, when " the Pharisees went out, and straightway with the Herodians took counsel against Him, how they might destroy Him."

Let us then observe this opposition, in order that we may consider the attitude of Jesus in the presence thereof.

The opposition is at once clearly revealed in the four words of criticism which were uttered. Observe how these words advance to the climax of the text.

" He eateth and drinketh with publicans and sinners " (2: 16).

" Why do John's disciples and the disciples of the Pharisees fast, but Thy disciples fast not? " (2: 18).

" Why do they on the Sabbath day that which is not lawful? " (2: 24).

" They watched Him . . . that they might accuse Him " (3: 2).

The first criticism was spoken, not to the Lord, but to His disciples concerning Him. The next two words were spoken, not concerning the Lord, but to the Lord concerning His disciples, and were undoubtedly intended to reflect upon Him for the influence He had been exerting upon them. In the last sentence there is no record of any word spoken; but a graphic fact is presented. Again they were in the synagogue,—a week later, as Luke declares,—and these men were silently and malevolently watching Him to see whether He would heal, that they might accuse Him.

With regard to the first of these criticisms, the occasion was that of the call of Levi, and the feast that followed. Jesus, passing along saw Levi (or Matthew) sitting at the receipt of custom, and said to him, " Follow me." Immediately he followed Him. Whether on the same day, or later, cannot be stated with any certainty, but the fact is recorded definitely that Matthew gathered together a number of people of his own order, and made a feast that they might have the opportunity of meeting with Jesus. Our Lord is seen accepting that hospitality of Matthew, and Himself becoming a veritable Host in the midst of these men, the gathered publicans and sinners, old friends of Matthew, a class held in supreme contempt by the religious men of the time. The Pharisees charged Him with entering upon a fellowship with sinning men, which was defiling.

While recognizing the fact of the traditions by which these Pharisees were bound, it must also be recognized that theirs was a very sincere difficulty in this regard, and in all probability their philosophy was perfectly sound, had they applied it to any other than Jesus. This was one of those occasions when our Lord made Himself, without patronage and without any appearance of contempt for the men among whom He sat, the common Friend of publicans and sinners. From the criticism of the Pharisees upon this occasion, and also upon other occasions, we have a picture which is still a startling one. Jesus is seen sitting at the feast with these men, without taking up toward them anything of the attitude of superiority, patronage, or contempt. They charged Him with cultivating a friendship with sinning men which, as it seemed to them, must be defiling.

In the second of the scenes, the occasion was the observance of some fast. The tenses warrant the declaration that it was not a general question merely, but that at the time some fast was being observed, which the disciples of John and the disciples of the Pharisees observed, but which the disciples of Jesus did not observe. The enemies of Christ came to Him thus again still strangely perplexed, and asked Him a general question, which nevertheless had a particular and immediate application. They charged Him and those associated with Him, with an absence of seriousness and solemnity. There were evidences on the part of His disciples of joyfulness and happiness. They were neglecting to fast, and were rather given to feasting. That was the second criticism.

The third incident was in the cornfields. His disciples began, not to pluck merely, but as they moved forward other evangelists tell us that they rubbed the ears of corn in their hands, and ate. That was the occasion for the third criticism. They charged our Lord with permitting His disciples to do secular things on a sacred day.

. In the last picture the occasion was again a Sabbath day in the synagogue. In that synagogue was a man with a withered hand. Here occurs one of those incidental things, which are so full of beauty in these narratives. Seeking to find an accusation against Him, His enemies nevertheless all unconsciously paid Him a supreme compliment. They associated Him immediately, not with the chief seat in the synagogue, but with the most needy man in the crowd. They expected He would do something for that man with the withered hand. They hated Him, but they were quick to know Him, and they watched Him that they might have their opportunity to accuse Him.

There was a new element of rooted objection to Himself now entering into their criticism. This opposition expressed itself in the most startling way, startling because the Pharisees took counsel with the Herodians. Here were two political parties in the State, always bitterly opposed to each other, now brought together. The Herodians believed in the government of Rome, in order that Herod's jurisdiction might be maintained. The Pharisees were against the yoke of Rome. Many and bitter were the disputes and quarrels between them. But the Pharisees went out and took counsel with the Herodians; they sank their political differences in their mutual hostility to Jesus; and they took counsel how they might destroy Him.

Now let us watch the Lord, and observe His attitude toward all this opposition; how He opposed Himself, His mission, and the meaning of His ministry, against

every successive form of criticism; until when these men
went out to take counsel against Him, He withdrew, and
left them. A fourfold charge had been made against
Him; first, that of a moral carelessness, in that He sat
to eat with publicans and sinners; secondly, that of lack
of seriousness, in that He encouraged His disciples to
violate a tradition by not observing a fast; thirdly, failure
to differentiate as between the sacred and the secular, in
that He allowed His disciples to do a thing, not in itself
wrong, but purely secular, upon a sacred day, in plucking
the ears of corn; and finally, by their very silence, and
the malevolence of their intention, these men declared
their conviction of His utter worthlessness, and that He
merited destruction.

First with regard to the charge of moral carelessness,
our Lord admitted at once, by the figure of speech that
He used, the moral maladies of the men among whom
He sat that day as Guest, or among whom He sat as
Host. That is seen in the answer He gave: " They that
are whole have no need of a physician, but they that are
sick." He thus immediately revealed Himself as conscious of the spiritual and moral disease of the men
among whom He sat. His sense of evil was not less
acute than that of His enemies. This was His answer.
He knew these men, their nefarious tricks, and their gross
life. There is no doubt that there was a good deal of
ground for the opposition of the Pharisees to these men.
They were debased men. Jesus admitted their moral
maladies, and then quietly, and without any argument,
assumed for Himself the authority and the ability of the
physician.

Thus He denied the charge of moral carelessness by
declaring that He cared so much, that He was there to
cure these men of their spiritual sicknesses. He revealed
the fact that the reason why He sat familiarly at the
board and condescended to the level of these men, assuming no attitude of superiority, patronage, or of contempt,

[54]

was that He was against the very things to which the
Pharisees objected, but that He was there as the Pharisees never could be, with the healing power of the physician. He declared in effect, when they criticized Him
for moral carelessness, that there had been committed
to Him the cure of souls, and that in order to cure them,
it was necessary to come into contact with them.

Observe our Lord's method in dealing with the second
of these criticisms. I have named this the charge of lack
of seriousness. Surely this is what these men meant.
The observance of the fast was always the time of
solemnity, and fasts had been multiplied far beyond those
commanded in the Law; occasions when men wore sackcloth, put ashes upon their heads, did not anoint their
faces, and appeared in the garments of mourning, in
sorrowful and solemn silence. They were doubtless observing such a fast on this particular occasion. But the
disciples of Jesus were not wrapped in sackcloth, nor had
they scattered ashes upon their heads. They were not
abstaining from food, but were filled with gladness and
joy. When they asked the question why His disciples
did not fast, these men were thus charging Him with
failure to realize the seriousness and solemnity of life.

In reply to this criticism, He at once adopted the figure
of the wedding, spoke of Himself as the Bridegroom,
and declared that these men could never be sad while
the Bridegroom remained with them. The adoption of
the figure was in itself a vindication of the right of His
disciples to be joyful. In those Eastern lands during a
period of seven days, all the friends of the bridegroom
were full of joy and merriment and laughter and songs
and gladness. When these men questioned the disciples'
attitude toward fasting, suggesting thereby that they had
no sense of the seriousness and solemnity of life, He did
not deny it. He admitted it, and said, "As long as they
have the Bridegroom with them, they cannot fast." Then
in an aside, He recognized the fact that there were days

coming to these men when the Bridegroom should be
taken away;—lifted away, snatched away, for such is
the word, a very significant word, having in it an element
of tragedy, a suggestion of violence. The choice of the
word was in itself a recognition of the purpose which
was already in the hearts of the men who were watching
Him. There was a reference to what He knew would
be the ultimate of their hostility, His taking away, His
lifting up, and that by violent and evil men. Looking at
these men who were criticizing Him, and knowing where-
unto their hostility would grow, He said: These men will
have their day of fasting presently when the Bridegroom
is taken away from them. This declaration was an
aside, and not the declaration of a final truth, for spiritually we have no place in that sadness, for the Bridegroom
is not taken away from us. He abides with us. Therefore our whole attitude toward life should be that, not
of men who fast, but of men who sit at the eternal
feast.

Our Lord immediately proceeded to illustrate this by
the figures of the cloth and the wine skins. New cloth
cannot be put into old. It will tear it. New wine cannot be put into old skins. It will burst them. In that
word our Lord claimed that He had come to initiate an
entirely new order of religious life and experience, which
would make necessary new methods of expression; instead of the fast, the feast; instead of the sackcloth, the
purple; instead of the perpetual and solemn melancholy,
a perennial and glad joyfulness. Thus, recognizing and
understanding the meaning of their criticism of the men
who were about Him, for the gladness of their lives,
and their refusal to fast, recognizing also that days of
sorrow were coming to them, He indicated in a prophetic
and illuminative figure the fact that presently there would
be for men the joy of gladness and song, and the necessity for sackcloth would forever pass away; the sackcloth in that day would be transfigured, metamorphosed

[56]

into the purple of royalty; all the underlying reason
for the fast being destroyed, the eternal feast would
begin.

The third charge against Him was that of failure to
distinguish between sacred and secular. " Why do thy
disciples on the Sabbath day that which is not lawful? "
The plucking of the ears of corn was not wrong in itself.
The rubbing of them, and the eating of the corn, was not
sinful. The wrong as these men saw it, was that the
disciples failed, under the influence of Jesus, to distinguish between that sacred day and that secular act; and
failed to realize the fact that the sacred must ever be
kept separate from the secular; that the secular, however
proper it may be, must be left when the sacred precincts
are entered. That was their criticism. I believe that
view still holds captive a great many to-day who think
they understand Jesus Christ, and His teaching.

Let us therefore carefully see how He answered them.
Incidentally, by the illustrations He used, He recognized
the reason of His disciples' action. They were hungry,
they had need of food. " David, when he . . . was
hungry, . . . entered into the house of God . . .
and ate the shewbread . . . and gave also to them that
were with him." In that illustration there was first of
all a careful understanding and recognition of the fact
that the reason why His disciples had plucked these ears
of corn, and rubbed them and eaten them on the Sabbath
day, was that of the perfectly natural hunger of the men.
Only as we see this aspect of this story do we reach the
real teaching of Christ on this occasion.

Then, by the two illustrations which He gave, which
flashed their light upon His disciples' action, and explained that action, He revealed the falseness of the di-
visions these men were making. Man is sacred in all his
being; sacred not merely in his spiritual nature; but
sacred as certainly in his moral and mental capacities;
and sacred also in his physical life. A call for food is a

healthy call, and a healthy call is a holy call; for health and holiness are identical terms. In our perpetual use of them we have divided between material and spiritual, but we of the Anglo-Saxon tongue have derived them both from the old word Halig, which means whole, complete. A cry for food is a sign of health, therefore it is holy. Anything that the physical demands is essentially holy. The wrong of life begins when men answer a perfectly healthy call, in ways forbidden. A cry for food is holy, it is sacred! Were it not so, in the economy of God He would provide that men never become hungry on the Sabbath day. The fact that hunger crosses the threshold on the Sabbath day demonstrates its sacredness, and no man can escape from that. Our Lord recognized the sacredness of man; and then particularly, condensed into brief words the whole law of the Sabbath day. The Sabbath is indeed sacred, but wherein lies its sanctity? It is sacred because it is made for man. Man was not made for it. It was made for man, to minister to his needs. Therein lies the sanctity of the Sabbath day. The ultimate and final sanction of Sabbath observance is that of its service to humanity. It is indeed sacred. It was made for man; it retains its sanctity as it serves man.

So the Son of man, Who came not to be ministered unto but to minister, is Lord of the Sabbath; and the Sabbath must serve Him as He serves humanity, and consequently must be compelled to the service of humanity. The hunger of the disciples on the Sabbath day was healthy, was holy, and therefore the Sabbath must not be allowed to interfere with the supply of the need.

Of course all intelligent beings will discriminate between the doing of that which is the answer to a need, and the doing of that which is the answer to a desire which is not created by essential need. We must distinguish for evermore between that which is right and that which is wrong on the Sabbath day, whether it be the seventh day of the week, or the first day set apart for worship and rest.

Our Lord however answered the charge of failure to distinguish between the sacred and the secular, by enlarging the area of the sacred, and bringing into it man with all his essential needs; for the sanctity of man is the final secret of the sanctity of the Sabbath. Therefore whatever is necessary for holiness and health, is sacred as is the hour of worship, and must be observed.

Finally we look at that synagogue scene, at the antagonism which no longer finds expression in words, but which was all the more dangerous because it had become silent; the antagonism which sought an opportunity for attack, watching Him, knowing that the man with the withered hand was in the synagogue, to see if He would heal, that they might find an occasion of accusation (a legal term), in order to His arrest, and that they might encompass His destruction. How did our Lord deal with this?

Let it be observed first of all that He gave them the opportunity they sought, and healed the man. Then notice that He compelled them to face actual and startling contrasts of motive, startling even until this hour if quietly considered. Observe then, with real care, the alternatives He suggested to these men. He said to them, " Is it lawful on the Sabbath day to do good, or to do harm? to save a life, or to kill? " The startling nature of the enquiry is only revealed when we begin to ask ourselves the question. We might be inclined to say, But are we forced to that alternative? Is there not a middle position we could occupy? We do not want to do good to that man because it is the Sabbath, but sincerely we do not want to harm him. We have no desire to kill that man, but we do not feel that to-day we ought to stretch out the hand to save him. Is there not a middle position?

Christ in effect said, There is no middle position in the

face of human disability and need. We do good to the
man when he is in need, or we do him harm; we help to
save him, or we help to kill him.

It is a stern, hard, and yet necessary standard. Is it
not still a startling one? There lies the man upon the
highway that runs from Jerusalem to Jericho, bruised by
the robbers. Take up a negative position; look at him,
and pass by on the other side. The man who does so
perpetuates his pain, and is guilty of the continuity of his
suffering. In the presence of human pain, in the presence
of limitation like this, there is this one alternative. In
effect Jesus said, Which shall I do? You are watching
to accuse Me. Shall I do that man good, or shall I harm
him by leaving him for another twenty-four hours in that
limitation, when I have the power to help him? Shall I
save him or kill him? Which shall I do? His action did not
depend upon their decision. He did him good, He saved
him. By so doing He separated between Himself and
them. He did good to that man, He saved him. They,
even though it was the Sabbath day, were trying to do
Him harm, and to kill Him. Even though it was the
Sabbath, presently they crossed the synagogue threshold,
and entered into unholy coalition in order to destroy
Him. The alternatives of Heaven admit of no compro-
mises.

Thus our Lord opposed to their criticism, the real
meaning of His mission from beginning to end. He had
come for the cure of spiritual malady. He had come to
create the reason for abiding and abounding joyfulness.
He had come to enlarge the area of the sacred, and to
reveal to men that man is sacred, and that the sanctions
of all ordinances are to be found in their ministry to the
well-being of humanity. He had come to men, to save
them; not to harm and kill them.

Such a meditation as this opens the door for much investigation by way of application. Are these criticisms
ever made of us, that were made of the Lord? The

question needs safeguarding by another. If they are
made, are they made for the same reason?

Are we ever charged with moral carelessness because
we are consorting with sinners? I am constrained to say
that I believe at this very hour one of the secrets of arrest, and one of the reasons for the condition of things
in the Christian Church that is troubling us in many
ways, is the aloofness of the Christian Church from sinning men and women. We still build our sanctuaries,
and set up our standards, and institute our arrangements,
and say to the sinning ones: If you will come to us, we
will help you! The way of the Lord is to go and sit
where they sit, without patronage and without contempt.
We may run great risks if we begin to do it. If we will
dare to do it some one will say that we are consorting with
sinning men, and that we are in moral and spiritual peril.
I am afraid, however, that the Church is not often criticized on these lines.

Are we ever criticized to-day for lack of seriousness
because we are joyful in the Lord? Ah yes, we may be
criticized for lack of seriousness because we are joyful
in other ways, and I am not sure that such a criticism is
not well deserved. There is a sense in which I fear that
we do lack seriousness. These men were not glad because
they were sharing in the frivolity of an age. They were
glad because they were with Jesus. That was the gladness which made men criticize them for lack of seriousness. Are we ever so criticized to-day? How little we
really seem to know of the joy of the Lord. I asked
Dan Crawford what impressed him most forcibly when
he got back to London after twenty-three years in the
long grass of Central Africa. He said, " The fact that
London had lost its smile. I stood on the bridges, and
walked along the thoroughfares, and looked at the hurrying peoples, and they all looked so sad." Is not that also
true of the Church? Would not the fairer criticism of
those who name His name to-day be not lack of serious-

ness born of joyfulness in the Lord, but lack of joyfulness in the Lord, expressing itself in depressing seriousness in the things of life?

Once again, are we ever criticized for our failure to distinguish between the sacred and the secular, because we are sanctifying the secular? We are criticized for neglecting the Sabbath, and rightly so perchance. I cannot tell. I cannot judge. You tell me of men who spend their Sabbath, and week-ends, motoring and playing golf. I say frankly, I have nothing to do with legislating for these men. I can pity them honestly and kindly and without patronage. I can pray for them. But unless there is the expulsive power of a new affection, I do not wonder that they do it.

My trouble is not with these men outside the Christian Church. My trouble is with men inside the Christian Church. Is there a sanctification of the secular that makes other men criticize us, or are we secularizing the sacred? Along these lines of investigation I think we may profitably press forward alone; and that for the correction and inspiration of our own lives.

Or once more, are men of the world ever saying that we are worthless because we rebuke their worthlessness? That is the story of the Son of God. The very character of Christ, the very attitude of Christ, the known purpose of Christ toward that man with the withered hand, made these men hate Him. They called Him worthless because they themselves were worthless. Are we ever criticized for worthlessness for these reasons?

A real fellowship with Christ must bring us into a partnership with Him in expression and experience. If by diligence we add to faith all the things implicated therein, we shall go with Him where He goes, do with Him what He does, for our emotional nature will be mastered by His compassions. That will inevitably mean that we are misunderstood as He was, hated as He was, and persecuted as He was. But it will also mean that through us needy humanity will be served and saved, as it was through Him.

The supreme value of our meditation is that of its revelation of the glory of Christ, the Servant of God; and in proportion as we desire to serve as we should, we must come into line, in fellowship with Him:

" O Who like Thee, so calm, so bright,
    Thou Son of man, Thou Light of light!
O Who like Thee did ever go
    So patient through a world of woe!

"O Who like Thee so humbly bore
    The scorn, the scoffs of men before;
So meek, forgiving, Godlike, high,
    So glorious in humility.

"O in this light be mine to go,
    Illuming all my way of woe;
And give me ever on the road
    To trace Thy footsteps, O my God."

" He appointed twelve."—MARK 3 : 14.

Mark 3 : 7–19a.

THE opposition to the Servant of God was by no means universal, nor indeed at the time was it general. Our Lord attracted men irresistibly, and among them He exercised a ministry of mighty and prevailing power. When the coalition of Pharisees and Herodians took counsel to destroy Him, He withdrew to the sea, and here again Mark summarizes the story of very much service in a few sentences. The multitudes grew in number, and gathered from all quarters. Not only did the Galilean crowds go after Him. There were also those who had travelled north from Judæa, and among them were some from Jerusalem itself. They came moreover from Idumæa, that is from Edom; from the region beyond Jordan, that is the region usually described as Peræa; and from Tyre and Sidon. From all these places they came, the fame of Jesus having travelled far and wide; they came to hear His words, observe His works, and share in the benefits which He was so lavishly conferring upon men. Those with plagues pressed upon Him, in order that they might touch Him, and receive His healing; wherever He went, unclean spirits recognizing His presence, confessed Him Son of God, only to be silenced and cast out from their possession of men. In order to escape a while from the pressure of these crowds, He secured a little boat from which, in all probability, He taught the people, and in which He may have sailed away to some other place. That, I think, is the inference of the story.

At this juncture He selected His apostles. Going up

into a mountain He called twelve from among His disciples. This was action in advance, preparatory to a
wider ministry, before the hour of His arrest and passion.
Hostility had manifested itself to Him in Judæa, and
He had left that region when John was imprisoned, and
had begun His ministry in Galilee. Hostility manifested
itself to Him in Nazareth, as He passed on His way to
Capernaum. In Capernaum itself it had already been
manifested when the scribes and Pharisees criticized Him
for forgiving sins, and it had grown until now the Pharisees and Herodians were taking counsel to destroy Him.
He knew that the hour would come when they would be
successful, for that was by the determinate counsel and
foreknowledge of God; and ere that hour arrived He
would increase the scope of His own ministry. This He
did by calling into yet closer coöperation with Himself a
certain number of men in order that they might exercise
an immediate ministry, and thus be prepared for that
larger ministry which should follow His exodus, and the
coming of the Holy Spirit.

The story then of this paragraph is full of value in
this matter of His appointment of some within the circle
of discipleship, to special relationship with Himself, and
to special service in fellowship with Himself. Already
all His disciples were witnesses to Him. Those who had
yielded their allegiance were those who spread His fame
far and wide as they told the story of what He had done
for them. It was His intention, as we know full well,
that to the end of time all His disciples should be witnesses for Him. Nevertheless, it was necessary, within
the circle of those earliest disciples, to call some into
special relationship, and into special fellowship in service.

Let us observe three things; first, His election of the
twelve, " He calleth unto Him whom He Himself would:
and they went unto Him "; secondly, His appointment of
those whom He elected, " He appointed them that they
might be with Him, and that He might send them forth

to preach, and to have authority to cast out demons";
and finally, His distinctions within the circle of the
twelve; three He surnamed, and the rest He did not.

First then as to this matter of our Lord's election of
the twelve. I have most resolutely chosen the word
" election " for it brings us face to face with the central
fact, a fact which is of supreme importance. The words
of Mark read thus, " He goeth up into the mountain, and
calleth unto Him whom He Himself would, and they
went unto Him." Now if we put that statement into the
order of its procedure, we must begin at the centre first,
" Whom He Himself would "; secondly, " He calleth unto
Him," that is those already chosen; and finally, " they
went unto Him," that is those chosen and called.

" Whom He Himself would "; that is, those whom He
preferred. The word suggests an active option resulting
from a subjective impulse. There is another word in
our New Testament which might be translated in the
same way, but which does not at all mean the same thing.
There is a verb which we translate " to will " which suggests passive acquiescence, the decision of the mind
which is the result of objective considerations, the thought
being that of disposition toward a certain action as the
result of facts without. That is not the word of Mark
here. This word suggests self-determining sovereignty,
choice based upon reason within personality. " Whom
He Himself would." He was entirely uninfluenced by
temporary appeals. No appeal that any man might have
made to Him would have influenced Him in the least.
No protests of inability that any man might have suggested would have changed His purpose. His choosing
was choosing from within, the choosing of His own
sovereignty; a choosing therefore in which He assumed
all responsibility for what He did. " He called unto Him
twelve, whom He Himself would." That is the fundamental fact.

His choice proceeded out of His infinite wisdom and

understanding. When He called them, it was not because they had asked to be called; and when He called them, there was no room for protests of inability. He assumed responsibility.

Those whom He Himself had thus chosen He called unto Himself, and by that call first set them free from all responsibility; and secondly, imposed upon them serious responsibility. He set them free from all responsibility. If there were any mistake, He made it. They were not responsible. If there were defects in them, He must deal with them and remedy them. They were not responsible. They did not choose to be His apostles, and at the last, in the Paschal discourses He said to them with infinite tenderness, and yet with wonderful illumination, "Ye did not choose me, but I chose you, and appointed you, that ye should go and bear fruit, and that your fruit should abide." That was surely a word of infinite comfort to those men to the end of their ministry. There is an infinite ease in doing things He gives us to do, when we can say to Him, Lord, we did not choose this. Thou art responsible!

And yet that call brought them into a place of very definite and real responsibility. It called them to confidence in the wisdom of His choice. How much these men must have needed this, in subsequent hours of fear and failure, of faltering and denial. It called them also to obedience to His commands, and therefore to yield to His power.

Think of the comfort of all this. Truly it was a strange and mixed group of men; not many mighty, not many wise; some of them full of that human force which compels attention, some of them unobtrusive and willing to be obscure. Yet they were His choice, and He chose them in the interest of the work. He had chosen them because they already had powers which He needed. He had chosen them because they were capable of appropriating the power He supplied.

[Mark 3: 7–19a]

In his *Theological Essays* R. H. Hutton has this most interesting paragraph:

"The chosen apostles themselves misunderstand and misinterpret their Master. Peter, after being told that his confession is the rock on which the Church should be built, is spoken of as a tempter and an offence to his Master, as one who savours not of the things which are of God, but of those which are of men. John is twice rebuked, once for his revengeful spirit, once for his short-sighted ambition. Judas's treachery is predicted. All the twelve are warned that they will fail at the hour of Christ's trial, and that warning, like the more individual prediction addressed to Peter, is certainly most unlikely to have been conceived after the event. In a word, from beginning to end of the Gospels, we have evidence which no one could have managed to forge, that Christ deliberately chose materials of which it would have been impossible for any one to build a great organization, unless he could otherwise provide, and continue to provide, the power by which that organization was to stand."

All that is true. When He chose those men He did indeed choose men utterly inadequate to the doing of His work, knowing that He Himself could empower them to do it; but it is also true that He chose men in whom there were capacities which He would sanctify and employ. That is a principle never to be forgotten. I sometimes hear it said that God chooses men entirely unfitted for certain work by nature, and fits them by grace. I deny it absolutely. There is no such discord between God's original creation of a man, and His use of him for the purposes of His work. How often have I heard it said that D. L. Moody was a man with no natural gift of speech. I deny it. Those who knew Moody best would agree that had he never been a Christian man he would yet have been a master of assemblies, an orator, sweeping and swaying men by the force of his natural eloquence. Upon that capacity God fastened, sanctified it, cleansed it, filled it with the true fire, gave him the godly vision, and made him the mightiest evangelist of the last century.

So, when our Lord chose these men, He chose them, knowing His power and their powers; and knowing that in the fact of their cession to Him, and His cession of Himself to them in the Spirit's fellowship, He had found the men best suited to the doing of His work.

Let us proceed to consider what Mark tells us concerning the appointment of the men thus elected. He appointed them to two things; first to be with Him; and secondly that He might send them forth to preach and to have authority to cast out demons.

The first was initial, preparatory, fundamental, necessary. He appointed them to be with Him. The immediate application of the words undoubtedly was, that He called them at this time in some senses—all the details of which we cannot explain, for we have no record—into closer association with Himself. He called them to a special training which was to consist of more intimate nearness to Himself. I am inclined to think that from this hour, He spent a great deal of time in private with them, gave Himself to them more completely than He had done before, and began that process which was so marked in the latter part of His ministry, of withdrawing Himself from the multitudes, and devoting Himself more and more to them. He appointed them to be with Him.

This, however, does not for a moment exhaust the meaning of the phrase. The very preposition made use of is illuminative. The preposition *with* indicates the very closest association, an association which inevitably and invariably issues in resemblance, and consequently in true instrumentality. They became men through whom He could act unhindered. In the mystic mystery of Pentecost they became actual members of His body, mastered by His intelligence, driven by His emotions, governed by His volitions. In this sense also He appointed them to be with Him.

[69]

In the last great prayer of Christ He made use of this same preposition several times. First, "And now, Father, glorify Thou Me *with* Thine own Self, *with* the glory which I had *with* Thee before the world was." That threefold use of that particular preposition illuminates its value in my text, " He appointed them to be *with* Him." Again, " While I was *with* them, I kept them in Thy name which Thou hast given Me: and I guarded them, and not one of them perished, but the son of perdition." And yet once more: " Father, I desire that they also whom Thou hast given Me be with Me where I am; that they may behold My glory, which Thou hast given Me."

I know how unsafe it may be to build doctrines upon prepositions, but there is much of suggestiveness in this; and in our Lord's use of this one in that great prayer, we have a revelation of union with His Father, of His giving of Himself to His disciples in the days of His flesh, and of His perpetual purpose for them that they should be with Him to behold His glory not in heaven only, but here in travail with Him, and presently in triumph.

Having appointed them to be with Him, He appointed them also to go forth to preach and to have authority to cast out demons. In a flash their relationship to Himself, to men, and to the underworld of evil is revealed. Their relationship to Himself was that He appointed them as His apostles. Originally the word means those who are set apart. Resultantly it means those who are sent forth. The suggestiveness of the word is that He only sends forth those whom He has set apart. This was their relationship to Himself. Wherever they went, and whatever they did, and whatever they said, they were His apostles, set apart to Him, and in the power of that setting apart, sent forth.

They were sent forth to preach. The word made use of here suggests that preaching which is the work of the herald. It was a common word in the Greek language,

and from Homer was used to describe the work of the
messengers of kings, magistrates, princes, military com-
manders, those vested with public authority. The word
always suggests formality, gravity, an authority that must
be listened to and obeyed. He sent that strange group
of men, so mixed and so varied and so lacking in strength
and wisdom, to preach.

He sent them, moreover, to have authority over demons; authority, not power; power was always His.
They had authority to speak in His name, so that His
power might become operative for the casting out of
demons, and the mastery of the underworld of evil.

He *appointed* them, and the very word made use of
here is poetic and beautiful with the poetry and the
beauty of Greece. Paul writing his Ephesian letter, said,
" We are His workmanship." That is the same root idea,
and might be translated, We are His poems. His work
is always a thing of beauty and a thing of use. His ap-
pointments are of the same character. Their appointment was infinitely more than official. It was an enabling.
His appointment is His workmanship.

This was the secret of strength in both applications.
He appointed them to be with Him, and because He appointed them to be with Him, they must be fitted for the
fellowship. Because He appointed them to service, they
must be strengthened for the service, difficult as it inevitably would be.

Thus we come to the last matter, one of interest and
suggestiveness, that of His distinctions. He surnamed
three of them, Peter and James and John. Our word
surnamed is the translation of a phrase, which quite literally means He imposed a name upon them; the phrase
itself suggesting a naming indicative of His authority,
and the outcome of their character.

With His naming of Peter, we are all familiar. It has
been the subject of many a consideration. He surnamed
him prophetically when He first met him. That was

Peter's introduction to Jesus. It came in that hour when Jesus, looking into his eyes said, " Thou art Simon the son of John: thou shalt be called rock." Later at Cæsarea Philippi, when Peter made his great confession, Jesus looked again into his eyes and said, " Blessed art thou, Simon son of Jonah." He named him rock—the symbol of strength and solidity—the most changeable and vacillating man among them.

Now let it be observed that He did not name him something that he could not be. There was no contradiction of the true nature of this man in this name. It was a contradiction of the experience of the man, but not of his nature. Peter stands out on the New Testament page as the elemental man, the man in whom all elemental forces were found. He was a man of intellectual strength; a man of emotion; a man of marvellous volitional powers; strong-willed and yet weak and frail; all the elemental forces there, but lacking cohesion, consistency, because lacking a principle, which would weld them into strength. To him Jesus said, I have chosen you, Simon, and I have appointed you to be with Me, and to preach, and to cast out demons, and I impose a name upon you that will indicate what you will become. Peter would never have become rock apart from Christ, but the capacities that became rock were in his nature. What Christ did was to take hold of the elemental capacities which were in him by his first birth, and by supplying the one thing he lacked, to weld them into strength.

James and John He surnamed Boanerges. Now it is generally imagined that Jesus called these men Boanerges because of what they were. As a matter of fact, exactly the same principle obtained in their case, as in that of Peter. He named them for what He would make them, Boanerges, sons of Thunder; a poetic description of force and high enthusiasm. The capacities were there, and yet how different these brothers were. John was poet, dreamer, visionary. Of James we know little, and in that fact there is a revelation of the man; he was quiet and retiring. Christ saw the capacities of the men, and named them Boanerges, sons of Thunder. James, when for loyalty to his Lord, he yielded himself and died by the sword of Herod; and John, when in the Isle of Patmos, he saw his visions and wrote, were true sons of Thunder.

There were a number not surnamed. Some of them we know. Andrew, the first enquirer; Philip, the first whom Jesus really called; Bartholomew, undoubtedly Nathanael, the guileless; Matthew, the publican. Here are also some new names. We have not met them before in our study of this Gospel. Thomas, we shall find him presently, the magnificent sceptic; another James, about whom we know nothing; Thaddæus or Jude, whom we shall hear speak once in the upper room; Simon the Canaanean, that is, the Zealot, a member of a very troublesome political party who had now become a Christian and doubtless would bring his enthusiasm into Christianity, as he ought to do. That is all we know about these men.

Yes, but there is one other, a tragic figure, Judas. As the rest, he was chosen, called, appointed to be with Him and to preach and to have power over demons. And as God is my witness I hardly know how to speak of this thing, this appallingly solemn fact that He appointed one to be with Him who never by any means came into that close and mystic association which was his appointment; appointed one to preaching, whose preaching if it ever began, ceased, and changed into betrayal; that He appointed one to cast out demons, who so failed to respond, that Satan entered into him. I do not think any words of mine are necessary. The appalling fact is one to be faced alone; and I resolutely leave it there for myself when I am alone, for you when you are alone.

The same Lord is still directly, immediately, choosing, calling, appointing. We cannot choose to be His apostles.

We must be His chosen, or we can never serve. I cannot choose to be a missionary or a Christian minister. I must be chosen. The restfulness of this consideration lies in the fact that His choices are right choices, and that His calls are vindications. If He has called me I know it, and if He has called me, He has chosen me.

Every day I live I wonder more why He called me; but I know He did, and therein is my rest, my peace.

Now for a solemn enquiry. I have emphasized the fact that none can choose to be minister or missionary. He must choose. This, however, leads on to the solemn enquiry as to whether perchance He has called and chosen, and there has not been obedience. I think this is a question that young men should be asking very seriously today everywhere. I cannot go to young men and ask them to become missionaries. They cannot choose to be ministers or missionaries. But I can and I do ask them whether the call has come to them. It may have come in some early morning hour of quiet communion, or in the appalling solemnity of some great convocation of the people of God; and yet they may have been busy ever since trying to persuade themselves that it was no call, listening to the voices of time and of the world and of earthly advantage.

Young men, my brothers within the Christian Church, young women, my sisters within the Christian Church, you cannot elect to serve. But if He has elected and called you, how solemn the responsibility that rests upon you. I pray you, be of good cheer, for if He calls it is because He has chosen, and your responsibility is only that of yielding. He is responsible. If it is a mistake it is His mistake. If there are difficulties in you, He knows them, He is responsible, He will deal with them. Blessed be God, He is able to deal with them; for He takes the weak things to confound the mighty, and the foolish to bring to naught the wise, and the things that are not, in order that He may destroy the things that are.

[74]

VII

"And He cometh into a house."—MARK 3 : 19b.

Mark 3 : 19b–35.

THESE words separate and connect two paragraphs, the first recording the special setting apart of the twelve, and the second telling of some things following thereupon.

The twelve had been chosen, called, and appointed by the Lord. They were now to be with Him in a new and special sense before being sent forth to preach and to have authority to cast out demons. From this time there was most evidently a deeper note in His teaching, and His operations brought out into greater clearness the forces which were against Him, and His power over them. From this point in the narrative of Mark, to the sixth verse of the sixth chapter, (after which follows the account of the sending forth of the twelve), we find recorded, in sequence, some of the events in which these twelve were " with Him."

After the solemn ordination on the mountain, the Lord and the twelve entered a house, probably still that of Simon and Andrew, which He seems to have made His home and headquarters. The marginal reading of the Revised Version, suggesting that these words should be translated, "And He cometh home," is indeed an illuminative one, for the phrase literally translated is, " He cometh into house "; not *the* house, or *a* house, but *into hŏuse*. It is a phrase suggesting the idea of home. The Greek word here translated " house " is one never used of a building merely. It was always used of a building inhabited; sometimes of the Temple as inhabited by God, sometimes of the dwellings of men as inhabited by men.

So the suggestion here is that He came home, and immediately the crowds congregated, and their demands were such that He and His disciples could not so much as eat bread. In that statement of Mark, there is a wonderful revelation, first of the attractiveness of Jesus; and then also, of His self-surrender. Wherever He was, they came with their sick and suffering, their sad and sorrowing; and He gave Himself to them.

Mark has not recorded for us all that transpired at that time. Other of the evangelists give more of His teaching. But Mark has given us the account of two matters which illustrate the opposition which Jesus encountered, on the one hand from His friends, well-meaning but nevertheless opposition; and on the other hand from His foes, by no means well-meaning, and quite definitely hostile.

It is important, therefore, in order to an intelligent study of the story that we observe the method of Mark, and the order of events. He records the fact that His friends, hearing of His doings, started out to find Him, and to put Him under restraint (verses 20, 21). This is a reference, undoubtedly, to His mother and His brethren. The literal translation of the words rendered " His friends " is, " They who were from beside Him "; that is, those who were related to Him. They, hearing of the unstintedness of His giving of Himself to the crowding multitudes, said, " He is beside Himself "; and they started to find Him, and to restrain Him; started probably from Nazareth, whither the news of Him and of His immediate activities had reached.

In the meantime, while they travelled toward Capernaum, both Matthew and Luke state that, there in the house, He healed a demoniac—Mark making no reference to the healing—and that gave occasion for the criticism of Himself and His work by the Jerusalem scribes, in which they declared that He had Beelzebub, and that by the prince of the demons He cast out demons. Then in the midst of His teaching, consequent upon that criticism, His mother and His brethren arrived. Matthew says "While He was yet speaking" His mother and His brethren came.

Let us observe then, the opposition which this paragraph reveals; dealing first with the opposition of His foes as revealed in the criticism of the Pharisees; and then with the opposition of His friends as revealed in the hour when His mother and His brethren arrived.

We have observed in a previous study the opposition that was offered to our Lord in Galilee. The first manifestation was in the house at Capernaum, when He had said to a man, "Thy sins are forgiven," they said, "He blasphemeth: who can forgive sins but One, even God." This was a perfectly sincere criticism, entirely justified if He had been such as they thought Him, merely a human teacher. None can forgive sins save God. That was the first manifestation of opposition.

The second manifestation was in Levi's house, when they criticized Him for consorting with sinners; and again, through His disciples, because they had not observed the fasts.

Then followed the opposition in the cornfields, when they charged His disciples with breaking the Sabbath as they plucked the ears of corn on their journey.

That opposition culminated with the scene in the synagogue when they watched Him that they might accuse Him, and He gave them the opportunity they sought, as He healed the man with a withered hand. The result of that healing was that of the coalition between Pharisees and Herodians, and their taking counsel together, how they might destroy Him.

In the interval between the hour when that coalition was formed and this, great things had taken place. Multitudes had come from north, south, and east, from all the country side, and had followed Him. Great wonders had been wrought, and the special note which Mark perpetually emphasizes, and to which we shall come for more particular consideration a little later on, was that of His power over evil spirits. There had been special and persistent exorcisms in the course of our Lord's ministry.

Before thinking of the criticism offered and the opposition manifested, it is well that we remind ourselves that nothing new had taken place. Only one more demon was cast out, one more man healed, restored; there had been one other putting forth of power, not in violation of order, but for the restoration of order on the part of our Lord. Therefore in the criticism of the Pharisees at this point we discover no criticism proceeding honestly against some new difficulty, but criticism proceeding out of the hatred for the Lord which had taken possession of their hearts. They had been watching for the opportunity. These Jerusalem scribes now uttered their criticism.

Observe with care, moreover, in the reading of the story that their criticism was twofold. It is important to see this, because our Lord answered the two parts of that criticism quite distinctly. The form of the statement by Mark makes this quite clear. They said, " He hath Beelzebub," and, " By the prince of the demons casteth He out the demons." Their criticisms declared first something concerning Himself, and secondly something concerning His work. As to Himself, they said, " He hath Beelzebub." As to His work, that particular work which He had been doing in the casting out of the demons, they said, " By the prince of the demons casteth He out the demons."

In our Lord's reply He dealt first with the second part of their criticism, that of His work; and secondly and most solemnly, with the first part of their criticism, that of Himself.

There is no need that we should dwell at any great length upon their criticism. They said, " He hath Beelzebub." The exact significance of that word Beelzebub it is impossible to decide. It may have meant quite simply "the lord of the house," a reference to the whole underworld of evil, and to the presidency over that underworld of one master. In that case it meant quite simply, "the lord of the demons," and was synonymous with the description that follows, "the prince of the demons." Translated, by a common use, it may have meant "the dung-god." The general meaning is plain. They declared that Jesus was possessed by, and under the mastery of, Satan; that He was acting in league with one who was the source of all uncleanness. They charged Him with being possessed by an evil spirit, supreme in uncleanness, the master and fountainhead of everything that was impure.

From that criticism of Himself to the criticism of His work was an easy stage, the second being a sequence of the first. "By the prince of the demons casteth He out the demons." This was indeed a subtle word. They declared, in effect, that in all these exorcisms He was trifling with men and with evil spirits for personal ambition. They declared that there was no beneficence in His activities, no compassion in the things that He was doing; that He was not casting out evil spirits because He compassionated the men whom they possessed, but that He was acting in the realm of which He was a native, the underworld of uncleanness. In order to attract attention to Himself, and so to gain for Himself some passing popularity, He was trifling with men, and was trifling even with that very underworld of evil.

We turn then to the answer of Jesus, and look at Him, listen to Him, as the Servant of God, as He is supremely set forth in these stories. Dealing first with the second part of their criticism, that of His work, He answered them negatively and positively, showing first the falseness of their philosophy; and secondly making quite clear the secret of His own power.

Showing first the falseness of their philosophy, He de-

clared the folly of their suggestion. They understood the
motive of Satan, personal aggrandisement and ambition;
but they were ignorant of his devices; they did not know
his method. When they suggested that Satan was trifling
with the underworld for purposes of personal aggrandisement, they were entirely ignorant of his methods. Our
Lord's words—so familiar that we may miss the pro-
fundity of their philosophy—revealed His perfect knowledge of the subtlety of His foe. He reminded them that
Satan does not fight against Satan, for in so doing he
would bring his kingdom to an end, and would frustrate
the purpose of his own ambition. If a house be divided
against itself it cannot stand, and perchance in that very
employment of the word " house " He was remembering
the significance of what they had said, that He was in
league with the lord of the house of evil. A house divided against itself cannot stand. " If Satan hath risen
up against himself, and is divided, he cannot stand, but
hath an end." So He immediately showed the folly of
their suggestion in that while assuming the motive underlying the mastery of the underworld of evil, they were entirely ignorant of the devices of Satan.

By that reply, moreover, the whole underworld of evil
is set in the light. There came a day when Paul the
apostle wrote, " We are not ignorant of his devices."
These men were ignorant of the devices of Satan. But
these devices were dragged into the light, and made clear
before the eyes of men by the very ministry of our Lord.
This is one instance in which we see Christ revealing the
fact that through these very men Satan was attempting
to deceive men about his own methods, in order ultimately to hold them within his grasp. In their suggesting
that Satan himself had been working the wonders of demon exorcism he was deceiving men as to his devices.
The earnestness and clarity of our Lord's reply was intended to silence opposition; and for evermore to set out
in clear outline, the revelation of the fact that at the heart

of evil is a perpetual untruth, and that Satan will for evermore proceed upon the basis of the lie that deceives and slanders men, and that slanders God.

He did not, however, leave His answer to this criticism at that point. In words, the ultimate value of which we shall only refer to, He declared the secret of His victories. Using a parable, He said that the strong man armed can only be defeated by one who is stronger than he. In that picture our Lord claimed that He was stronger than the strong man armed. The strong man armed is Satan himself, the master of the underworld of evil, holding its hosts of opposition under his control. But the One upon Whom they had been looking, to Whom they had been listening, Whose works they had been discussing, against Whom their hearts were now moving in hatred, because they were unable to understand Him, and were not honest enough to follow Him, claimed in that hour to be stronger than the strong man armed; and declared that every exorcism that He wrought was the result of His power, which was superior to the whole underworld of evil.

Then passing to the first part of their criticism which was far the more serious, He uttered these words which are so full of appalling solemnity: "Verily I say unto you, All their sins shall be forgiven unto the sons of men, and their blasphemies wherewith soever they shall blaspheme; but whosoever shall blaspheme against the Holy Spirit hath never forgiveness, but is guilty "—suffer a change in the word " guilty "—" is held by an age-abiding sin"; and therefore cannot be forgiven. We have no reason whatever to imagine that these men had committed that sin, but they were in the danger-zone, they were approaching the sin.

Let us approach the meaning of our Lord here by an ordinary, every-day illustration. The ultimate sin which any man commits against his brother is that of the mis-interpretation of his motive. The one sin against my brother that can never know forgiveness is that I wilfully misinterpret his motive. If we could but remember that, from how many blunders should we be saved! A man may criticize my method, he may show how my action does not harmonize with my profession. I may attempt to show him how his method does not harmonize with his profession. I may say of this man, who in the political or religious world differs from me, that I hold his policy to be entirely wrong, but I have no right to say that his motive is impure or unholy or wrong. God is the God of motive. By Him alone are motives measured and weighed.

If this is a superlative fact in the realm of human interrelationships, then we begin to see what was happening here, and why our Lord's words were so severe. They were now attempting to account for His motive; they were invading that inner, secret, lonely, holy sanctuary of the reason why He did what He was doing. They did what men always do when they invade that sanctuary. They carried into it their own pollutions, their own distorted senses of values; and all unconsciously they read into the reason of the doings of Jesus, the reason that was prompting them at the moment. They, and not He, were in league with the devil. It is almost always so. I very rarely hear a man criticize the motive of another man without being at least suspicious that he is attributing to the other man the inspiration of his own activities.

These men had now invaded that realm. All their previous opposition had been against Himself, as to His methods, but this invaded the realm of motive where in His case the Holy Spirit was supreme. He had taken no journey and sought no rest, He had eaten no meal save in communion with God the Holy Spirit. He had healed no sick soul save as the result of unutterable and inexpressible anguish, the anguish of God which atones for human guilt. He had cast out no demons save by the finger of God. When these men suggested that the

motive of His activity was that of league with unutterable filthiness, with the source and origin of all uncleanness, can we wonder that—not on His own behalf, but
on behalf of eternal right, and the principles that must
constitute the foundations of the Kingdom of God,—He
made a protest so severe and so solemn. They were in
the danger-zone, approaching a blasphemy against the
Holy Spirit, which is only committed by men who have
so yielded themselves to the mastery of unholy things,
that they fail to detect good when they see it, and so
attribute the results produced to a deeper evil, and declare that the producer is in partnership with Beelzebub.
That is eternal sin, which in the nature of it never can be
changed, and consequently for which there never can be
forgiveness. We have no reason to believe these men
had committed that sin in its finality, but they were coming into its region. Our Lord at that moment was looking on, as He ever was, to His larger day of ministry, to
that ministry which should succeed His Cross, Resurrection, Ascension, and Pentecost, to that ministry in the
midst of which we live our lives; rejoicing in the fact
of the wider and more intimate and marvellous ministry
that followed Pentecost, more intimate and more marvellous than that of the days of His flesh. Jesus lifted His
eyes, and looking to those days when the Spirit should be
poured in fulness upon men who should continue His
work in spiritual power and without geographical limitations, said, In that hour it will be possible for men to
sin a sin for which there shall be no forgiveness.

We now pass on to look at the opposition of His
friends. Quite literally, as we have said, the phrase " His
friends " means " they that were from beside Him."
Wycliffe translated with great accuracy, " His kinsmen ";
and Tyndale, employing a colloquialism of the time, " they
that belonged unto Him," His own blood relations, undoubtedly His mother and His brethren.

It is interesting to observe in passing that this is the

first appearance of Mary since Cana, when Jesus had said to her, What is there between thee and Me; and indicated that there were things in Himself that she did not apprehend at the time. This is also the first appearance of His brethren since they travelled with Him from Cana to Capernaum in that early year of His ministry. Now they are seen coming to Him. Their complaint was that He was beside Himself. This was their interpretation of the ceaselessness of His activity. Their criticism was not directed against the particular work He was doing, but that He was doing so much. They were not concerned as to His motive. That, they were not questioning. They were there believing that One Who would so give Himself to great motives as to have no time for eating or rest, must be beside Himself, and their intention was one of solicitude. They wanted to save Him, to restrain Him. In that spirit they travelled; how far we do not know; perchance from Nazareth. So far as we have any right to measure the emotion of Jesus by our emotion,—and we have some right, for He entered into our humanity—this opposition was surely harder to bear than the opposition of the Jerusalem scribes; more difficult to contend with. One was an opposition resulting from malice; the other, opposition resulting from love; the first that of those who were against Him because they were out of harmony with His purity; the second that of those who would try and save Him from folly, and take care of Him.

Jesus looked round about upon the twelve; upon those men who were with Him. Think what He saw. All the subsequent story will reveal it. He saw one man who, mastered by fear and saved by cowardice would swear in the darkness of the night that he did not know anything about Him; and He saw ten others who in the ultimate hours of His agony would run away. But He saw men who in the deepest fact of their lives—that very realm of motive—were consecrated to God and to Him.

He saw all the possibilities of failure and knew how they were all to work out. But He found that central fact, the motive; He invaded that realm which none other could invade, and He said, Behold My brethren, born for My adversity. Behold My sisters, born for all sweet confidences and sympathy. Behold My mother, born for all comfort and solace. " For whosoever shall do the will of God, the same is my brother, and sister, and mother."

He thus revealed a spiritual relation so high as to be infinitely above the affinity of blood relationship. He declared that in these men He found His true comfort and solace; not in those who tried to save Him from the unceasing pressure of the path of duty, but in those who were going to tramp the pathway with Him; and who, even if for a little while they would leave Him, would come back again, and presently count it all joy that they were considered worthy to suffer shame for His Name. To this high relationship Mary and His brethren also came after a while, but not immediately.

Our Lord has passed beyond this opposition now, even with regard to His earthly ministry. In the light of the accumulating and accumulated testimony of two millenniums, no sane critic to-day suggests that He was in league with the devil; or that He was mad. Oh! there are other ways of dealing with the difficulties now. They get rid of the devil, and get rid of these stories of exorcisms! Yet mark it well, for it is a significant and valuable fact, that when those who are unable to believe the things that some of us verily do believe, when they have sifted and attempted to destroy the documents, the Lord emerges, and they still hold Him in reverence, and suggest no complicity with Satan and no madness.

But the principle of opposition revealed persists against His disciples to-day. The first of these lines of criticism is rarely if ever boldly advanced. We are not often charged definitely with being in complicity with the devil. But the same thought is subtly suggested even to-day

when it is affirmed that the motive of Christian service
is self-aggrandisement.

The second is more subtle, and is more persistent.
Our friends still say " He is beside himself." What a remarkable fact it is that even within the Christian Church,
ties of blood relationship constitute terrible hindrances to
Christian service. Men to-day never seem to think that
out-and-out, passionate, and sacrificial devotion, suggests
madness in any realm, except that of the spiritual. No
man suggests that the scientist, so devoted to his science
that he will give himself to its operations and shorten his
life, is beside himself. No one suggests that the soldier
who gives himself to the high places of the field, and
sacrifices life in the interests of his country, is beside
himself. No man thinks that the explorer who shortens
life by his intrepid daring is beside himself. No one
imagines that the commercial man who is so devoted to
the amassing of wealth that he shortens life, is beside
himself. No! this suggestion is still retained for those
who make their service for the souls of men sacrificial.

Let all such be comforted. They are in holy comradeship! At the same time let them endeavour resolutely to
be of the number of those who have the highest affinity
with the Son of man, because they are devoted to the
will of God; who will not try to hinder Him in sacrificial
service, or to save themselves therefrom, but walking
with Him the rough road, will find larger life in the
shortening of the present.

VIII

Mark 4: 1-34.

As the text suggests, our theme is that of the parabolic
teaching of the Lord. This is the special subject of the
first thirty-four verses in the fourth chapter of Mark.
The whole paragraph contains three parables of the Kingdom: those of the Sower, the Development from the
Blade to the Full Corn, and the Mustard Seed. The
paragraph opens and closes with declarations that our
Lord employed the parabolic method. " He taught them
many things in parables." " With many such parables
spake He the word unto them, as they were able to hear
it: and without a parable spake He not unto them; but
privately to His own disciples He expounded all things."

In the course of the paragraph there are two sections
dealing with the reason and purpose of that method
(verses 10–12 and 21–25). The first of these explana-
tory passages is somewhat obscure and creates a difficulty.
I propose, then, first to state the difficulty; secondly, to
consider it with some care; in order that thirdly and
finally, we may make some deductions from our study.

The difficulty is caused by the way in which Mark records the fact that our Lord employed this parabolic
method. It is quite evident that at this point in His
ministry our Lord adopted this method as He had never
done before in His dealing with the multitudes. From
this time to the end of His public ministry He followed
it almost exclusively. Prior to this time He had upon
occasion made use of what may be described as parabolic
illustrations. For instance, when speaking to the woman

of Samaria, He referred to the water of life springing up unto age-abiding life. Again in the same connection He spoke to His disciples of fields white to harvest. At Nazareth He made use of the parabolic proverb, " Physician, heal thyself." To His disciples He had said, " I will make you to become fishers of men." In the course of the great Manifesto He had employed the parabolic symbolism of salt, light, and house-building.

The first full parable that Jesus ever uttered—all three evangelists agreeing—was that of the Sower. Recognizing the fact, then, that we are now at the parting of the ways in the method of His ministry so far as the outside world was concerned, and that from here to the end, when addressing Himself to the multitudes, He spoke in parables—as Mark specifically declares, " without a parable spake He not unto them "—it is pertinent that we should inquire concerning the reason of this method, in order to the following of our Lord upon the pathway of His public ministry as revealed in Mark.

Let us further prepare for our inquiry by reminding ourselves of the nature of the hour in the ministry of Jesus, and the condition of affairs in which He was now situated.

It was the hour when opposition was becoming far more definite and hostile. We have observed the growth of that opposition. In the Galilean ministry it was first manifested in the house at Capernaum when He forgave sins, and the scribes challenged Him, saying, Who is this that forgiveth sins? None can forgive sins save God. Then in the house of Levi He was criticized for consorting with sinners, and for permitting His disciples to neglect the ceremonial fasts. Later in the cornfields He was criticized for permitting His disciples to pluck the ears of corn for the satisfaction of their hunger. On another Sabbath in the synagogue He healed the man with a withered hand, and the result was that Pharisees and Herodians took counsel together how they might destroy Him. Yet once more, and finally, in the house at Capernaum they had definitely declared that He had Beelzebub, and that by the prince of the demons He cast out the demons; and He had answered them with words among the most solemn that ever fell from His lips.

Our Lord was exercising His ministry in the midst of this atmosphere of growing hostility and opposition, coming from the rulers, but undoubtedly affecting the multitudes that were still gathering about Him. We have seen how He looked at those men in the synagogue, and that He was filled with anger as He looked at them, the reason of His anger being that He was "grieved at the hardening of their heart." That is a most significant declaration in its application to our present study. They were hardening their hearts against Him, and at this point He began to use the parable definitely, and of set purpose.

This brings us immediately to the difficult passage. " When He was alone "—separated from the multitudes " they that were about Him with the twelve asked of Him the parables. And He said unto them, Unto you is given the mystery of the Kingdom of God: but unto them that are without, all things are done in parables: that seeing they may see, and not perceive; and hearing they may hear, and not understand; lest haply they should turn again, and it should be forgiven them."

No careful student of that passage has read it without at some time feeling the difficulty of it. This difficulty lies in its apparent meaning, which is that the Lord adopted the parabolic method in order that these people might see and not see, might hear and not hear, lest they should turn, and should be forgiven.

There have been two methods of dealing with that difficulty. Devout, earnest, sincere, and loyal expositors of the passage have declared that this is true; that even though we cannot understand it, and may find ourselves in revolt against it; not upon the basis of our own reason, but because it is out of harmony with the whole revelation of God in Christ, we must nevertheless accept it as true, that at this point for some reason, He did adopt in His teaching a method which He intended should result in hindering these people finding forgiveness.

The other method of dealing with the difficulty has been that of declaring that it is not true, that it is a mistake; therefore the passage is untrustworthy, and is to be eliminated.

The second method of reasoning is impossible to me. As to the first, I would ask, Is the difficulty due to what the passage actually says, or is it due to long-continued misunderstanding and misinterpretation of it?

There are some preliminary things to be considered as we look carefully at this matter. First, the narrative of Mark is condensed. This particular passage is evidently very much condensed. The parallel passage in Luke is even more condensed than that of Mark, so that there the same difficulty seems to be suggested, if not stated in such obtrusive form. But the account of the beginning of the parabolic method, and our Lord's interpretation of its meaning as recorded in Matthew is very much fuller.

Secondly and therefore, the three narratives are needed for an interpretation of what our Lord said. Carefully putting their testimony together, we shall necessarily be nearer a full understanding of our Lord's teaching.

The last preliminary word is that the subject as presented by Mark is not exhausted in this one paragraph (verses 10–12). The second paragraph (verses 21–25) is needed, for that also deals with the reason for our Lord's parabolic method.

To turn to the paragraph itself, the disciples' inquiry first arrests us, showing that they were face to face, not with the difficulty presented to us by these paragraphs, but with the fact that our Lord did here and now adopt a new method of teaching. He had asked for the little boat, and His disciples, at His request pulling a short distance out from the shore, He sat in the boat, and to the multitudes gathered on the beach, He spoke the first full, and formulated parable, that of the Sower. When He had finished, Mark says that " when He was alone, they that were about Him with the twelve, asked of Him the parables." That is a perfectly accurate statement, but somewhat ambiguous. Matthew simply says that they asked Him why He spoke in parables. That statement illuminates this, and reveals the fact that these men noticed He spoke in a parable and when they were alone, that is, while still in the boat, but privately, they asked Him why He did so. This inquiry He answered immediately in the words that follow.

We turn then to the answer. The first part of the answer is contained in these words, " Unto *you* is given the mystery of the Kingdom of God; but unto them that are without, all things are done in parables." This was a revelation of His intention at that moment to confine Himself to the parabolic method. It is interesting, as well as valuable and important, that we should remember, what we have already noted, that the record of His discourse, as Mark gives it, is not as full as that of Matthew, but is fuller than that of Luke. There are differences in all, but the fundamental affirmation is given by each of the evangelists in almost the same words: " Unto you is given the mystery (or mysteries) of the Kingdom of God: but unto them that are without, all things are done in parables." Unto you is given the mysteries, the hidden things, the secret things, the profound things, the ultimate meaning of things; but to those that are without, is given the parable, the picture. Thus when they asked Him the reason of the parabolic method, He first said that the difference in method was due to the difference in relationship between Him and men. To His disciples He could tell secrets, and make known mysteries. To the people without, who lacked the capacity to understand, He could no longer tell the mystery, reveal the secret, or

[91]

utter the profound thing in definite speech. For them, therefore, the parable, the picture was necessary.

Our Lord then proceeded to explain His reason for adopting the parabolic method. If we only had the passage in Matthew, I venture to suggest that the difficulty would not be present to our minds.

Let us read it:

"Therefore speak I to them in parables; because seeing they see not, and hearing they hear not, neither do they understand. And unto them is fulfilled the prophecy of Isaiah, which saith:

"By hearing ye shall hear, and shall in no wise under-
    stand;
And seeing ye shall see, and shall in no wise perceive:
For this people's heart is waxed gross,
And their ears are dull of hearing,
And their eyes they have closed;
Lest haply they should perceive with their eyes,
And hear with their ears,
And understand with their heart,
And should turn again,
And I should heal them."

In that answer is emphasized our Lord's revelation of the reason for the adoption of the parabolic method. He adopted it because He was surrounded by people who had eyes, but could not see; and ears but could not hear; neither could they understand; and they were blind and deaf and dull because they had become gross of heart, and had wilfully and resolutely shut their ears, and closed their eyes, lest they should turn and be healed. Lest the light should lead them back to God, lest the truth proclaimed should produce conviction, they had resolutely shut their own eyes. Therefore Jesus used the parabolic method, not in order to blind them, but in order to make them look again; not in order to prevent them coming to forgiveness, but in order to lure them toward a new attention.

Now while this is perfectly plain in Matthew's record, at the first, it does not seem to be so evident in the passage in Mark. Therefore we return to it.

In the twelfth verse we read:

"That seeing they may see, and not perceive; and hearing they may hear, and not understand."

Is that the same statement as in Matthew? That question must be faced. Matthew reads: "Because seeing they see not, and hearing they hear not, neither do they understand." Mark reads, and the translation is quite to be trusted here—"that seeing they may see, and not perceive; and hearing they may hear, and not understand." These being two reports of the words of Jesus on the same occasion, one must interpret the other. Shall we then adopt the statement as found in Matthew, that He employed the parable because these people seeing, could not see; and hearing, could not hear; or shall we adopt the apparent meaning of Mark, that He used the parable here in order that seeing they might see, and yet not perceive; and hearing they might hear, and yet not understand? It is impossible to say that on the surface, they convey the same idea. Which then interprets which?

I believe here that Matthew must interpret Mark, because Matthew's treatment is in consonance with the whole fact of the mission of Christ in the world. He did not come for judgment, or to make it impossible for men to see and live; but for mercy, and so to make it possible for men to see and live. I do not, however, personally think that we are driven to the alternative of supposing that there is disagreement. I believe rather that Mark's is a very much condensed report of what Jesus said, and that our difficulty is created entirely by that condensation.

Let us look at the particular declaration of Mark again.
" That seeing they may see, and not perceive." Our Lord
was presenting a truth concerning the Kingdom of God
in parabolic form to these men that they may see it, but
not perceive it. He was hiding *the mystery of the Kingdom* from these men, not *the fact of the Kingdom*. He
was presenting the truth concerning the Kingdom to these
men in parabolic form that they might hear, and yet not
understand the deep, hidden mystery of the Kingdom of
God. In other words, our Lord was now adapting His
method to the strange and appalling attitude of mind
which had filled Him with anger, which anger was the
outcome of grief. He saw them hardening their heart,
and refusing to listen to His teaching, and consequently
He now adopted a method by which He would show them
as much as may be seen, in order to attract them, by
hiding from them those deeper, mysterious things which
were giving them offence and driving them away from
Him.

Then the question naturally arises, What about the remainder of the verse, "Lest haply they should turn
again"? This is a partial quotation. We have therefore
no right to link the "lest haply" with the statement of
the reason of our Lord's parabolic method. It must be
linked with that whole quotation from which it is taken,
which Matthew records fully, and Mark does not. The
"lest haply" does not refer to any action of Christ or of
God, but to the action of the men themselves. Not that
He adopted the parabolic method, *lest haply* they might
be forgiven; but that He adopted the parabolic method
because they had shut their own eyes, *lest haply* they
should be forgiven. The "lest haply" does not indicate
the purpose of Jesus in the parabolic method, but the
attitude of soul that made the parabolic method necessary.

To ask one other question. Why then did He hide
from these men the mystery? After He had finished His

parabolic teaching in the presence of the crowd, He expounded all things to His disciples, but why not to the crowds? Why did He hide the mystery from them?

At this point the second paragraph in our chapter becomes valuable (verses 21–25). Here again we have the two thoughts of the first paragraph, seeing and hearing. The lamp is for seeing; the truth is for hearing. Our Lord deliberately declared that the reason for the hiding of the mystery from the crowd was in order to its ultimate revelation. The man who hardens his heart against the great things Christ has been saying, and closes his eyes, Christ will now lure by a picture which conveys to him no revelation of the secret and profound things, but which is in itself true to those secret and profound things. He put the limit, not to bewilder men, but to enlighten men; and if they will but be lured by the parable to inquire concerning the thing hidden from them, there may be ultimate revelation. *Nothing is hidden save that it might be manifested; nothing made secret save that it should come to the light.*

Immediately at the close of His first parable, He said, " He that hath ears to hear, let him hear." That was the word to the multitudes. Now, in talking to His disciples, He repeated it. " If any man hath ears to hear, let him hear." The parable hides the mystery, does not declare the underlying principle of truth and life. But let these men hear the parable, and with what measure they mete it shall be measured to them. Their attitude of hearing shall create the ultimate result. It shall be measured to them again according to the way they measure. If they will hear honestly, even though for the moment the parable has hidden the mystery, through the door of the parable they will find their way to the mystery. Our Lord was now adopting a method, not of preventing these men coming back to Himself and God; but was employing the last and only method possible in public teaching for luring them toward the things which they would not receive in their nakedness, and in the unveiling of their essential glories. Therefore He adopted the parabolic method.

The last word of explanation here is an important one. " He that hath, to him shall be given; and he that hath not, from him shall be taken away even that which he hath." Matthew places that quotation earlier in the discourse. He introduces the answer of Jesus by that quotation. Mark concludes with it. This word marks the difference between the disciples and the multitudes. The disciples have; these men have not. The disciples have gained what they have by obedient relationship with Him as King; to them, therefore, can be given the mystery. But the men who have not come into that relationship, who have not obeyed His first teaching, if now they refuse the parabolic teaching, ultimately there will be taken away from them even that which they have.

Thus our Lord is seen at the parting of the ways, adopting the new method of the parable, not to prevent men coming to Himself, but to lure them and win them. So the beneficence of the parabolic method is revealed.

Can one believe otherwise? When later on these men, still in hostility, bitterly criticized Him for eating and drinking with publicans and sinners, and in answer thereto our Lord spoke to them the matchless parable of lost things; the lost sheep, the lost silver, and the lost son, it is unthinkable that Jesus was adopting that method to prevent men reaching the Father. He was luring men who would not listen to the essential truth, with pictures. To men who would not believe in the meaning of His Shepherd ministry, nor in the declaration concerning the Father's interest in men, nor in His declaration concerning His Father; to them He gave pictures to explain His mission, not to prevent their coming, but to hasten their steps, and lure them toward the heart of God.

In conclusion, let us make some deductions. The method of Christ with rebellious souls who have become gross of heart, dull of hearing, wilfully blind, is the hiding of the mysteries which would affright and offend them and the presenting of pictures which invite and suggest. If they will answer the invitation of the picture, and follow its suggestion, lo! they will find themselves face to face with the mystery.

Therefore the parable is ever an open door to the mystery. The mystery is not stated within it, the profound and underlying secrets are not therein declared, but they are involved. If men will but consider the picture, they will be compelled to inquiry, and if they will inquire, He will answer, and will lead them beyond the picture to the fact behind, through the parable to the mystery of life.

Now let me remark in this connection that that method is vaster and more perpetual in the Divine economy than that of the actual parables of our Lord. When He adopted the parabolic method at this dividing of the ways in His ministry, and followed it to the end, it was not something new, but something perpetual and persistent. Whatever the writer of the proverb may have meant, there is remarkable significance in the first proverb in the collection made by the men of Hezekiah's days. " It is the glory of God to conceal a thing; but the glory of kings is to search out a matter " (Prov. 25:2). There is the whole principle in a flash. There is a crystallized statement of God's perpetual method. It is the glory of God to conceal. He does so first, because things concealed are things that men at the moment cannot look at, understand, or accept. He conceals them in the vesture of the material, the passing, the parabolic. But the glory of kings is to search out the matter, and a man demonstrates his true kingship as obeying the suggestion of the picture and the parable, he presses to the heart of it. Whenever he does that, God Who has concealed the matter, answers him in revelation.

That is God's method in all creation. It is the glory of God to conceal a thing. Imagine how much God concealed from man in this earth, when He made it. We live in an age of discovery. What is discovery? Revelation, always! The glory of kings is to search out a matter. But God has hidden all they are searching out. Why did He conceal it? Why does He still conceal it? Because men are not prepared for revelation at the moment, and they must find their way to the secret and hidden things, through the processes of suggestion that are made.

There is another illustration, more supreme, more tremendous; absolutely final and inclusive, most familiar, and yet most mysterious and wonderful. "No man hath seen God at any time; the only begotten Son, who is in the bosom of the Father, He hath declared Him." Jesus was the final parable. Let John, who wrote these words ultimately, tell us what happened. We looked at Him, our hands handled Him, and then we found the mystery, the Word of life, the Logos of God.

When Jesus looked around, and saw the grossness and hardness of men's hearts, He turned to parables, Himself being the supreme parable. He uttered parables, as He had come, "God contracted to a span," to woo rebellious hearts back to the heart of God, Whom they could not, or would not know. He gave them parables to woo their rebellious hearts back to Himself, Whom they were about to refuse. It is the perpetual method of God.

Then let us dare to use His method, never forcing the mysteries of our faith upon unwilling souls, as necessary to salvation; never demanding in the first place from gross, deaf, blind men and women that they accept doctrines of Deity, of Resurrection, and of Atonement, which men cannot understand. Let us rather lure them back by pictures which are true to the mysteries, and which must inevitably lead on to those mysteries.

IX

"Who then is this, that even the wind and the sea obey Him?"—Mark 4:41.

Mark 4:35-41.

THIS was the question of a great fear. The statement of Mark, which our translators have rendered, "They feared exceedingly," quite literally rendered is, They feared with a great fear.

Moreover this fear was not produced by the storm, but by the calm. Whatever fear they had in the presence of the storm was lost as the greater fear and consternation took possession of them, when the storm was suddenly hushed and ended. In the question, therefore, we discover the effect produced upon the twelve by what the Lord had done. The stilling of the storm was a sign granted to the twelve only, the men who at this time were "with Him," by His appointment, being specially trained for work to which presently they were to be sent.

Mark was most careful to link this wonderful stilling of the storm with the day of parabolic teaching, that day of wonderful teaching, when Jesus requested His disciples that they should cross to the other side, and when their compliance with His request was ready and immediate. As Mark graphically states it, they took Him "as He was" in the boat; that is, without making any change of situation, without making any special preparation for crossing over, or for being away for any length of time. In all probability the phrase "as He was" also suggests that He was tired with the strain and tension of that day, the crowds pressing upon Him, and the pouring out of Himself in parabolic teaching, followed by the private exposition of His teaching to His own disciples.

[99]

The boat put away from the land in the quiet and the calm of the evening. Almost immediately they were in the midst of the storm, one of those furious storms that still sweep so suddenly from the mountains and lash the sea into turmoil and unrest, storms which Rob Roy has described for us so graphically as to enable us for all time to understand this story better. As he has said, the wind, having gathered force, seems literally to tumble in avalanches upon the water, and beat it into wildness. The word that Mark used here means more than an ordinary storm, it means a furious storm.

There, in the hinder part of the vessel, with His head upon the cushion (not *a* cushion, but the only one there), Jesus was asleep. The disciples were filled with perturbation. The storm undoubtedly was of unusual severity, for these men were sailors who understood the management of their craft; but they were at their wits' end, and at last made their way toward the sleeping Jesus, and waking Him, said to Him: Master, is it no concern to Thee that we perish? Then quietly rising from His slumber, He looked out over the storm-tossed waters, and addressed the wind with anger: "He *rebuked* the wind." This is a very strong word. One of the earliest translators rendered it, "He menaced the wind." Morison, with that quaint accuracy which characterized him, says that the real force of the statement is, He rebuked the wind, and then addressing Himself to the sea, said, Be muzzled. The peculiar quality of what happened was that of the suddenness of the change. The wind ceased; and the sea, which in the ordinary course of events would be a long time sobbing itself back into quietness, was almost immediately—to use the forcible thought of the Greek word—beaten back into levelness. Over the sea, and away to the mountains, and everywhere, with sudden swiftness there was quietness and calm. Then, looking at the disciples, Jesus said to them, "Why are ye fearful? Have ye not yet faith?" They then forgot all about the terror of the storm in the new fear, a great fear, an exceeding great fear that possessed them, a fear that had at its heart a sense of awe. They said one to another, " Who then is this, that even the wind and the sea obey Him?"

The story is suggestive in a hundred ways. Perhaps every preacher turns to it sooner or later, some often in the course of a life's ministry; and yet it is ever fresh, fascinating, forceful. It is so full of suggestiveness that it has inspired the poets also, and we have a rich collection of hymns expressive of its varied values. The story has values which make for new strength and new joy, however tempest-tossed man may be.

The first value of the event to the twelve is revealed in this question, "Who then is this, that even the wind and the sea obey Him?" To understand their question we must observe with some care what they observed, the things that gave rise to the question. We will try to observe them from their standpoint as though in very deed we were with them in the boat and passing through their experiences. What did they see that day in Jesus that made them ask the question? The question was new, and one compelled by some new manifestation. These men had been with Him now for some time. They had seen Him in many circumstances. They had heard many different tones in that voice which in itself was all music. Yet something happened which made them say, Who then is this?

Then secondly, in order to understand them, we must pay special attention to their question. These remarks will indicate the lines of our meditation. First, let us see Jesus as the disciples saw Him that day; secondly, let us see the disciples as they are revealed by the question they asked.

Jesus as the disciples saw Him. For the sake of brevity, I will summarize everything by saying they saw Him asleep, and they saw Him awake.

They saw Him asleep? Let us look at Him as they thus saw Him. He had been teaching. The day had come to its close, the shadows of the evening were about them, but He had requested them to cross to the other side of the sea. With alacrity and immediateness they had yielded to His request, and the boat was moving away. They saw Him find His way to the after-part of the boat, and pillow His head upon the one cushion there, and go to sleep. They saw a Man tired, feeling the strain of suffering, conscious of the drain made upon Him by the success of those gathered multitudes, and the opposition which was growing against Him. He was asleep. He needed sleep; and He was able to sleep. That in itself was a sign that He was a Man of perfect physical health, and of mental peace. Mark their own word when they presently came to Him. Have You no concern? That was exactly it. He had no concern, and was at peace. He was a Man therefore of spiritual holiness. These are the elements that make for sleep. A man who is in physical health, without mental concern, and at peace with God, will sleep.

We have seen Jesus asleep. Responsive to their touch and their cry, He awoke. The rush of the storm, and the sweep of the wind did not wake Him; but the touch of the trembling hand, and the cry of men in trouble, did. The moment they touched Him, and said, " Teacher, carest Thou not that we perish?" He was awake. There is no need to lift that thought to any higher level than that of His glorious humanity. That does not deny His Deity, but it does help us to see what we supremely need to be reminded of—the perfection of His humanity. We have seen something of this glory in a mother, whom all the noise of traffic will not waken, but who will be aroused by the sigh of a baby. This was supremely manifest in the Lord, for all the excellencies of motherhood were also in Him. Thus awakened, He looked out upon the storm, unperturbed in His own soul; and with authority He rebuked the winds, and said to the sea, "Peace, be still!"

Without laying undue emphasis upon the fact, it is interesting to notice in passing that in His dealing with the storm upon this occasion, our Lord employed exactly the same method as when dealing with demons. For the sake of illustration, glance back at the story of the first Sabbath morning in Capernaum. Then a demon cried out and disturbed Him in His teaching: "What have we to do with Thee, Thou Jesus of Nazareth. Art Thou come to destroy us? I know Thee Who Thou art, the Holy One of God." Jesus listened to the words, and rebuked him, employing exactly the same words. This fact is suggestive. It does seem to suggest that there was something in that storm of the nature of the storms that swept upon Job in the olden days, which were caused by the prince of the power of the air, the spirit that works in the kingdom of darkness. I will not argue it, nor dogmatize about it; but I cannot understand Jesus speaking evidently in tones of anger to a wind. He rebuked the wind, and the word suggests anger. I cannot understand Him saying to the sea, Be muzzled. I believe that He knew that the storm was due to the spirit of darkness, to the underworld of evil.

Dismiss that thought if you will, and simply look at the actual fact, that He rebuked the wind, and it ceased; and then spoke to the sea, and it beat itself back into levelness, and was calm.

Then while their hearts were filled with wonder at the deed, they heard Him reproving them: "Why are ye fearful? Have ye not yet faith?"

Mark the strange merging. The disciples saw a tired Man asleep. They saw a Man so tremendous in power, that the wind that tossed the sea into fury ceased; and the sea, tossed into fury, was immediately calm. What wonder that they asked: "Who then is this?"

We have more than those men had. We have the story

in the light of subsequent events. Observe the things which they did not see, which they could not observe, for they themselves must be observed also. They saw the tired Man suddenly rising from the slumber made necessary by His weariness, and hushing the storm to rest. What can we see? We see the mighty One Who can hush the storm to rest, confronting the human soul, and saying, " Why are ye fearful." In other words, it is suggested by this story that the problem that confronted God was not that of stilling the storm on the sea, but that of stilling the storm in a human soul, and that is a harder work for God! With a word the storm on the sea is over, but even He must ask these men, " Why are ye fearful? Have ye not yet faith?"

In that question there is reminiscence of the way along which He had led them, of the things He had said to them, of the things He had done, of all the pathway along which they had travelled. We see the mighty One limited in the presence of a human soul; but not ultimately, nor finally. Before He has finished He will also bring peace there; but He had not yet accomplished it, in the case of these men. For the moment we see men, to whom this very operation of peace brings no peace, but a new fear.

Let us look then at the disciples themselves as they are revealed by their question. We must observe them in the immediate experiences of the storm; in the sign that was given to them by the stilling of the storm.

Look first at the start they made. Wondering at His wisdom, after the day of parabolic teaching, doing His behests with eagerness, they immediately put out to sea. Then, suddenly, the storm came. At first they forgot everything in their terror in the presence of the storm, for they were reduced to the point of hopelessness. The waves beating into the boat, threatened to engulf it; it seemed that all must be over; nothing could save them; they were going down; they were going to perish; there was no help for it; this was the end of everything! Then they woke Him. Here we must watch them with great care. They remonstrated with Him in protest, not expecting that He would do anything. We have generally been inclined to interpret this story by saying that they woke Him in order that He might still the storm. Nothing of the kind. They were intensely surprised when He did still the storm. When they said, " Carest Thou not that we perish," we need to be very careful to understand what they meant. They were not protesting against Him for being careless that *they* were perishing. They were protesting against His lack of concern in view of the fact that they were *all* going to perish, Himself amongst the number. Their " we " referred, not to the disciples only, but to all who were in the boat. To take their words exactly as they were uttered, this is what they said: Is it no concern to Thee that we perish? Not, Art Thou neglecting us? But, Thou art not perturbed in an hour like this, when the boat is in peril, and our lives are in peril, and Thy mission is in peril, when we are all about to perish beneath these waters which in the morning will be blue and placid again, with all the enterprise of the Kingdom buried beneath them? Is it no concern to Thee that we perish? It was not a request to Him to do anything; but a protest against His apparent indifference.

Then He awoke, and they watched Him. They heard His angry rebuke, His authoritative command. They heard the rushing and moaning of the wind cease; and they saw the waves beaten back into levelness.

Then He startled them more than ever. He turned round and reproved them, "Why are ye fearful? Have ye not yet faith?" No word of comfort this, but a word of reproof! If this story had been a fabrication, it would never have entered into the heart of man to make Jesus speak that word of rebuke! He rebuked them, and they were startled; so startled were they, that they feared with a great fear. It was not the storm that filled them with fear, but the calm, and what He said to them.

"Who then is this?" said they. "Who then"—in view of this rebuke—"is this, that even the winds and the sea obey Him?" These facts demonstrated His right to rebuke. Evidently He was justified in sleeping. They had no right to awaken Him; and they ought to have known that they had no right to awaken Him, or else there is no meaning in His rebuke.

What then were the ultimate values of this event, and what the place that this scene really occupied in our Lord's method with these men, and in His training of them?

The first value is that of the question which they asked; in the fact that they were compelled to the attitude of mind that expressed itself in that question. They had discovered in their Master, in that hour of stress and strain and storm, followed by quiet and peace and calm, followed again by strange and new rebuke, an authority and a power, demanding a more intensive discipleship; and that more intensive discipleship had its manifestation in the question, "Who then is this?" We must get nearer to Him! We must find out more about Him!

This was a fine attitude of soul to which He brought these men by that event. All down the centuries again and again He has brought men to that attitude through storms. "Who then is this, that even the wind and the sea obey Him?" The attitude of mind that inspired the inquiry is the first value of the experiences through which they had passed.

The second value is that of the necessary effect upon the past, and upon the future of His ministry, produced by the things that had happened that day, by that actual stilling of the storm, and by His strange rebuke of them. In that hour there was a seal set upon the authority of all He had been saying. Among other things, in that hour there was a vindication as well as an illustration of

His parabolic method. He had been employing the parable in all that long day of teaching. They had challenged Him as to His reason for employing the parabolic
method, and He had answered them. Here was an illustration in their experience. This also was a parable, a
parable not in words but in deed, intended to explain and
correct an attitude in their own lives. It was a parable
made necessary by their dullness; seeing, they did not
see; hearing, they did not hear, neither had they understood; or, they never would have awakened Him. But
because they were blind and deaf and dull, He gave
them a parable by stilling the tempest; and having done
so, suggesting the reason of His absence of concern, and
the meaning of His sleeping, and why it was unnecessary
to wake Him; then He rebuked them, and left upon
their souls the impression of the teaching of the parable.
He exercised this parabolic activity of power, in order
to remove the dullness that made it necessary; and in that
hour there was a vindication of what He had said about
His parabolic teaching; and thus a new authority was
set upon all His teaching by reason of what He had done.

From that time forward the event became to them, and
not to them alone, but to all the Christian Church—our
sermons, expositions, and hymns bearing witness—a
source of strength in days of stress and storm. Can we
think that these men could ever forget that scene? There
was another occasion when He came to them in the
night, over the sea and through the wind, and that also
was for them alone. Neither of these wonders of the
deep were wrought in view of the multitude, but for these
men alone. The sea is always typical of the possibility of
storm, even when most beautiful, as it is lulled to quietness and rest. The sea is ever the symbol of peril. At
last the seer in the island washed by the sea, wrote as one
of the ultimate things of the final order, " There shall
be no more sea." To repeat our question therefore, can
we imagine that these men who were with Him that day

in the boat, ever forgot the spiritual values of that event, and the fact that He slept at the heart of the storm? Could they ever forget that when they went to Him, He woke and ended the storm?

I do not think that His waking and ending of the storm was the value of the lesson to them. I think the chief value of the day's experience was its revelation of the fact that there was no need to wake Him; that

"No waters can swallow the ship where lies
The Master of ocean, and earth, and skies."

They certainly did learn that in days of stress and strain and storm, if they cried out, He would end the storm. Yes! but the deeper thing they learned was this; that no storm can wreck the programme of God; that though all hell be let loose, and though it have power over elements, and events, and the hearts of men, and the passions of the world, to stir them into storm, and wreck the apparently frail bark where Christ lies asleep, it is all useless. If He be there, all is well!

That is the profoundest lesson of all. I am not prepared to say that these men learned it so perfectly as always to live in its power; but whenever they failed, He would help them, and the memory of it and of His rebuke would come back.

"With Christ in the vessel,
I smile at the storm."

That is not waking Him! Can I smile at the storm with Christ in the vessel? I am not sure that I can; but I ought to, and I want to. I believe it is one of the profoundest lessons of life, whether in regard to personal experience, or world-wide affairs. There ought to be no panic in the heart of a man, when he knows Christ. We may be sure that Christ is at the heart of every storm. He apparently sleeps in the hour of our anxiety. We go to Him, and say what these men said, and as others have said, Carest Thou not that we perish, Lord? What art Thou doing?

" See round Thine ark the angry billows curling."

We are in danger of being swamped. Everything is going wrong!

All such panic is unnecessary, and unworthy. The Lord is at the heart of the storm, and we may rest in Him, and smile at the storm. It is, perhaps, more easy to believe that about the world, than it is about our own life! It is a curious fact, but it is quite true. We can often trust Him for the world, more readily than for ourselves. Does Christ seem asleep? Ah! but He *is* there. If we would see the greatest things we had better not waken Him. It will be great if He will hush the storm! But there are greater things. What are they? Watching Him through the storm. That is what He wanted these men to do. In proportion as we believe this, we ought to have no panic.

Though nearly two thousand years have run their course, and in some senses we know more than these men, we are still driven to say, Who then is this? In the answer to that question is the secret of rest. In proportion as we really know Him, in that proportion we shall be quiet. It was Jeremy Taylor who said that we are far safer in the middle of a storm with God, than anywhere else without Him. And that is what we need to learn and to remember, that we may be at peace, and that we may coöperate with Him.

X

"There met Him out of the tombs a man with an unclean spirit."—MARK 5:2.

Mark 5:1-20.

BY these words our attention is immediately fastened upon our subject, that namely of our Lord's dealing with demoniacs.

That special importance attaches to the subject is evidenced by the fact that Mark has given so much space to this particular story, relating it with much more of detail than either Matthew or Luke, who nevertheless both record the miracle.

The subject has arisen before in the course of these narratives. On the first wonderful Sabbath in Capernaum, in the synagogue in the morning, Jesus healed a demoniac, and still others in the evening of the same day (1:23-27, 32-34). Mark records the fact that as He journeyed through Galilee He constantly did the same thing (1:39). Mark also declares that in the course of His ministry "the unclean spirits, whensoever they beheld Him, fell down before Him and cried, saying, Thou art the Son of God. And He charged them much that they should not make Him known" (3:11-12). In the choosing of the twelve also, He appointed them to have authority ultimately to do the same work (3:15). Moreover, He had answered the declarations of the Jerusalem scribes on this subject with great solemnity, and solemn warning, as they declared that by the prince of the demons He cast out the demons (3:22-30).

Our story is significantly the next in order. As we proceed with our study of the Gospel we shall touch it again and yet again; when He sent out the apostles, He gave them this authority (6:7 and 13); when He healed the daughter of the Syrophœnician woman (7:25–30); when at the foot of the mount of transfiguration He healed the boy (9:17–29); when John reported that one, not of the twelve, had been casting out demons (9:38); in a final reference to Mary of Magdala, out of whom He cast seven demons (16:9), and last of all in the commission as Mark recorded it (16:17).

In this story of the man in the country of the Gerasenes the subject is evidently purposely dealt with most fully. The case was a remarkable one in many ways, and Mark recorded it with much of detail. Matthew alone tells us that there were two men. Both Luke and Mark refer to one only, evidently because the case was a notorious one in itself, and the healing of the man therefore was all the more wonderful. The words of the text quite literally rendered are, " There met Him out of the tombs, a man *in* an unclean spirit." Dr. Morison says that the suggestiveness of the expression is that " the demoniac in the man was more conspicuous and obtrusive than the man's own manhood." Our Lord here came face to face with one of the most terrible cases of demon-possession. The special nature of the case, and the prominence thus given to it, compel special attention to the subject. I propose, therefore, now to deal generally with demon-possession, and to consider the illustration particularly as it bears on the subject.

The testimony of the sacred writings to the existence of spiritual beings is unequivocal. Behind that testimony I do not go. The whole Bible recognizes this world of spiritual beings, and the fact that under certain conditions, and for certain purposes, they have access to men. The testimony of the Gospel narratives to the fact of demon-possession, and to the further fact that our Lord, during the course of His earthly ministry exercised authority over demons, which He manifested by casting them out of human beings, is equally without question. At the commencement of our study of this Gospel I drew attention to a book published in 1864, on Progress in Revelation, being the Bampton Lectures by Bernard, in which book attention is drawn to the fact that this seems to have been one of the dominant notes in this Gospel according to Mark.

The things that precede this particular story, leave the impression upon the mind that our Lord was constantly coming into contact with these demons, in men, women, and children; and that He ever acted with authority and with power over them.

Some objections have been raised to this view. It is said that our Lord did not know the truth about these cases. That I am not going to argue, for it involves our Christology, and I cannot accept that definition or interpretation of the Gospel stories.

It is suggested that there was no such thing as demon-possession, but that He adapted His language, using the method of expression of His age, well knowing that these people were not really possessed by demons. For me personally this charges Him with giving countenance to superstition, and I cannot accept the interpretation.

It is suggested that the language of the records is that of the writers, who have thus explained certain things which Jesus did; that He never really talked with demons as the narratives would lead a plain man to suppose, but that He did produce upon a madman a certain effect of quietness and peace, and that the disciples interpreted what He did in the way in which we have read the stories. That, for me, would destroy the authority of the writings in every particular, and I should immediately say of my New Testament, there is nothing here upon which I can depend.

Therefore, dealing no longer with objections, let us face the subject. In order to its intelligent consideration it is important that we should observe a distinction which

[Mark 5 : 1-20]

is made in the English Revision, in the marginal notes, between a devil and a demon. The American Revisers have brought the correction into the actual text. It is a very important change, and one that must be borne in mind. As a matter of fact, the word translated " devil" as a substantive, occurs thirty times in the New Testament, but always in reference to Satan. It is found adjectively three times in the pastoral epistles, always in reference to men. In the New Testament then, taken as a whole, the word " devil " is always used of one strange, mystic, awful personality, whom we speak of as Satan. The word translated " demons" is used repeatedly. It was a common word at the time, a word with which men were perfectly familiar. It may be a little difficult for us to interpret its meaning to-day, although we know of its use, at the time. Confining ourselves to the New Testament, we find that the synonym for demon is always either " evil spirit" or " unclean spirit."

It is important in the second place that we should recognize all that the New Testament reveals, as to the relation between the one who is described as " the devil," and those who are referred to as " demons." In that controversy between our Lord and the Jerusalem scribes, which we have considered, they charged Him with casting out demons through Beelzebub, whom they named the prince of the demons, thus revealing the popular view and conception. It is to be borne most carefully in mind that in our Lord's answer to what they said, an answer characterized by the utmost solemnity, He did not correct that view. He accepted it, and based His argument upon its accuracy, as He declared that if Satan cast out Satan, then his kingdom is divided; admitting therefore that very conception which they held, of a great underworld of evil spirits or demons, controlled, marshalled, ordered, governed, so far as such words can be used in that connection, by this one of whom they spoke as Beelzebub, the prince of the demons.

THE GOSPEL ACCORDING TO MARK

[Mark 5 : 1–20]

The mission of Jesus Christ was once expressed by an apostle in these words, " He went about, doing good, and healing all that were oppressed of the devil," the reference being to the healing of sickness and to the casting out of demons; and the entire conception being that of this world under the control of this one personality. Our Lord made no contradiction of this; but accepting it, in all His dealings with demonized men and women, proceeded upon the assumption of the accuracy of that view.

Let it at once be said there is nothing final in the New Testament as to whom these spirits really are. The old view was that they were the spirits of men. The view of Greek philosophy was that these were the spirits of those who lived in the Golden Age. They were not looked upon as necessarily evil in all cases. Hence there was demon-worship, the worship not necessarily of evil spirits; but of the spirits of those who had existed in the Golden Age. That view, or a modification of it is held to-day by some. Both Pember and Gall in their most interesting books, have suggested that these spirits were those of pre-Adamite man, of a race that fell before the story as recorded in Genesis. I but refer to these things in order to say that they are speculations with more or less likelihood of being true. Certainly when considering the subject, the weird revelation of the New Testament should be remembered, that these spirits were always seeking some material resting-place, always hankering after some material instrument through which to act, and in which to dwell. Nothing can finally be said concerning this, but it is repeatedly revealed.

There is also the generally accepted theory that these spirits are angels who were involved in the primal fall, when Lucifer, son of the morning, himself became the arch enemy, the prince of the power of the air, the god of this world.

The New Testament is quite clear as to the existence of these spirits, quite clear as to their access to humanity,

[114]

quite clear in its revelation of the fact that their access
to humanity always meant harm wrought in human life,
both in intention and purpose. The pictures that the
New Testament presents of demonized humanity are
very terrible ones. Here once more let us halt for a
definition. Our phrase " possessed of a demon " does not
occur in the New Testament. The phrase is really " demonized man," or one who may be called " a demoniac."
While not desiring to build anything final upon that distinction, it is well to bear it in mind, because when
speaking of a man being demon-possessed, we have our
own imagination as to what that means. Let us then
correct, or hold in suspense our imagination by remembering that the actual word of the New Testament is not
" demon-possessed," but " demonized "; a man under the
influence of one or more of these evil spirits. The possibility of this is clearly taught in the New Testament.

It is taught also by modern experience, especially by
the experience of missionaries in certain lands. They
testify that to-day they find exactly the same conditions
as those described in the New Testament; and they add
to that testimony the fact that they also find the name
and power of Christ, are sufficient for casting out these
demons, and setting people free.

The purpose of demon-possession, so far as the demon
is concerned, is always that of finding an instrument.
The power of the demon is acquired from without, and is
terrible in its finality. There is no single instance in the
New Testament which suggests that a spirit of good takes
possession of a human being, other than the Spirit of
God. There is no single suggestion of a spirit taking possession of a human being in order to the enlightenment,
healing and uplifting of that human being. There is no
case in the Bible of men finding communion with spirits
who are in themselves good and pure and holy, save
the lonely exception of the appearance of Samuel to
Saul.

What is revealed as to the condition of the man thus demonized? First of all, that he had passed to the place of terrible isolation; he was living among the tombs, in the region of death, as far as possible from his fellow beings. Secondly, that he was characterized by terrible lawlessness, breaking through all restraint. Thirdly, that his whole experience was one of restlessness, crying out night and day. Fourthly, that it was one of suffering self-inflicted, cutting himself with stones. Finally, that it was one of menace to all men,—as one of the evangelists records—so that it was not possible for men to pass by that way. The picture is a terrible one of the ultimate effect of the possession of a human being by an evil spirit.

What is here revealed as to the demons themselves? Perhaps the most suggestive thing,—and it is not peculiar to this story—is their recognition of Christ, the obeisance they yielded to Him. This man, seeing Jesus from afar, as our translation says, hastened to Him and worshipped Him. The word worshipped may simply mean that he yielded obeisance to Him, bowed in His presence; but what he said suggests that attitude of worship in the presence of Christ. The question asked was a strange and startling one: "What have I to do with Thee, Jesus?" Or, What is there to me and to Thee, Jesus? That is, What have we in common? Then came that strange word, so constantly recurring when evil spirits came into the presence of Christ, "Thou Son of the Most High God." Then followed the plea of the evil spirit: "I adjure Thee by God, torment me not"; and the weird request. "He besought Him much that He would not send them away out of the country" says Mark; and Luke says, "They entreated Him that He would not command them to depart into the abyss." At the last moment they clamoured that if they were to be driven out from possession of this man, they might enter into the swine; thus manifesting their desire for some material instrumentality in order to the satisfaction of some craving of their nature.

Look at the story once again in order to observe the dealing of Christ with this demonized man. In answer to the challenge, " What is there to me and to Thee? "— the man speaking, and yet voicing the demon,—Jesus said, " Come forth thou unclean spirit out of the man." That was the word of quiet authority, which impressed the disciples, who listened and observed. In the first morning scene in the Capernaum synagogue, they were amazed, not that He cast the demons out, for the scribes also were doing this, but that He did it with a word, and with apparent ease, with an authority which the demon immediately recognized and obeyed. So in this case He spoke the word, " Come forth, thou unclean spirit out of the man," and the word was enough.

In the next place, in answer to the plea of the evil one, " I adjure Thee, torment me not," Christ asked a question: " What is thy name? " Here perhaps we are at the point of special arrest. The careful reading of the story convinces me that our Lord was not asking the demon his name, but the man; thus recalling him to the sense of personality. I believe that the question was asked with infinite tenderness. The Lord spoke to the man as he was emerging from the terrible control that had wrought havoc in his life: " What is thy name? " He was answered by the spirit of evil, which nevertheless was an answer revealing the man's agony, and sense of hopelessness, " My name is Legion, for we are many." It seems to me that in that answer also there is evidence of the man himself, wakened to a sense of his own personality. " *My* name is Legion, for *we* are many." Notice the awakened sense of personality, " My name," and then the swift return to the terrific sense of mystery that had blighted and ruined his life, " we are many."

When the spirits made their request that they might enter into the herd of swine, Mark says, " He gave them

leave "; Matthew records His answer in one word,
" Go! " The answer of Jesus, which was permission to
the evil spirits to enter the herd of swine, was also His
word of judgment on them; for the herd, possessed by
the evil spirits, perished in the waters, and so were lost
to the demons, who passed on into the abyss.

I am not going to enter into any discussion of the old-
time difficulty, the controversy between Huxley and Glad-
stone, about that herd of swine. Suffice it to say that our
Lord was exercising His ministry in Jewish territory, and
even if Josephus is right, that this was a Greek city, it
is nevertheless true that our Lord was dealing with the
children of Israel, and in the destruction of the swine
He was rebuking their indulgence in a traffic absolutely
forbidden.

The Lord's last word to the man was this, " Go to thy
house unto thy friends, and tell them how great things
the Lord hath done for thee, and how He had mercy
on thee." Thus the whole incident was set in the light
of the purpose of the ministry of Christ; the compas-
sionating of man, and his deliverance from all evil domination. Thus also the whole purpose of demon-possession is revealed, as being that of the spoiling of humanity.

The last scene is one full of sadness. It is that of the
people as they besought Him to depart out of their coasts.
They saw the man, sitting, clothed, and in his right mind;
but they would dispense with such benefits rather than
have their gains interfered with. Christ is seen therefore, taking boat and passing back to the other side.

What value has such a consideration for us? I suggest first of all that the fact of the incorporation of these
stories in the records is proof that they are not without
value. They serve first as an unveiling of the underworld
of evil; and secondly, as a revelation of our Lord's power
over that underworld.

But it is objected that there are no such cases now.

That is a hasty conclusion. I have already stated that the testimony of missionaries as to their experience in what we call heathen lands at this time, is unequivocal. I suggest also that the whole of the phenomena of spiritualism is closely allied; and that the moment the word "medium" is employed, the word "demonized man" or "demonized woman" may be substituted. Christians make a terrible mistake when they laugh at spiritualism, and treat it as a fancy. It is a reality. Men *are* holding traffic with spirits, and obtaining answers from the spirit world; and yielding themselves thus to the control of spirits, they become mastered by spirits, and the media through which the spirits actually speak. But the whole realm of spirits, with which men thus communicate, is the realm under the dominion of Satan.

Admitting, however, for the sake of argument, that we have no such manifestations to-day in our own land, as those which the Gospels describe, the question arises as to whether this also is not a method of Satan. To-day, in this land, in the places where the Gospel has been preached, and where therefore the common level of spiritual intelligence,—quite apart from the intelligence of definitely Christian people,—is far higher than it can be in places where the Gospel has not been preached; the very fact that there are no such manifestations proves the subtlety of Satan. In such places he has girded himself as an angel of light, seducing men by evil spirits that come to them, as if they were spirits of God.

The underworld of evil spirits still exists. It is still true that "our wrestling is not against flesh and blood, but against the principalities, against the powers, against the world-rulers of this darkness, against the spiritual hosts of wickedness in the heavenly places." But it is also true that the power of the Lord, and His authority over the whole of this realm abides; and therefore there may be for us perfect and constant victory over all the power of evil spirits as they approach us from without;

and moreover, in and through His name there may be
for us perfect authority and power for the exorcising of
evil spirits from other men, if we will but place ourselves in true relation to the Lord Himself.

To quote again from Paul's language in his Ephesian
letter, in order that we enter into the conflict with this
underworld of evil, it is necessary that we should "put
on the whole panoply of God, that we may be able to
stand against the wiles of the devil." We fight our way
toward the ultimate victory through unseen forces and
foes; the principalities and powers, that are under the
control of the arch-enemy of the race.

But if we recognize the foe, let it be none the less our
business to remember the power of the Lord. When the
apostle wrote, "We are not ignorant of his devices," he
wrote as one who had come to a true understanding of
the whole underworld of evil, into which he looked with
intrepid eyes, and to which he perpetually made reference; and that understanding resulted from the light that
Christ had brought to him.

It is for us therefore, to study these stories, not as
though we were face to face with exceptional things of
long ago, not as though the adversaries therein described
did then exist, and now are non-existent; but as those
who take their way toward the perfecting of the realization of the Kingdom of God on earth amid these hosts of
darkness.

O'er this whole realm of darkness also our Lord and
Master has sovereign rule. As our trust is in Him, and
we are yielded to Him, we in this regard also, may be
more than conquerors.

Only let us ever remember that if

> "Hell is nigh, . . . God is nigher,
> Circling us with hosts of fire.
> For lo! to faith's enlightened sight
> All the mountain flames with light."

XI

" One of the rulers of the synagogue, Jairus; . . . and a woman."—MARK 5 : 22, 25.

Mark 5 : 21–43.

AMONG all the stories of the ministry of our Lord, none, in certain regards, is more beautiful than this of two sorrowful souls who found their way to Him, and were comforted.

It is one story. Matthew, Mark, and Luke each record it in the same way, telling how, while Jesus was on His way to the house of Jairus, the woman came to Him; and, from the viewpoint of Jairus, hindered Him; but from the standpoint of Jesus, enabled Him to help Jairus.

Taken thus, as one story, it is supremely a revelation of the sensitiveness of the Servant of God to human sorrow; and of His ready, almost eager response thereto.

In language, most simple and most natural, the suffering ones are presented to us. To read this story naturally, is inevitably to be brought into very close sympathy with these two suffering people. In proportion as we have trodden the sorrowful way, and ourselves have known anything of pain, we read these stories intelligently, and are carried immediately over the two intervening millenniums, to Jairus and to the woman; for their successors are with us yet.

Such emotional sympathy prepares us for the apprehension of the tenderness and strength of the attitude and activity of Jesus, as the result of which peace and joy took the place of turmoil and sorrow in the experience of these two people.

In the country of the Gerasenes the Lord had manifested His power over demons most remarkably. Then, by the strange and inexplicable mystery of human nature, requested by the inhabitants, He had departed from their borders, crossing back with His disciples over the sea which He had so recently hushed into rest. On the other side great multitudes gathered about Him, and He continued His work. The word that Mark employs here is a very suggestive one; the multitudes "thronged Him," the exact thought being that of actually pressing upon Him. It was impossible for Him to move easily, they crowded Him so. When presently He started with Jairus, they still thronged Him, jostled Him, not with intentional rudeness, but with a great anxiety to be near Him. These multitudes were curious, interested, and crudely sympathetic; and yet entirely ignorant of all the tenderness and compassion of His heart, or of the capacity of that heart for love.

The disciples were with Him also, the twelve who were appointed to be with Him; and this as every other incident had its bearing upon their training and preparation for the work that lay before them. They were loyal-hearted and yet very ignorant, so that presently when He asked that strange question, "Who touched Me?" they did not at all understand Him; and when later He lifted to life the little damsel, they were amazed.

This is a great scene. I like to dwell upon it. If I were an artist, I would try to paint the picture of this crowd, some of them with happiness on their faces, others with sorrow; mothers perhaps lifting their bairns up that they might see Him as He passed; eager men jostling Him, getting a little ahead of the rest of the crowd to look back into His face. It is a great human picture.

Let us leave them all, the crowds and the disciples, and fasten our attention upon the central figures in the picture; Jairus, the woman, and Jesus. We will attempt carefully to look at Jairus, and understand his sorrow; to look at the woman, and come into sympathy with her desolation; in order that with reverence we may watch the Lord in the presence of such sorrowful folk, our predecessors in the experiences of pain and loneliness.

We will try first to imagine Jairus and the mother of the maid. The mother did not travel with Jairus, to persuade Jesus to come. She stayed where mothers do, by the side of the child in her illness. She is only mentioned in the story once, and would not have been mentioned then perchance, except for the understandingness of Jesus; for when presently He came to the house, He took into that inner chamber Jairus and the mother. Thus then they are first presented to us; Jairus in the presence of Jesus, the mother at home by the side of the damsel.

How many can really see these people? How many know the parental love that is here revealed? It is strange, mystic, different from all other loves, having qualities that are all its own, so fine, so subtle, so delicate, that any words by which we try to describe it seem coarse, hard, and inadequate!

Jairus employed a phrase which had at its very heart, a sense of proprietorship: *my little daughter!* Ah! we may love all children, all the bairns may seem to us the special messengers of God to mortals; but there is a difference. Parental love has within itself an almost terrifying, and yet most exquisitely tender sense of responsibility. If a man shall say to me, It is your duty to do thus or so, I shall challenge him for his reason; and if he shall reply, For your own sake; I may answer, Stand out of my sunlight, and do not interfere with me! But if he shall say, For the sake of that boy in your home; he has conquered me, he has mastered me! Oh! that strange agony in the love of parent for child, that makes the parent ever tremble! "*My* little daughter." That is a picture in itself. Luke records the fact that she was an only daughter, and that she was twelve years of age. Twelve years of sunshine, twelve years of music in the home! She had come to that wonderful age which to-day we

are describing as the period of adolescence, when will is
becoming supreme, and choices and elections are being
made alone, when all life seems to be breaking from bud
into larger blossom with the potentiality of fruitage.
Twelve years of age!

Then the sorrow is revealed in the one graphic sentence: "My little daughter lieth at the point of death."
The cloud is over the home! Silence is within the home!
Nothing need be added! Jairus stands forevermore as
a type.

Then we turn to look at the woman, for deep as is
the sorrow of Jairus, there are deeper depths here.
Home, society, and religion, are the great things in the
real life of all true womanhood. Of these home is first.
From the connection I do not propose to omit the word
society. I am using it in the sanctuary, and therefore
using it correctly, not with reference to that most ve-
neered and rotten thing that we call society, but in its
true sense, the social circle of life. The inner sanctuary
of religion is always open to true womanhood, and into
its mysteries she again and again finds her way with
light and experience such as others do not know.

Now look at this woman. She was suffering from an
ailment which had weakened her, and was in itself destructive. That, however, does not tell the story of the
depth of her sorrow. We must look at this woman in
relation to her own age, and to those very things to
which I have already made reference, as the things of
her full and beautiful life. All women suffering from
hæmorrhage in that age were suspect. Consequently, by
the very law of her people, she was divorced from her
husband, and could not live in her home; she was ostracized from all society, and must not come into contact
with her old friends; she was excommunicated from the
services of the synagogue, and thus shut out from the
women's courts in the temple. Hers is indeed a pathetic
figure! Twelve years in which the passionate desire, not

so much—unless I misunderstand this story and misunderstand women,—for her healing, as for restoration to all those places of life which were her joy, home, society, and religion. Twelve years of agony, physical, mental, spiritual, in which she had poured out her wealth in the attempt to regain her health, with no success. As Mark, with bluntness puts it, she "was nothing bettered, but rather grew worse."

In the case of Jairus, twelve years of sunshine suddenly devastated, with the death of the bairn. In the case of this woman twelve years of suffering, gradually issuing in weary desolation.

Now let us observe the Lord. We have been following Him through these holy fields. We have, with the multitudes, been amazed by the wisdom of His teaching; we have been watchful in the presence of His power. We have seen Him dealing with the vast underworld of evil, casting out demons. Now let us look at Him in the presence of these people of sorrow.

Both these people came to Him. Jairus came to Him with public request; the woman came to Him in a private approach. The man came to Him in the midst of the crowds asking Him definitely and openly that all might hear, that He would come and help him. The woman came; and how she did so, I can never quite understand. How difficult some of us, in full vigour and health, find it to get through the crowds of London. Think of this jostling crowd of eager people thronging Him, and then of this woman, weak and wan and worn and emaciated, with twelve years of suffering. Yet she reached Him! She came, and she came quietly. She touched Him. The word "touched" really does not convey the true thought. It was not a delicate touch; it was the clutch of the hand of despair. The woman in this thronging pressing crowd said, If I may but snatch at it, if I may but clutch it, I shall be healed! So she came.

Mark, with that bluntness which is often so full of the

poetry of revelation, simply tells us that when Jairus had made his request, " He went with him." Notice the immediate response. That cry from the heart of Jairus had touched the soul of Jesus. " My little daughter is at the point of death." The compassion of Jesus was not for the little daughter. He is never touched with pity for those who die. It is for those who live. It was the agony of the father and mother that appealed to Him.

On the way He delayed. That is the second thing to notice. He went; but He tarried. The woman had touched Him. Power had gone out to her healing, and He tarried. Why not pass on? Why did He not go on? Not merely in order that He might talk to the woman. That assuredly; but this also; He knew that at the house of Jairus the child lay dead, and He knew perfectly well that those messengers were already starting to tell Jairus the sad news. He paused to lead Jairus into an atmosphere in which it would be possible for him to believe; when the news came that it was too late. He paused for Jairus's sake. Yet if I were painting the picture I should try to represent Jairus as impatient! Why does He tarry so long? My child is dying!

In a few moments there came the last blow on the father's heart, " Thy daughter is dead! Why troublest thou the Teacher any further?" It was necessary that Mark should write this, " But Jesus, not heeding the word spoken, saith unto the ruler of the synagogue." Let us, however, dare to be dramatic, and leaving out the explanation, see what happened. Christ had just said to this woman, " Daughter, thy faith hath made thee whole; go in peace." Then the messengers came; " Thy daughter is dead. Why troublest thou the Teacher any further?" Then said Jesus, " Fear not, only believe." Thus the voice of the uttermost desolation was immediately followed by the voice of the uttermost consolation. Yes, but how could Jairus believe the thing that was said? There was the woman; something strange had happened

[126]

to her. She declared she had been made whole by a touch, and He had said, " Go into peace." There was a method and a purpose in the halting of Jesus. There is always a meaning in His delay. Out of the delay will come help, out of the darkness will come light. It is always so with this Christ of ours.

Then He came to the house, and no words of ours are needed to describe the scene. It is so full of exquisite beauty. Listen to His first words: " Why make ye a tumult, and weep? the child is not dead, but sleepeth." That is God's outlook on death. He said the same thing when Lazarus died, and then because they could not understand Him, He had to say plainly, " Lazarus is dead," accommodating Himself to the ignorance of the human outlook upon death. So He said to these people in the house, The child is not dead; she is asleep.

Then there flashes out in the story a touch of dignity and authority. When they laughed Him to scorn, He put them all out, and taking with Him only Peter, James, and John, and the father and mother, He came in and took her by the hand; and dropping into Aramaic (for I believe He spoke in Greek, and the very reason why the Aramaic is retained for us here is to show that He adopted the language of the inner home circle, those diminutives which are the very essence of love) ; He said, " Talitha cumi." Damsel arise, is a harsh translation. The real meaning of the word is, " Little lamb, arise." He took her by the hand, and He said, " Little lamb, arise."

Then He gave her back to father and mother. Poor little lamb! He gave her back to tears, He gave her back to pain, He gave her back to sorrow. Not out of compassion for her did He bring her back, but out of compassion for them. So after all, my little lamb, that He took, was better off than she was, though I have been left lonely through many years. It was the father's heart that appealed to Him. He gave him back his child. It was the mother's heart that moved Him, and He gave her back the little one. Oh! it was all right with the little one also, undoubtedly so, in the long issues, but He brought her back to sorrow.

Now let us watch Him with the woman. One or two things are brought together here so closely that we hardly notice that they are together. " She felt in her body that she was healed. . . . Jesus perceiving in Himself that the power proceeding from Him had gone forth." That is the whole story. She touched. They said, How sayest Thou, Who touched Me? The multitudes throng Thee, and press Thee. Ah! yes, my brethren! Augustine long ago said of this story, " Flesh presses, faith touches." Crowds jostle Him, but agony and need touch Him; and He can always distinguish between the jostle of a curious mob, and the agonized touch of a needy soul.

He is still making that distinction. He is always asking the same question, " Who touched Me? " So many people jostle Him, crowd Him, press on Him. We are really interested. We love to hear about Him. We enjoy—terrible word—the service! But, thank God, there is always some soul who touches Him, and reaches Him. Whenever a soul does that in desperation, as the last possible thing—He answers. He knows the touch of need, and responds to it.

Then the woman who had touched Him, must come and tell. She must confess, not for her own sake, nor for His sake only; but principally for the sake of Jairus. So as the result of His question, she came and told Him all the truth. Then, looking into her eyes, He said, " Daughter." This is the only occasion on record when He used this particular kind of endearing epithet, to a woman. " Daughter . . . go into peace "; not " in peace," but " into." All the land behind for twelve years had been wilderness, a land of darkness and desolation. Now He said: Daughter, go into peace. Thou hast been divorced from home. Come into My home.

Thou hast been ostracized from society. Come into closer
kinship with Me. Thou hast been excommunicated from
the rites of religion. Come into fellowship with the One
Who brings thee to God. " Daughter, go into peace."

She is moving away. Where is she going? Perhaps
back home, perhaps back to friends, perhaps back to the
synagogue next Sabbath. I do not know. This I know,
she is going into peace! What does it matter if she is
never readmitted into the synagogue? She is in peace.
She is His child.

What are the permanent values of these stories? In
this particular unveiling of Jesus we have a revelation of
His extreme sensitiveness. Oh, the ugliness of human
words when we try to talk about Christ! I want some
new language. Sensitiveness is indeed a beautiful word,
and yet it is not rich enough to express the thought. In
Him sensitiveness was responsiveness, quick, immediate,
full, generous, magnificent. Then again we have here a
wonderful revelation of the understanding of Jesus. I
think that is one of the most wonderful qualities in human love and friendship. Understandingness! That is
why He tarried to talk to the woman and help her. That
is the meaning of the very word upon which we have
already dwelt. Daughter! So much was not said; and
consequently so much more was said! Perhaps the most
beautiful sacramental symbol of His understandingness
in all the narrative is its last touch. The dead child was
lifted by His hand. She arose to life at the music of His
voice. Then He commanded that they should give her
something to eat. If we had been inventing this story
we dare not have added that. Even now we are a little
afraid to believe it. But He is God; He knew that the
little child wakening back after the long unconscious
slumber, with the little body thrilling with new life, was
hungry. Give her something to eat. With a touch gentle
enough for a little maiden's dimpled hand, and with a
voice musical enough to bring the sweet spirit back from

the far-off place, He did not forget that she wanted something to eat. Oh, the understandingness of Jesus!

Yes, but, you say, my child died, and I lost her! Yes, but, you say, I am not cured. I am still suffering! How shall I reply to that kind of statement? Reverently I say in answer; even though our children went, and He did not let us have them; even though we were not cured, and long, long suffering runs on, there is something to be sure of. Seeing that we have had that unveiling of Him; we know His heart and therefore are sure of His sympathy.

There is another thing to remember. Many children are raised up even yet. Do not put these stories back two millenniums. That one lassie that God took out of my home I did so want to keep; but she went. But I have other bairns in the home who have seemed to be as near the end as she. I asked for them, and they are with me yet. He still touches the little hands, and raises up the children. He still heals, and He has cured many a soul of bodily infirmity.

Therefore we know that those who are not raised up or cured, are still in His love. Therefore that which happens to them is best for them, and must be best for us. He did not let me have my lassie. He took her. Then that was best. I do not quite see how, for me, and yet I am sure it was so. If He Who can, does not, then it is better so!

He can raise up that child you have left at home sick. But perhaps over against the ability of actual power there is the disability of some larger meaning of His grace for you and for that child.

So we thank God for these pictures. This Jesus is here now;

> "The healing of His seamless dress
>   Is by our beds of pain.
> We touch Him in life's throng and press
>   And we are whole again."

XII

"He could there do no mighty work."—Mark 6: 5.

Mark 6: 1–6.

Matthew and Mark tell the story of this second visit of our Lord to Nazareth. Luke records the first visit, about a year earlier, at the beginning of His more public ministry in Galilee. There is an evident difference between the two stories. On the occasion of the first visit He went to Nazareth unaccompanied by His disciples; on this Mark distinctly declares "His disciples follow Him." On that first occasion He wrought no miracle; on this He laid His hands upon a few sick folk and healed them. On that occasion, when with madness they attempted to cast Him from the hill, He immediately departed from the neighbourhood; on this, He seems to have tarried in the adjacent villages.

During the interval between the first and second visits His fame had grown, and His power had been yet more wonderfully manifested. But recently His mother and brethren had travelled together from Nazareth to Capernaum to dissuade Him from continuing His arduous labours. They said, "He is beside Himself," and for very love of Him they attempted to persuade Him to return with them to Nazareth, and to quietness; but He had declined to do so.

Now, just before sending out the twelve who had been with Him in preparation for their work, He returned to Nazareth, taking them with Him. Thus the men appointed to coming service, who since He had appointed them to be with Him for special training, had seen Him, in the exercise of His power, Master in every realm of human experience, now saw Him in a situation where "He could do no mighty work." It was a new revela-

tion to them of His limitation. They saw Him in such
conditions that all the power that had been so remarkably
manifest—spontaneous, victorious, and irresistible—was
now inoperative. This also was part of their training.

Let us first attempt to understand the unbelief of the
Nazarenes in its manifestation, in its cause, and in its
effect; then in the light of that consideration, glance at
some phases and manifestations of modern unbelief.

First then, the unbelief of the Nazarenes in its manifestation, its cause, and its effect. The story, brief as it is,
reveals first, what these men knew of Jesus. They were
attempting to reconcile that which was immediate with
that which they knew of Him before this time. They
were in His presence, facing what they had heard from
Him, what they had seen Him do, or more probably, what
they had heard that He had been doing. Then they were
thinking of Him, as they had known Him during those
years in which He had lived amongst them.

They asked two questions. First, " Whence hath this
Man these things? " and secondly, " What is the wisdom
that is given unto this Man, and what mean such mighty
works wrought by His hands? " The two words, " what
mean " have been introduced by the translators. In all
probability they are helpful, but we may substitute two
others, and read thus: " What is the wisdom that is given
unto this Man, and *what are* such mighty works wrought
by His hands? " That carries the real thought of their
question more correctly to our minds.

There are two questions. " Whence hath this Man
these things? " Secondly, What are these things? What
is the wisdom, and what are the works that He is doing?

The questions which follow reveal the reason of the
first two. " Is not this the carpenter, the son of Mary,
and brother of James, and Joses, and Judas, and Simon?
and are not His sisters here with us? "

All this story is perfectly natural, tragically natural!
Nazareth was a town, probably of about ten thousand in-

habitants, one of those towns where every one knows every one else, and every one knows every one else's business, as a rule a little better than people know their own business! So they said of Jesus; this is the carpenter; the Man we know so well; His mother, and brothers and sisters are here with us.

We will now invert the order of our consideration, coming secondly to what they mentioned first. What did these men know of Jesus? They knew first, that He was one of a most ordinary family in Nazareth. They knew His brothers, they knew His sisters.

They knew also that He was " The Son of Mary." When He visited Nazareth a year before they did not say that. Then they said, " Is not this Joseph's Son? " Now they said, " Is not this the carpenter, the Son of Mary? " While not daring to dogmatize at this point, I am going to suggest a question. How much of suspicion and contempt may have lurked behind that particular description of Him? I do not think there can be any careful reading of these narratives, without recognizing that there were those who fastened upon Jesus an insufferable and intolerable stigma. There was another occasion upon which He was speaking of His Father, God, and the Father of the men by whom He was surrounded. They said unto Him—and there is the accent of a great satire and bitterness in it—" We were not born of fornication." I believe the sword that pierced through the soul of Mary was partly the fact that she also had to share the tragedy of misunderstanding, in the presence of the most infinite Mystery in all human history.

Then they knew Him as " the carpenter," the Man to Whom they had gone when they had required that yokes should be repaired, or ploughs refashioned; the carpenter Whom they had employed to attend to their houses, and probably to build them. These were the things they knew about Him.

But they now knew other things about Him. They

[133]

knew that He was a worker of powers. It was impossible
to deny it. They admitted it.

Perchance His working of powers was but the report
which had come from other places, but they knew Him
as a teacher of wisdom. On that very Sabbath they had
listened to Him once more, and were amazed at His wisdom.

Now look carefully at the story. Observe their mental
activity in the presence of what they knew, and their
consequent mental attitude. I have already drawn attention to the fact that they asked two questions, and we
want to understand them. They said, "Whence hath
this Man these things?" Whence hath *this* Man—
what man? This Man we know so well, Whose brothers and sisters are with us, the carpenter, the Son of
Mary; this Man Who has lived in our town, by our
side. We have observed no halo about His brow, no
sign of supernatural glory; He is one of ourselves;
whence hath this Man *these* things? Now mark the
second question. What is this wisdom, and what are
these works?

Lurking beneath these questions was a suspicion, which
ultimately became a conclusion, that the wisdom which
had amazed them, and the works that had filled them with
astonishment, resulted from His complicity with the underworld of evil. The wisdom was patent, the works
were evident! How did He get this wisdom; how did
He do these works? They said in effect; They are not
His own, these works; the wisdom He utters is not His
own. What is the secret of it all? Had they decided that
the secret was that of His fellowship with God, that
He was an instrument of God, that God was working
mighty works through Him, that God was giving Him the
wisdom which fell from His lips, then they had not been
offended in Him. They were offended in Him because
they came to the conclusion that He was in complicity
with the underworld of evil.

This was no new thought. It had been declared before. There were those who affirmed that by the Prince of the demons He cast out the demons; that He was in very deed an instrument of the underworld of evil. Now in Nazareth we detect the same line of thought, and the suspicion suggested by the question became their conclusion. " They were offended in Him," they were scandalized in Him, they tripped over Him and fell, for He was a stumbling-block in the way. They were scandalized in another sense. They were refusing to submit themselves to His wisdom, or to the appeal of His works, because, seeing that they thought they knew all about Him, they thought that these things could not be from above, but were from beneath. So wrought the minds of these men in Nazareth.

We come now to consider the cause of their unbelief. What brought them to this decision? The solution is not far to seek. It may be found in the words of our Lord upon this occasion, and in words that He uttered upon a similar occasion in Jerusalem, not to His fellow townsmen, but to the men of light and leading who were face to face with the same problem. In order to understand this unbelief, I shall make my appeal to the words He spoke here, and to the words He spoke upon the occasion referred to, in Jerusalem.

" A prophet is not without honour, save in his own country, and among his own kin, and in his own house." These are words which we constantly quote, and therefore I need not tarry with them, but will take the ugly heart out of the centre of them, and say that Jesus affirmed that the reason for their unbelief was that of envy, of the difficulty of acknowledging the superiority over themselves of one of their own number. That needs no exposition. We understand it so well. It is a part of humanity's inherent vulgarity, which persists through all the centuries, and is as powerful to-day as in Nazareth in the olden time. It is part of humanity's contempt for

itself, in which humanity imagines that it thinks highly
of itself; the inability to believe that the man who
worked by our side could ever be our teacher. We know
all about him, and therefore we cannot believe in him.

Observe then some implicates of this attitude as revealed here in Nazareth. First—and this is patent—
its unreasonableness. There were the facts, the wisdom
which they admitted, the powers which they acknowl-
edged; but they refused the appeal of the wisdom
and of the works. What reason was there in such
refusal? Mark the falseness of the attitude. The
only escape for them was that of attributing good to
evil. These good things came out of evil. This wisdom, which they admitted, came from the underworld
of evil. Yet listen once again to these men of Nazareth,
and notice the reaction of their criticism upon themselves.
He is one of us, therefore He is incapable of being an instrument of good! Mark how their criticism of Him,
had they understood it, was condemnation of themselves.
This man, who has worked by my side, cannot teach me
anything. Why not? Because he is on my level. Then
you can never teach any one anything. This man who
comes from our village, cannot come back to our village
and teach us anything. Why not? Because he is one
of us. Then the whole community labours under the disability of being unfit for doing anything that in itself is
great. Oh! these critics of Jesus in Nazareth! How
tacitly and unconsciously they were confessing their own
limitations.

But we have not touched the deepest note. It seems
to me that Jesus was very tender and patient with these
provincials. He did not say the deepest or profoundest
or most searching thing there. He reserved it for Jerusalem. There came a time a little later on when He was
in Jerusalem, and there in the midst of its light and culture and refinement, in Jerusalem as here at Nazareth,
they asked the question, Whence hath this Man the let-

ters, never having learned? In Nazareth, the little provincial town, they said, "Whence hath this Man these things?" But in Jerusalem they did not ask the question in that way. In Jerusalem they said, "How knoweth this Man the grammata, the letters?" As they might say to-day, Whence hath this man culture, never having been to Oxford or Cambridge, to Yale or Harvard? That is exactly the spirit of the enquiry. Oh, how it persists! There are some men preaching to-day who have to live in that atmosphere of criticism, and will do so, to the end.

But get behind their criticism, and see the marvel of it; that the Galilean Peasant Who astonished the Nazarenes, astonished metropolitan Jerusalem also, astonished them particularly in the realm of their own thinking. When Savonarola began to preach in Florence, people would not go to hear him, for they were offended at his Lombard accent. The people were living under the sway of Lorenzo de' Medici, in that wonderfully cultured age when Cardinal Bembo warned his clergy against studying the epistles of St. Paul, lest they should spoil their style! Dwight Lyman Moody beginning to preach in London, London was offended at his American accent. That is illustration by contrast. When Jesus went to Jerusalem there was no accent that marked Him as provincial. When Moody began to preach here, some people were offended at his grammar, or lack of it. When Jesus went to Jerusalem they said, "How knoweth this Man the letters, having never learned?" The Nazarenes and the men of Jerusalem, the provincials and metropolitans, were in the same difficulty. Whence? When Jesus accounted for the fact in Nazareth He said, "A prophet is not without honour, save in his own country." When He accounted for it in Jerusalem, He said: "My teaching is not Mine, but His that sent Me. If any man willeth to do His will, he shall know of the teaching, whether it be of God, or whether I speak from Myself."

Now with that word of Jesus in mind, we leave these metropolitans, and go back to Nazareth, and ask, what was the cause of the unbelief? Mark this tremendous thing. Jesus said in Jerusalem that willing to do God's will, created the capacity for detecting the Divine authorship and authority of what He said. He that wills to do the will of God shall know! Perhaps Jesus never said a more daring thing than that. In that word He challenged the attention of men to the end of time, declaring that wherever a man is found who in his heart wants to do the will of God, when that man hears His teaching, he will know it as the voice of God. In that word there is involved a revelation of the cause of their unbelief. The central motive of life was wrong. These men were not living solely to do the will of God. That they were not doing the will of God is not the point. Jesus did not say, He that doeth the will of God shall know; but, " He that willeth to do " it. There is a man who is not doing the will of God, but he wants to do it. Christ said, I can reach *that* man with Divine authority. Christ did not say the perfect man is the one who will know; but the man who wants to be perfect. His appeal was to the underlying motive, passion, desire of the heart, however it might be crippled, broken, paralyzed; for if the desire be there, said Christ, I have that to which I can appeal; and he who has such desire is the man who will discover the authority of My appeal.

These men in Nazareth were without that desire; the central motive of life was wrong. Instead of wanting to do the will of God, they wanted to please themselves. Consequently they were blinded in their outlook, and therefore were unbelieving.

Finally, then, what was the effect of their unbelief? Here we face at once the mystery, marvel, wonder, and solemnity of the whole meditation. " He could there do no mighty work." That is the paralysis of omnipotence. Why could He do no mighty work there? Because God

was excluded from the central desire and motive of life;
and as a result the men were degraded; when the light
of His wisdom and His works flashed upon them, they
loved the darkness, and hurried back into it, refusing
the light, and so God was shut out anew. "He could
there do no mighty work."

In this connection we find another of the most arresting statements of the New Testament. "He marvelled"
not *at* their unbelief; but "*because* of their unbelief."
Their unbelief was not the object of His marvelling; it
was the cause of it. If you are inclined to think that
is a distinction without a difference, I admit at once that
there is a sense in which the unbelief itself was an object. But He marvelled not at the fact, but at the nature
of it. Their unbelief opened up a far wider range;
and when I read that He marvelled, He was astonished
because of their unbelief, I begin to wonder over what
area His thinking ranged, when His soul was thus astonished. Perfectly understanding the unbelief, He marvelled at it; knowing its genesis He marvelled at it;
knowing its paralyzing power He marvelled at it.

I think there is a clear light on this in the Old Testament in one passage which, in some respects, has no relation to this story. Jeremiah in one high and exalted
hour of prophetic insight, said this most astonishing
thing: "My people have changed their glory for that
which doth not profit. Be astonished, O ye heavens, at
this, and be horribly afraid, be ye very desolate, saith
Jehovah. For My people have committed two evils; they
have forsaken Me, the fountain of living waters, and
hewed them out cisterns, broken cisterns, that can hold
no water." From that terrific passage in Jeremiah, take
out once more the central word, that daring thought
which assaults the soul, and almost makes it breathless.
"Be astonished, O ye heavens, at this;" be horribly
afraid, ye very heavens, at this; be ye desolate in the
presence of this! "He marvelled at their unbelief." It

[Mark 6: 1-6]

was God's astonishment in the presence of the unutterable and appalling folly of human unbelief.

The final effect of their unbelief was that He left them, never to return. Yet mark the discrimination of His grace. There were a few sick folk, whose longing eyes were fixed upon Him, and from whose hearts there came to Him an appeal, and He healed them! There He could do no mighty work; and yet so fine in its discrimination, and so quick and sensitive in its operation was the power of His infinite grace, that in the town hardened in its unbelief, paralyzing His own power, where there were weak hearts trembling toward Him, He laid His hands upon a few sick folk, and healed them.

We turn from this meditation upon the strange story of Nazareth, and think of modern unbelief. I am at once halted by my term. Modern unbelief? We are to-day a little in fear of the word modern; indeed, we are a little inclined to pay homage to it. I am getting somewhat tired of the modern mind, and the perpetual burning of incense to the modern mind, this eager, fitful anxiety to accommodate faith's declarations, and the whole Biblical revelation to the modern mind.

What is the modern mind? What is the meaning of the word modern? *Modern* simply means of the present time; *modernus,* of the present time; coming from that very simple Latin word *modo,* which means *just now.* Sometimes it is translated, and suitably so, *only;* sometimes *but.* Supposing we substitute some of these words, the *modern* mind, the *just now* mind. That is better. We are getting nearer to the meaning! The very word, modern, contradicts the idea of finality. It has, moreover, very close association etymologically with other words from which it seems to be entirely severed at the present moment. Modern has very close association with *moderate,* and *modest.* We are apt to forget this sometimes.

However modern the mind may be, and however much

[140]

we may burn incense to it, we need carefully to remember the continuity of some elements in men, and in the human mind. We need to remember the persistent place and importance of motive in mental activity. We need also constantly to remember that in all mental activity there is an alternative motive; the motive of truth, or the motive of casuistry. Behind that is the motive of God, or the motive of self. Thus the modern mind, and modern unbelief will be found very near akin to that modern unbelief of Nazareth.

What does modern unbelief know about Jesus? What are the established things from which neither faith nor unfaith can escape? There is first, the fact of the association of Jesus with persistent spiritual revolutions, secondly the association of Jesus with persistent, moral transformations; and finally the association of Jesus with persistent, material betterment. We name the name of Jesus. We remember it first as the name found in our New Testament. We then think of the name to-day, held in high reverence. From that first use of it by the men of Nazareth, until this latter use of it, it has had associated with it these things, spiritual revolutions, moral transformations, material betterment of the people.

One other thing modern unbelief must acknowledge. All these facts are related to the Jesus of the New Testament. All the results which are so rapidly covered by the phrases, spiritual revolutions, moral transformation, material betterment, have followed where the Jesus of these Gospel narratives has been preached and known. These results are not due to the Church as an ecclesiastical organization. These spiritual and moral and material results are not due to the theologians. They are due to Jesus, to the Jesus of the Gospels. It is as men have read these stories, and have seen Him, have listened to these very words, that these things have happened; and that through all the running centuries.

Remembering these facts, observe the attitudes of modern unbelief. Modern unbelief admits the first three, spiritual revolutions, moral transformations, material betterment, but denies the fourth; it is busy denying these very stories of the Gospels.

But mark where that kind of unbelief is leading men. They are not making the blunder of the Nazarenes of attributing good to evil. It is too late in the day to make that blunder. Modern unbelief is seeking to reconstruct the cause; admitting these results, it is offended in Him. It takes Jesus and the Gospel stories, and says, No, no, these things cannot spring from such an One. The ground of its mental operation may be covered by declaring that on the one hand it denies all the supernatural elements; and on the other—and this is the very latest phase—it denies the natural elements. Modern unbelief says first of all, that these stories of the supernatural are not true. Then modern unbelief is left to face facts without a sufficient cause, for if this Jesus be not as these Gospels represent Him—of our humanity, and yet other than our humanity, closely and intimately related in some infinite mystery to the Godhead and to our human experience, while yet for ever standing separate therefrom —if He be not the Logos incarnate, Man born of the will and power of God alone, then I am not surprised that modern unbelief says that these results cannot have sprung from such an One, and so comes at last to this final deduction, the denial of the natural, declaring that Jesus did not live.

Then what must unbelief do? Modern unbelief is seeking among the things of spiritual darkness, moral turpitude, and material degradation, for the things that change the darkness into the light, the turpitude into morality, and the degradation into liberty. Modern unbelief is face to face in that search with an impasse.

What is the effect of modern unbelief, wherever it asserts itself? This, " He could there do no mighty works." Modern unbelief without Jesus can work no

spiritual revolution, and produce no moral transformation; and therefore in the long issue will produce no
material betterment. All attempts to better the condition of humanity fail save as they are under the mastery of moral conceptions; and moral conceptions perish
save as they result from spiritual inspirations.

We remind ourselves to-day, that His wisdom under-
lies all modern thinking, and His mighty works have
moulded all modern history. That wisdom is found in
the speech of Jesus as recorded, and in those very works
in the presence of which men are stumbling to-day; in all
that "He began both to do and teach."

We ask anew, Whence hath this Man these things?
We affirm our belief in His own answer as John records
it, both in regard to the teaching and the doing. Hear
then these words of Jesus. "The very works that I do,
bear witness of Me, that the Father hath sent Me."
Hear Him again. "My teaching is not Mine, but His
that sent Me."

Then, by the works and teaching of long ago; proceeding in their prevailing power through every successive century unto this moment; these being the things that
inspire the best thinking of the age, and formulate its
highest activities; by these things we affirm Him still,
this Man of Nazareth, the Sent of God, and therefore the
Saviour of the world.

XIII

" And the apostles gather themselves together unto Jesus; and they told Him all things, whatsoever they had done, and whatsoever they had taught. And He saith unto them, Come ye yourselves apart into a desert place, and rest a while. For there were many coming and going, and they had no leisure so much as to eat. And they went away in the boat to a desert place apart."
—MARK 6: 30–32.

Mark 6: 7–56.

IN these words we have the account of how the first apostolic mission ended. They constitute the minutes of a meeting for report and review, most probably held in the month of April.

The story of this first mission of the twelve is told by Matthew, Mark, and Luke, in each case with arresting and notable brevity. Mark and Luke each give a clear and concise statement of the facts, while Matthew gives some particulars.

It is at once an interesting and important story. Its brevity is part of its value. There can be no better vantage ground for considering the story, than this report of the gathering which followed the mission.

According to His appointment, these men had been with Him for a period of training, at least about a year. From that moment when from among the number of His disciples He selected twelve, and appointed them to be with Him in order that ultimately He might send them forth to preach and to cast out demons, that period had passed. During that time they knew that they were being prepared to be sent away from Him to do His work. They had been observing Him at His work, and listening to His words. In that period they had seen His power

[144]

manifested in every department of human life. They had observed the wonderful ease with which He had healed physical infirmity, the majesty with which He had cast out demons; in full and final authority, they had watched His working in the spiritual realm, forgiving sin, and bringing peace to the conscience. They had finally seen Him unable to do anything, His power paralyzed; He could do no mighty works in Nazareth because of their unbelief.

Then the hour had arrived when He had sent them forth, the men who had been with Him so constantly; sent them away to be His representatives, to say the things He had Himself been saying, to do the things He had Himself been doing. On their return this gathering was held. Let us then consider the report of the apostles; the response of the Lord; and then look at the things immediately following, as recorded in this chapter.

First, with regard to the report of the apostles, note that it is not printed. There is no account of anything they did in detail, no mention of any place to which they went definitely, no record of any discourse that either of their number delivered, no story of any interesting incident. That is the first arresting fact.

Yet the essential things are revealed. The story begins in the sixth chapter of Mark, at verse seven, immediately after a declaration which in the arrangement of the Revised Version is put with singular aptness, quite alone. Verse six is divided, almost strangely divided, and yet very properly so. The last part of the verse reads thus, "And He went round about the villages teaching." This immediately followed His rejection at Nazareth. It is a lonely little paragraph, hardly a paragraph, a sentence merely. For the illumination of that sentence we need the longer paragraph and more detailed declaration which is found in the Gospel of Matthew at the close of the ninth chapter, where Matthew also draws attention, not to any one particular occasion, but to the general ministry

of our Lord, to that itinerating ministry which Mark dis-
misses in this brief sentence. Matthew declares in that
paragraph that He went about all the cities and villages,
teaching in their synagogues, preaching the Gospel of the
Kingdom, healing all manner of diseases; and that when
He saw the multitudes He was moved with compassion
for them, for they were as sheep not having a shepherd,
distressed and scattered. In that declaration of Mark, so
briefly made, without note or comment or explanation, in
the light of the fuller declaration of Matthew, we have
discovered the inspiration of the apostolic mission. It
was that of the King's compassion for His people. He
saw them as sheep without a shepherd, that is as a mob,
disorganized, lacking the true principle of government;
for the shepherd figure in Biblical literature, and in all
Eastern literature, is the true figure of the kingly position.
Here the King, rejected of His own, is seen moving
through the villages and cities, and moved with compassion for the people as He saw them, distressed, scattered
sheep without a shepherd, a people without the true central authority which is based upon love, expressing itself
in righteousness.

That was the inspiration of the apostolic mission. It
was as the result of this seeing of the people that Jesus
called the twelve whom He had been preparing, and
immediately enlarged the sphere and scope of His own
ministry, by calling them to share His ministry and His
power. Our Lord was labouring under limited and strait-
ened circumstances; and in order that more of the villages might be reached, that more of the folk of the
cities might hear the message; that the proclamation of
the Kingdom—with its exhibition of power in the wonders wrought, in the exorcising of demons, in the healing
of the sick—might have a wider area, He sent these
twelve men out.

We also have here a revelation of the nature of their
mission. There are distinct differences between their

[146]

mission and ours. There are also fundamental similarities. In their case the mission was limited, and their material equipment was a limited one. Later on our Lord changed that entirely. The instructions given to them here regarding hospitality were instructions that marked the transitory nature of their stay at a place, and the necessity for pressing on quickly that ground might be covered. Also they were strictly charged, as Matthew tells us, not to go to the Gentiles, nor to enter into any city of the Samaritans. They were limited to the house of Israel. These are things in which this particular mission differed from that which is now the full mission of the Church.

But the mission upon which these men were sent was a most important one. They went in His name; thus they were apostles now who never had been before. They had been disciples, but now they became apostles, men sent in His name, to represent Him, having entered into the fellowship of His authority because they had His message, and because they had the power that He had given them to do His works. They were sent forth with a definite message, " the Kingdom of heaven is at hand." They had given to them, special powers over the underworld of evil for the casting out of demons, and to heal the sick.

These men were sent out two by two. Our Lord never sent any man alone to a difficult sphere of work. We have often done so, and do it yet, and in that way wander from a fundamental principle. We will presently glance back at Matthew's Gospel, and see the couples as they went on that first missionary journey, a passage full of light and suggestiveness.

What do we know of their work? No place is indicated, no journey described, no discourse recorded, no special day referred to, no interesting incident recounted. But we are told certain things.

First they preached that men should repent. That is

a declaration that needs careful consideration. It does not mean that they told men to repent, but that they preached in such a way as to produce repentance. While this is a brief sentence, how much there is suggested by it, of personal conviction, of earnest statement, of argument, of appeal. They so preached that men should repent.

Their going was that of faith. They had nothing to prove to them that they possessed the power except the Lord's own word spoken, until they demonstrated their possession of it in the presence of demon-possessed men and women. A little later in His ministry, when He sent out the seventy, they came back amazed at the results themselves, and full of joy that " the demons are subject unto us." One cannot read this story without feeling that when first one of these twelve men stood confronted by a demon-possessed man, and commanded him to come out, it was a venture of faith.

One other thing is revealed here; the effect produced by their mission. The statement is a little involved, and the greater fact is declared in a secondary sentence. This is the summary of the whole effect that their mission produced: " His name had become known "; and as a result, " King Herod heard "! What then was the result of this first apostolic mission? The cumulative and sufficient answer will not take any count of the number of demons cast out,—there are no statistics; will not take any count of the number of people healed,—there are no records; but the answer is this: " His name had become known." He was given a wider area through which He was known, a larger space in which He bulked, as the result of their work. Every evangelist gives as the central evidence of the spread of the fame of Jesus, that of the terror of Herod. With the story of Herod I am now not interested, save as it has a bearing upon this meditation. Here however are two evidences of the victory of the apostles; the first being that " His name had become known "; secondly, that the incarnation of all evil, vulgarity, and sin, trembled, even though he sat upon a throne. Such were the effects produced.

The second thing to observe in the consideration of this report of the twelve is that they told the Lord all the things that they had done, and all the things that they had taught. Imagine those six reports, not written but spoken. Let us look at these couples as they were given by Matthew. Notice the grouping.

" Simon . . . and Andrew his brother." Andrew was the first disciple of Jesus. Simon was his brother, whom he had brought to Christ. They had been somewhere working together; we do not know where.

" James the son of Zebedee, and John his brother." John had been with Andrew when Andrew first followed the Lord, and I think he went and found James. That is speculation, and may be dismissed. These brothers went together. What they did we do not know. I can believe they had some fiery times, these Boanerges men!

The next two; Philip, who was the first disciple whom Jesus definitely called, and with him Bartholomew. This man Philip went and found Nathanael. So Philip, the quiet man, always on the outskirts of the crowd, helpful, sympathetic toward the strangers, and Nathanael the guileless, went somewhere; we do not know where. I think their meetings were much quieter than those of the first and second couples.

" James the son of Alphæus, and Thaddæus." No one knows much about them. There are always two or three people in the Lord's elect company whom no one knows much about; but *He* knows all about them.

" Thomas, and Matthew." Thomas the sceptic, which simply means the man who looks at things from a distance, and investigates them. Matthew, the man whose business it was to keep accounts and give records. They went together, and I do not think that I could describe their meetings.

[149]

Then there were two others, "Simon the Canan-æan," the Zealot, the member of a hot political party, and "Judas Iscariot." These were the couples.

Now they had all returned, and were giving in their reports, and they told Him all that they had done. There is no list of deeds, there is no schedule of results. They went over with Him the things they had said. They told all to the Lord from Whom they had received their message, from Whom they had derived their power, to Whom alone they were responsible. Those reports would probably be very varied. I am glad that they are not printed. We might have had a School adopting the methods of James and John, the School of Boanerges; and another adopting the methods of Philip and Nathanael, the School of the quiet men; and so on. In the telling of everything to the Lord, and in His presence, they would discover the necessity for the man who goes about quietly, the Nathanael type of man; and the men who move like thunder-storms, James and John!

So we come to the second suggestion of the text, that namely of the response of the Lord. "Come ye yourselves apart into a desert place, and rest a while." As we read the words we should be careful lest we rob them of all their beauty by wholly spiritualizing them. Of course they have spiritual significance and intention. But to interpret them in the true sense, we need to go back in imagination, and look at the scene. Look into the face of Jesus, into those wonderful eyes that we have never seen with eyes of sense, but yet know so much about, those eyes which are always looking. The New Testament is full of the seeing and the looking of Jesus. He looked upon these men and listened to them. He noted the fact of their physical weariness, and began there. "Come ye yourselves apart into a desert place, and rest a while"; and we will not go anywhere, where we have to walk; let us get into the boat, and go over the sea. So they went. The rest was mental; no teaching

[150]

for a little while and no thinking. The rest was spiritual; no conflict with the underworld of evil for a while, and no praying for a little.

What were the conditions? They were to go with Him. They were to go themselves. They were to go apart. They were to go to the desert place. What a revelation is this of the understandingness of Jesus. What a revelation it is of the tender character of Jesus. Some people do not understand this, because they are well and strong, and are fit and eager for service. There *are* men and women who understand! He knew that these men were tired, and He said, Come and rest a while. Never mind any more journeyings for a little time. Do not think; do not pray for a little time. Rest!

If the story is a revelation of His understandingness, of His care, I go further and say it is a stupendous revelation of His wisdom. It is a rebuking revelation to some of us. Recently I came across this little paragraph from Amiel:

"We must know how to put occupation aside, which does not mean that we must be idle. In an inaction which is meditative and attentive the wrinkles of the soul are smoothed away. The soul itself spreads, unfolds, and springs afresh; and, like the trodden grass of the roadside or the bruised leaf of a plant, repairs its injuries, becomes new, spontaneous, true, and original."

So Jesus said to these men: "Come ye yourselves apart, and rest a while." Did they rest? The first thing was the boat, and a short voyage and not in a modern Atlantic liner! It was a voyage to Eastern Bethsaida; for there are two places of that name, one in the northeast, to which they went; and the other on the western shore of the lake. It was a voyage of ten or twelve miles of quietness and bodily rest.

But when they came to the desert place crowds were waiting. Then Mark records that He, the King Who had sent them forth, and Who having received them and their report, had called them to rest, was moved with compassion for that waiting crowd; because they were as sheep having no shepherd. The inspiration that had sent them forth was still burning within the heart of the King, and He gave Himself to teach the multitudes. The disciples did nothing. They were resting, as they watched Him, for Whom there was no rest, until He had accomplished His mission finally. They watched Him Who had to say in answer to criticism, "My Father worketh even until now, and I work." They watched Him give Himself once again with unstinted sacrifice to the crowds. But they were resting. Oh yes! they had their rest. I think I know enough of how they felt that day. It was a wonderfully restful time, such as that man, whose work is preaching, has, when he sits quietly down in some little village chapel, and listens to another man breaking the bread of life. No responsibility; just the quiet rest of it all. Oh yes! they had their rest. I have often said they had no rest; and thought they had not, until I began to look more carefully. They had their rest, but He did not. There was no resting time for Him during the days of His flesh.

But now glance at the two pictures which immediately follow; the story of the feeding of the five thousand, and the story of the storm.

When the day was far spent the crowds that Jesus had been teaching became a responsibility. The disciples said to Him, "Send them away, that they may go into the country and villages round about, and buy themselves somewhat to eat." That was the voice of the apostles. They said, "Send them away"; but Jesus said, "Give ye them to eat." Then the apostles spoke again, "Shall we go and buy two hundred shillings' worth of bread, and give them to eat?" It was the inquiry of protest. Jesus said, "How many loaves have ye?" They replied, "Five, and two fishes." And He said, "Bring them hither to Me." The results were that the multitudes were filled; and the disciples gathered up twelve basketfuls.

The story of the storm is one concerning these men, in the way of His will. He asked them to enter the boat, and cross back again to the other shore. They went. Remember that the way of His will was the way of the storm. He sent them into the storm, and there is a strong word used here concerning that storm. We have translated it " distressed." Far more literally we may render, They were " *tormented* in rowing." Why did they not turn back to the other shore? The wind was contrary. There was the difficulty. The wind was blowing off the shore to which He had commanded them to go. It would have been the simplest thing to tack, to put about, and run before the wind. But no! they must not do that. Why not? He sent them in that direction! They were tormented in the very path of obedience. But it was also the way of His power. He came after them. The wind was contrary to Him also, but did not hinder Him. The waters were storm-tossed for Him also, but they constituted the pavement of His victorious footsteps. When presently He was in the boat, the storm ceased.

Now look at the apostles, and mark the things that are said concerning them carefully. They were amazed. Why were they amazed? Mark says that it was because " They understood not concerning the loaves." These were apostles, not outsiders. Then why was it that they understood not concerning the loaves? Mark tells us that their heart was hardened; which means that they were dull, stupid, and therefore did not understand the miracle of the loaves, and consequently they were amazed at His mastery of the elements.

Now in all this my purpose has been that we should see the apostles. It was an interesting and revealing meeting when they told Him all they had done, and all they had taught; and the things following are equally interesting and revealing. So these were the apostles;

these men, who when they had been on that mission and returned, could only say in the presence of the hungry crowd, Send them away to buy; these men, who when Jesus told them to do the most natural thing, and feed them, argued, Shall we go and buy two hundred shillings' worth of bread; these men, who when He mastered the supernatural personally and for them, were amazed; these men who did not understand; these men who were dull and stupid! These were the apostles. Thank God! I think I can pray now, and go on a little longer. They were *His* apostles. He chose them, and He makes no mistakes. Consequently what is the ultimate truth that breaks upon the soul after such a consideration? That in all our service we must say, " Not unto us, O Jehovah, not unto us, But unto Thy name give glory."

He chooses, Oh gracious thing! He equips, Oh most wondrous thing! He uses, Oh amazing thing! He gives rest, and He patiently bears with all inability to understand Him in the presence of the hungry multitude, and all the inability to understand Him when He masters the waves and the winds. Oh tender and beautiful thing!

My deliberate conclusion is that the report is hardly worth printing; and it never is! It would be well for us if we told the Lord more often what we do and teach; and told each other less often.

XIV

" Ye leave the commandment of God, and hold fast the tradition of men. . . . Full well do ye reject the commandment of God, that ye may keep your tradition."
—MARK 7 : 8, 9.

Mark 7 : 1–23.

THE narrative of these first twenty-three verses of the seventh chapter of Mark's Gospel stands in striking contrast to that of the last twenty-seven verses of the previous chapter. That was the story of the gathering to the Lord of His apostles. This is the story of the gathering to the Lord of His adversaries. The respective beginnings show this. " And the apostles gather themselves together unto Jesus." " And there are gathered together unto Him the Pharisees, and certain of the scribes, which had come from Jerusalem." The first was the gathering of friends whose mission was to help Him. The second was the gathering of foes, whose purpose was to hinder Him.

That this story is of special importance there can be no doubt. These men who gathered to the Lord came officially from Jerusalem. The sending out of the twelve had drawn new attention to Jesus, impressing even Herod in the royal palace. The movement in Galilee was evidently growing, and that rapidly. The religious leaders in Jerusalem were perturbed, and sent a deputation to investigate. The occasion of controversy, apparently a trifling one, was nevertheless a most revealing one. In it, the religious ideal for which these men stood, is clearly manifested. The way in which our Lord dealt with them is singularly arresting in its anger, satire, directness, and scorn; and in that careful explanation of the meaning of His method which He subsequently gave to His disciples.

THE GOSPEL ACCORDING TO MARK

[Mark 7: 1–23]

In this incident two opposing ideals of religion are seen coming into conflict; that of the Pharisees and scribes, and that of Jesus. Theirs was that of the punctilious observance of traditions; His was that of simple obedience to the commandment of God. He shocked them in the habits of His disciples; they shocked Him in their disregard of the will of God.

Now there is a sense in which this story does not startle us. This is due to the fact that this whole question of ceremonial washings appears to us as patently futile, and we have a sense of real satisfaction in the way in which our Lord dealt with these men. But in that very feeling of satisfaction there is peril. It may be that our satisfaction results from a very superficial understanding of what our Lord really meant. If we can disengage the elemental principles from the incidental circumstances, we may be startled, perchance, quite as much as these men were.

If our Lord were here to-day in bodily form, He would not say to us the things He said to these men, because we should not say to Him the things they said. But I am not at all sure that He would not shock very many of those who bear His name, not so much by what He would do, as by the apparently religious things He would not do. That method of statement may bring us nearer to the real meaning of this story.

Let us then endeavour to understand this clashing of ideals revealed in the controversy between the deputation from Jerusalem, and Jesus. This we will do by considering, first, the history and intention of tradition; secondly, the genesis of obedience to tradition as Jesus laid it bare on this occasion; and thirdly and finally, the effects of tradition as our Lord revealed them.

It is pertinent therefore to our enquiry that we first simply ask what was meant by tradition upon this occasion, and in this atmosphere. What were these traditions to which our Lord made reference, not here alone, but again and again in the course of His public ministry, always in order to denounce them? They were precepts orally transmitted, illustrating, applying, expounding the written law. Some of the later Jewish teachers of that period claimed that the traditions were orally given by Moses. Earlier teachers had claimed that the traditions came from the elders who were associated with Moses. I am not proposing to argue this matter, but simply say that neither position was warranted.

The history and development of the traditions to which our Lord made reference here, and to which these men themselves made reference, were largely Pharisaic. The whole Pharisaic movement was born in the period of Jewish history, of which we practically have no record in our Bible. It was born of an intensely religious conviction. It is sometimes said—and the definition is more accurate than we are always willing to admit—that the Pharisees were originally the Puritans of their age. In that period the people had been gathered together and localized at Jerusalem, under different leaders; and Babylonian and Greek influences were threatening altogether the lonely separateness of the Hebrew people. The Pharisees were men who at this time had banded themselves together to maintain, by all means in their power, the distinction between the Jewish people and the nations surrounding them.

There arose at the same time the order of the scribes, who were always associated with the Pharisees. Not all scribes were Pharisees, and not all Pharisees were scribes; but there was the closest association between them. The work of the scribes was that of taking the law of God, illustrating it, and applying it to local circumstances, and local situations. As men enquired: What does the law of God mean for us at this point, or this juncture? the scribes interpreted the law of God.

Gradually they formulated precepts to meet the new conditions. These precepts constantly increased in number, in an attempt to keep pace with the ever-growing complexity of the conditions of life, until there had grown up a great body of traditions; traditions which in the first place were intended to be interpretations of the law, and applications of the law to local circumstances; traditions which in the second place became interpretations of traditions, and applications of traditions; and traditions in the third place, which were interpretations of interpretations of interpretations of traditions! So the movement ran, until there existed between the people of God and the law of God such a mass of tradition, that the law of God itself was out of sight, and practically forgotten.

Into the midst of this ideal of religious life Jesus came. The intention of tradition was that of the maintenance of religion. Here therefore we must make a very necessary distinction, which distinction our Lord made so graphic and patent in the words of our text, between the traditions and the law of God. That distinction must be made even in the highest realm of the consideration of tradition. The law of God must be kept separate and apart, quite alone from any human interpretation of it, which is a tradition. The law was given, and men in such sincere and devout ages, obediently desiring to maintain the law, interpreted the law to men. That was tradition, human tradition, human interpretation of the law.

To leave the Hebrew atmosphere, it may be that some may think this can have very little application to us. Certainly in the beginning of the Christian era, within the Christian Church, there were very few traditions. Those early Christians lived in such close relationship with the first Christian movement, that traditions were very few. That is wonderfully illustrated in the book of the Acts of the Apostles, in which—if there be one thing that is more manifestly and gloriously surprising than another—is seen the freedom of life in the Spirit. A particular Church doctrine cannot be based upon the Acts of the Apostles. A formulated creed cannot be found in the Acts of the Apostles. The warrant for any particular liturgical service cannot be deduced from anything there written. The Spirit is the Spirit of freedom, the Spirit of love, Who fulfils Himself in a thousand ways, but has always the one life. As the book of the Acts is read from that standpoint, we are greatly impressed with the fact that if we would make our appeal for anything that is traditional, we cannot go to the book of the Acts of the Apostles for our confirmation.

But traditions came within the Christian Church; they grew in number, and had exactly the same intention, that of maintaining the strength and character of the life. Systematic expressions of the belief of the Christian Church are but systematic expressions of belief, and are to be numbered among the traditions of the Christian Church; sincere, wonderful, but human interpretation only. When some man or number of men, some college, apostolic band, or council of the Church, gathered together and formulated into definite expression the doctrines of the Church, they were giving their traditions, and human interpretations. So also came in process of time certain definitely declared forms of Church polity, as men wrought out the things they believed concerning the true method of the government of the Church, in order to its fulfilment of life and service. Thus there grew up in process of time such forms of Church life as differed from each other by traditions. That most wonderful of all, the Book of Common Prayer, is one of the more modern illustrations of what I mean. It is a wonderful compilation! It is impossible for any man to join in a service where it is used without feeling that he is being brought into the true atmosphere of reverent worship; but it is a tradition, a set form of worship arranged by men.

Sometimes these traditions take other forms: uniformity of dress, modes of common speech; until the Church of God to-day is a mass of tradition, conflicting, contradictory, as great as were the traditions that had covered up the Hebrew religion in the time of Christ.

Here again the necessary distinction must be made between the revelation which is given to us, which is authoritative and final; and these traditions. The revelation is that of the Old Testament Scriptures interpreted by the New, and never apart from the New; and that of the New Testament Scriptures, in their revelation of Christ, and in their declaration of the principles of Christian service in the great writings of the Apostles and others. We must remember to distinguish between these, and traditions which are but human interpretations of them. Every creed of the Church, Athanasian, Nicene, or any other, is but an attempt to interpret the things of the Oracles of God; reverent attempts, made necessary in some hour of crisis, when for the crystallization of truth into the phrases and terms of the hour, men were making an attempt which had to be made; but after all, they were human interpretations, and nothing more.

Notice in the second place, what our Lord said to these men concerning the genesis, not of tradition, but of obedience to tradition: " Ye leave the commandment of God, and hold fast the tradition of men." This is a most startling announcement. He declared in that statement that the movement which leads men into subjugation to tradition is one of departure from the commandment of God. Directly a precept made for an occasion becomes a binding tradition to be subsequently obeyed, it is evil. Directly a creed formulated for an hour is crystallized into that which is to dominate the thought of men for subsequent ages, it is a curse. Directly a form of worship, or a form of church organization made necessary by the exigency of an age, is stereotyped into something that is to arrest the mind and soul of men perpetually, it becomes an evil thing. Men only submit to such when they pass out of immediate relationship with God. The in-

dividual soul never submits to the partial human interpretation, if that soul is living in immediate fellowship with
God. The corporate Church of God, living in fellowship
with the living Head, knowing His truth and righteousness and prevailing power, will never suffer itself to be
brought under the trammels of human teachers or the
arrangements of human office-bearers. Ever and anon
we have seen such a corporate Church of Jesus Christ,
almost always to be spoiled within a decade by tradition.
The first movement toward the mastery of the soul by
tradition is the movement of that soul away from immediate, direct, first-hand fellowship with God.

All this line of thinking is illuminated strangely and
wonderfully by the habit of Jesus. Follow Him along the
way of His earthly ministry, from that strange and wonderful hour when hearing the voice of the Hebrew
prophet, He emerged from the silent seclusion of Nazareth, and commenced the work of public teaching; and
watch Him carefully. The whole truth may be summarized by declaring that Jesus violated these traditions
systematically, intentionally, resolutely. Gather out the
instances which reveal His attitude toward the Sabbath,
and it will be found that the first cause of quarrel between Himself and the rulers was His violation of the
tradition concerning the Sabbath.

Then observe that again and again, in spite of the objection which they raised, which was bitter with the bitterness of great anger and hatred, He resolutely set Himself to do the same thing, over and over again. He
wrought His wonders of healing on the Sabbath, violating
their traditions, and trampling them under His feet,
shocking them with the irreligiousness,—as it seemed to
them—of His attitude toward the Sabbath.

I am not for a moment inferring that our Lord violated
the Sabbath. He never did so; but He violated their
false conceptions concerning it. He flung Himself persistently, in habit, word, deed, and attitude, against all

those traditions that stood between the soul of the people and their God.

Let us come away once more from the immediate and the incidental, and see the application of this teaching. In the examples already taken, mark the continuity of religious principles. No man who is living in true fellowship with God will consent to be mastered mentally by any creed that ever yet has been prepared for him. The proportion in which a man knows the high life of fellowship with God, is the proportion in which he knows that no creed his brother may write for him, no creed he may write for himself, can be final. No man or company of men, no Church living in true fellowship with God, will consent that its polity be stereotyped, or will confuse form with power, or life with the method of its expression. I have sometimes said, and shocked some of my friends by saying it, that I could hold a brief for every known form of Church polity on the basis of the New Testament. I could argue at length, if not eloquently, for Baptists. I could do the same for Presbyterianism, for Episcopalianism, and of course for Congregationalism. And I never forget that my argument would be based upon this fact, that life is more than a form of expression. Life may change its form of expression under different circumstances, with the coming of different needs. Consequently I can never quarrel with my brethren who are not following my conviction so far as Church polity is concerned. But I must never allow myself to be mastered by any polity when it interferes with my relation to life in the Lord Jesus Christ. Depend upon it, the souls who are enslaved by some form of ecclesiastical polity are weak and anæmic. The soul of man has immediate, first-hand fellowship with God. I hold that to be peculiarly true of any order of service that ever yet has been arranged for the worship of the saints, of any uniformity of dress, or manner of speech that has been adopted by the saints.

This teaching of Christ flings itself with force against every habit of excommunication on the basis of human creeds. It makes its undying protest against the habit of isolation on ecclesiastical grounds. It denies the possibility of stereotyped orders of service, so that there is no room for the movement of the life of God. It smiles with patience on all peculiarities of dress and modes of speech that are supposed to be symbols of sanctity, and of relationship to Christ. And the smile is not satirical, it is sympathetic.

Further, in this word of Jesus spoken long ago, there is a deeper note. He revealed here not only the genesis of obedience to tradition as being that of departure from God; but He revealed in the most startling way the effects of obedience to tradition. All we have already said needs qualification by way of explanation. His violation was not for the sake of violation. He only violated the tradition because it violated the law which it was intended to honour.

As we come to the remainder of this story, we hear the things He said as they reveal the real reason of His satire, His anger, His ruthless violating of all human traditions. He made it perfectly clear first of all that the tradition of man misses its own aim. Men are still defiled, wash they never so often. The inner life is never reached by external ceremony. External observance is only valuable as an expression of an inner life, and the expression of the inner life cannot be stereotyped. Consequently if the tradition be made, that there must be ceremonial ablution before men eat a meal, what is the value of it? Unless the ablution be an outward physical sign of inward spiritual cleansing, it is worthless. When the washing of baptism is the outward and physical sign of the inward and invisible grace, then it is useful and in its proper place. But when a man shall imagine that the ablution, the washing of baptism makes him a child of God, an inheritor of the Kingdom of heaven, he is mastered by a

tradition that is blighting him, and robbing him of the
faith he desires to realize, and misses his aim.

More than that, it stultifies its own purpose. The law
of God, which tradition was intended to interpret and
maintain, is insulted by it. Here again is an illustration
with which we are very familiar, and yet how much light
it throws upon the time in which Jesus lived, and then
upon our own times. Their tradition was that a man
might escape responsibility for father or mother by declaring that that which he could give to help them, was
Corban, dedicated, given to God. Look at the picture
Christ presents. A man who had a responsibility in
material things, for a father and a mother, escaped his
responsibility by declaring that that which might have
helped them was dedicate to the Temple. Oh! the anger,
the scorn of Jesus! He says, " Full well do ye reject the
commandment of God that ye may keep your tradition."
The deepest thing any human life knows of a man's relationship to God—his duty to father and mother—is to
be violated in the interests of his duty to God; and this
is what tradition does! Thus Jesus declared that men
are brutalized by tradition. Men mastered by tradition
become the slaves of these human interpretations, and
the very springs of compassion are dried up, and all the
finest parts of the nature are destroyed. Thus religion is
destroyed, when men are mastered by traditions.

These things persist. However excellent the intention
of tradition, however valuable the precept in the hour
when it was formulated for a local circumstance or condition; if that tradition take the place of the law of God;
if that opinion of the past interfere between the soul and
its immediate contact with God; if that expression of
truth, or order of Church government, or method of worship coming from the past, exclude the soul from immediate fellowship with God, make impossible that hearing
of the soul that catches the wind that bloweth where it
listeth, destroy that freedom of life that only comes where

the soul has direct access to God; then the tradition blights and blasts, however good its first intention may have been.

So finally, looking at the whole scene of the past, again being arrested by the earnestness of Christ here, by the directness of His word and the almost fierce invective of it, and the satire of it; let us remind ourselves that Christ's conception of religion as that of the direct obedience of the soul to the direct law of God, is the only one which can ensure to the soul its full realization of its own life. It is only in proportion as we individually find our way into that relationship which our Lord came to make possible as Saviour, and for evermore interpret through the Spirit, that life can be fulfilled.

This conception of life is at once difficult and easy. It is difficult. It seems to us so much simpler to live by rule than by principle, so much easier to find human sanction than to discover the will of God, so much easier to take an order from priest, or pope, or council, than to discover the will of God. There are moments of stress and strain when almost every man, while not likely to become a Romanist, wishes he could persuade himself to be one! If we only could make ourselves believe that the word spoken to us by another were the infallible word! But we cannot! It is against that pernicious tendency that Christ flung Himself. We must deal with God directly, immediately. The moment we admit any kind of tradition, or the exercise of authority that is based upon tradition, to come between the soul and God, we are impoverishing the soul, rendering it anæmic, weak, sickly. This conception of life is difficult.

But it is also easy, because when once the soul dare break through the trammels, and become utterly careless of human opinion, and walk with God, it finds a path of reason, a path of power, a path of joy. I repeat, when once a soul dare break through the trammels. That is the point of difficulty. We are so much in the power of

tradition that there are some who dare not stay away
from a service because people might imagine they were ir-
religious! I believe there are a great many services most
regularly held, that Jesus Christ would never attend!
What we need to-day, if I know the temper of my own
time, and the spirit of my own age, more than anything
else is a return to that fine independence of soul which is
created by loyalty to the Saviour and King, that brings
men and women back to God, bursting the bonds and
trammels of tradition.

In the moment of the soul's yielding to Him, will come
the great hour in which the world will see the Kingdom
of God, and the glory of its King. Let us become free-
men by becoming His bondslaves. Let us know the destruction of every yoke of bondage, by wearing the one
yoke that He places upon us. Let us practise our bondage, and so realize our freedom.

XV

"He hath done all things well."—MARK 7 : 37.

Mark 7 : 24–8 : 26.

IN this paragraph we have the story of the last things in the public ministry of Jesus, prior to the confession of Peter at Cæsarea Philippi, and the new teaching and method which followed that confession.

The story contained in this paragraph may be divided into two parts. The first gives the account of a Gentile ministry of Jesus which was new, and must have been startling to His disciples, and to others. He travelled north, away from the earlier scene of His labour, so far as Tyre, and there He healed the daughter of the Syrophœnician woman. Then, proceeding still further north, and bearing to the northeast, He came to Sidon, travelling in a southerly direction through Decapolis, the country of the Ten Cities, all the while in Gentile territory, exercising a ministry among these Gentiles similar to that which He had been exercising among the Hebrew people. All this is contained in chapter seven, from verse twenty-four to the end of the ninth verse of chapter eight.

The second part of the paragraph, commencing at the tenth verse of chapter eight, and ending at the twenty-sixth verse, takes us back again into a hostile atmosphere. As He returned across the sea to Dalmanutha, He was immediately met by Pharisees and Sadducees demanding a sign. Then, once more crossing the sea in company of His disciples, He warned them, and dealt with their blindness. The brief story ends with the account of their arrival on the other side—on the northeastern shore of the lake—again in Gentile territory, and the opening of the eyes of the blind man.

The text, " He hath done all things well," is resolutely

borrowed from the context. The words were spoken by the Gentiles, and had special reference to the healing ministry which Jesus had been exercising in Decapolis, of which Mark gives no account, but which Matthew records quite clearly, and to this wonderful miracle, the opening of the ears of the deaf man, and the straightening out of his twisted tongue. It was in the presence of these evidences of His power that these Gentiles said, " He hath done all things well."

If, however, I admit that I resolutely borrow the text from its context, let me hasten to add it is not ruthlessly so taken; for accepting the conclusion of these Gentiles, I propose simply to make a wider application of it; to let this declaration cover the whole of these events, and so form a fitting conclusion to that survey of the public ministry of our Lord which at this point ceases. By its use in this way, I desire to fasten attention upon Him.

In these events we see Him in His relation to humanity in its varied needs. We will take that outlook, ignoring the racial division which we have already recognized as between the Gentile and the Jew; simply looking at Him as He stands confronting these varied phases and illustrations of human need. Such a meditation will constrain us at the conclusion to return to the text and say, " He hath done all things well."

We know these stories, and are indeed very familiar with them. We glance at them once again, desiring, as we move in front of the pictures they present in imagination, specially to observe the need represented.

The first picture is that of the Syrophœnician woman. Out of the mass of detail that we have here in Mark and in Matthew, let us attempt to gather the central value. The revelation of need supremely represented here is that of the sorrow of a mother. Any careful reading of the story must bring something of pathos into the voice, as the account is read of how the woman besought Him that He would cast the demon out of her little daughter.

Leave the Lord out of view for the moment, and all the difficulties which gather about the story, and see that one woman in agony about her child. Admit the disabilities under which she laboured, which these evangelists are both careful to point out, Mark speaking of her as a Greek, which simply means a Gentile, and not a Greek only, but a Syrophœnician. Matthew does not speak of her as a Gentile, neither adds the fact that she was Syrophœnician; but, taking the more general term, he at once says a Canaanitish woman. Humanity is revealed as we look at the woman, and the elemental superiority to racial disadvantage is seen in the agony of the mother-heart. Oh yes, she was a Greek, and not a Hebrew, but she was a mother! She was a Syrophœnician, a Canaanitish woman, one of the accursed race, but she had a heart, and it was a mother's heart! There, flashing out on the canvas, is this revelation of a touch of humanity that is independent of advantage, and superior to disadvantage, mightier than racial differences; and in the wail of the woman we have the cry of the heart of a mother.

The next picture that Mark gives, is that of a man deaf, and having an impediment in his speech. This is a picture of personal disability. The whole point of the picture, however, as it occurs here in the Gospel, is not that of the man's personal disability. It is rather that of the fact that this man in this Gentile region was brought to Jesus by his friends. It is never safe to base too much upon the argument of silence, but at least it is an interesting fact to note that the man made no appeal to Christ. He did not come to Christ on his own initiative. His friends brought him, and besought Jesus that He would touch him. So while the man stands central in the picture, in some senses, I look again, and in the sympathy of these men for their friend, men outside the company of Israel, outside that racial relationship which was religious in its function, I see something human. I am again im-

[169]

pressed by the elemental superiority over racial disadvantage. Oh, yes, these men were Gentiles, but they were
men. Oh! yes, these people also probably were of the
Canaanitish race, but they had sympathy in their heart;
witness their effort to bring their friend to Jesus.

The next picture is one full of life, colour, and movement. It is that of a great multitude, at least four thousand people, gathered together; and it is a picture of
these people hungry. Do not spiritualize the word too
soon. There are spiritual values undoubtedly in these
miracles of feeding, but let us begin on the true level—
a literal hunger, a physical hunger, a need for food. The
hunger of these people was the outcome of their attrac-
tion to Jesus, and their determination to stay by Him.
Mark the words of Christ, "because they continue with
Me now three days, and have nothing to eat." Here was
a situation of real need, arising within the material and
the physical. These people were hungry, and it was the
hunger of health, and thus ought to be met and satisfied,
lest journeying back, they faint. This was an experience
of physical weakness!

The next is a very different picture. It is that of a
deputation, an official deputation, almost certainly, of the
Pharisees and Sadducees. Mark says " Pharisees " only,
but comparing the account with Matthew's Gospel, which
is necessary for the understanding of some subsequent
things, we find the Sadducees came with them, demanding
a sign from Him. Who were these men who came to
Jesus? The religious leaders of the hour, the men who
were religious teachers in Jerusalem, the spiritual rulers
of the people, men whose office it was to interpret to the
people the law of God, to reveal to the people the way
and the will of God.

They were in conflict with each other, these Sadducees
and Pharisees. The Pharisees stood for the spiritual
ideal of religion. While they trammelled that ideal by
tradition, and hindered its working, nevertheless they

[170]

stood for spiritual things; or if we may borrow, for the
sake of illustration, a somewhat questionable word, they
stood for the supernatural in religion. On the other
hand, the Sadducees were the rationalists, who denied
angels, spirits, resurrection, everything in the nature of
the supernatural. The Sadducees were men who believed
in a religion that was entirely ethical, and who never
admitted the relation of the ethical to the spiritual. The
representatives of these opposing parties came together
to Christ to prefer the same request. The thing they
asked was a sign from heaven.

What is the supreme revelation of this picture? It is
that of spiritual inferiority in spite of advantage. That
statement is only forceful as it is immediately put back
into contrast with what we saw concerning the Syrophœnician woman. In the case of the woman we saw the
elemental need of humanity superior to all social and
racial disadvantage. In these men we see deterioration,
and failure, and spiritual inferiority, in spite of religious
advantages. Here were men asking for a sign, who had
seen His signs; men who had listened to His words, and
followed Him from Judæa and from Galilee; men who
had watched the working of His power in the marvels
that He had wrought, had seen Him healing disease,
casting out demons, raising from the dead; and infinitely
more wonderful than all, banishing the power of sin, forgiving it, and demonstrating His right and authority to
forgive in the results that followed. They had seen Him
dealing with every form of human malady, material,
mental, moral. Yet these men said: " Show us a sign."

Once again I pass on, and the next picture is that of
the disciples, alone with Jesus in the boat, for I think the
warning and the conversation took place as they crossed
over the sea to Bethsaida. This is a picture of the misunderstanding of the loyal-hearted. It is a picture of
men who loved the Lord, and were loyal to the Lord, and
as He Himself with infinite grace did say upon a later

occasion, men who abode with Him in His temptations; but they had not understood Him. As they crossed over the sea, Jesus warned this little group of His disciples, His apostles, "Beware of the leaven of the Pharisees." They immediately connected His reference to leaven with material bread. They said, "We have no bread." Now what they really meant by that I cannot tell. It may be some one can tell me! I have been trying to find out how they connected the word of Jesus with bread. If I judge by the Lord's answer it is as if they thought He was rebuking them for carelessness; for in effect He said, Do you not yet see that I am able to provide for that physical need? Why should you trouble about that? Did I not feed five thousand and four thousand?

Yet I am still in some difficulty. What did they imagine He meant by the leaven of the Pharisees? Did they imagine that the Pharisees were going to take their meal and put leaven into it? Or was there in their mind some lurking suspicion that when He said, "Beware of the leaven of the Pharisees," He was giving them a new ceremonial addition to the law? I do not know. Speculation is unprofitable! I cannot see the connection between what He said and what they thought. The fact remains that, when Jesus uttered that which He evidently felt was a greatly-needed spiritual warning, His disciples, His loyal-hearted ones, those who loved Him, thought about bread.

There is one other picture. Arrived at Bethsaida again, they brought to Him a man suffering personal disability, a blind man. Once again the central value of the story is that it is a revelation of the sympathy of His friends, for they brought Him to Jesus.

Now let us look again at these stories. What did Jesus do with that woman in whom there was manifested the touch of true humanity, the agony of the mother's heart? In considering what He did for her, first look at the result. That may not be a proper line of consideration,

yet I think it is. The result was what the mother found
when she got back home. She found the child laid upon
the bed, and the demon gone out. To know what He did,
we must see that child as the mother left her, contorted,
twisted, and then lying on the bed, quiet, restful. That is
what He did for her. To look at the result first is to be
better qualified to see the process. Is not that the solution of many of the things of this life? I think so. I
think when at last we really see the result, we shall not
be so perplexed about some of the processes.

From the standpoint of the result, let us observe His
method, and observe it most carefully. It did look hard.
It did seem severe. First, He was silent. He did not
answer her. Then He said to her, " Let the children first
be filled; for it is not meet to take the children's bread
and to cast it to the dogs." But did He really say this?
Listen to Him again, and notice that He said to her,
" Let the children first be filled." That in itself was suggestion that others might be fed after the children were
fed.

Then we have not a word conveying the exact equivalent in our language to a word in the Greek here. He did
not say, " It is not meet to take the children's bread and
cast it to the dogs." To put it into colloquial English, He
said, " It is not good to take the children's bread and cast
to the doggies." There is a difference here. There are
dogs *and* dogs; and there certainly were dogs *and* dogs
in Palestine. There were dogs fierce and wild, marauding
beasts; but there were also the dogs of the household, the
diminutive dogs, that had their place in the household,
that had their place in the dwelling. This word the Master used was one of these diminutives; and there is so
much in diminutives! No one can use them without there
being tenderness in the voice. I claim that tenderness for
Jesus here. He said, " It is not meet to take the children's
bread and cast it to the doggies." There is at least something in that tenderness. Ah! to us it may seem harsh to

[173]

refer to her even in that way; but mark what He did for the woman. Put the apparent severity of His method by the side of what He did. He set her free from the trammels of a false view of privilege. When she first called to Him she called to Him as the Jewish Messiah. " O Lord, Thou Son of David, my daughter is grievously vexed with a demon." She was asking some pity from a Hebrew Messiah, she herself being a Gentile, and He answered upon that ground. If she appeal to Him as Hebrew Messiah He will say Nay. So she was brought to cry to Him out of her elemental humanity. " Lord, help *me* . . . for even the doggies eat of the crumbs which fall from their masters' table." Then He said, " For this saying go thy way; the demon is gone out of thy daughter." Thus, whereas He said the apparently severe thing, He admitted her immediately to the privilege of a child. There is a word of Paul in his Galatian letter, having a profounder application than I am now going to make of it, but in some ways the dealing of our Lord with this woman is a wonderful commentary on this word of Paul; " For in Christ Jesus neither circumcision availeth anything, nor uncircumcision, but faith working through love." That is what happened in the case of the woman; faith working through love. Christ had told her that it was not good to give the children's bread to the little dogs; and faith wrought through love, and He treated her, not as a dog to whom the crumbs were to be given, but as a child admitted into all the privileges of the family.

Thus our Lord showed that in Him all racial barriers were broken down, all racial privilege was as nothing; that where the soul in its elemental human agony approached Him in faith, He answered. It was a foreshadowing of the Acts of the Apostles; of what Peter and others had to learn afterwards.

But look at Him again. I will take the second and last pictures, and put them together, because they are so much alike in certain ways. He was dealing with two men, a dumb man and a blind man. Now it is noticeable—and all students of these stories are arrested by it—that our Lord was adopting new methods in His miracles, or seemed to be doing so. He took the dumb man apart from the crowd, put His fingers into his ears, and touched him with His own spittle, sighed, and said, Ephphatha, and the man's ears were opened. Even more remarkable was the case of the blind man, where His working of the wonder seemed to be gradual; first of all the anointing with a touch, then asking him, "Seest thou aught?" and after the answer of the man, "I see men, for I behold them as trees, walking," the touch of the hands, and full recovery. In these two cases we see a process of healing.

Do not let us imagine for a moment that in these methods of Jesus we have any revelation either of weakening power on His part—for that has been suggested— or of the adoption of new methods and the banishment of the old, for this also has been suggested.

In these two stories we have wonderful illustrations of a perpetual fact in the method of Jesus with human need; the fact that He adapts His method to the peculiar circumstances of need of the one with whom He is dealing. I am quite convinced if we could perfectly know these men we should discover the reason for the method. In each case Christ adapted Himself to the need of the man. This was also finely illustrated in the case of the woman.

In all these stories Jesus approached human need full of resources. There was no necessity, as far as He was concerned, to heal by any kind of means; no necessity to keep that woman waiting for a moment for the healing of her child; but there was profound necessity for everything He did in the case of the people who came to Him. If at your leisure you will go through the Gospel stories, and the cases in which Jesus dealt with need—

I am not now referring to the spiritual needs, but to the
needs met by these very miracles—you will discover, perhaps to your amazement, and certainly to your profit, that
He never did anything the same way twice. There was
infinite variety in all His dealings with men. He never
healed more than one blind man in the same way. He
never cast out the demon from more than one man in
the same way. There was always a difference, and in
the difference is a wonderful revelation of the variety of
the experiences of human need, and consequently a wonderful revelation of our Lord's adaptability to that variety of experience.

All of which is at once a revelation of the Lord, and an
indication of the true line of Christian service. If we are
really going to deal with men in the name of Christ and
humanity, we cannot deal with all men in the same way.
Inasmuch as the material miracles of Jesus are all parables of spiritual value in Christian service, as I watch the
Lord I understand that when I talk to one man of his
spiritual need, and try to help him; and then to another
man of his spiritual need, and try to help him; if I approach the two men in succession, having arranged everything as to my method of dealing with them, the probability is that I shall not help them at all. The Lord
never did a thing twice in the same way. He was not
changeable therefore, but changeless; absolutely true to
the underlying principle that every human life is lonely,
separate, peculiar, and must be separately dealt with.
Christ never deals with men *en masse*. He deals with
men one by one.

It is an old proverb, and a foolish one, that God made
Oliver Cromwell, and broke the mould. I join issue with
what is inferred when men say that God made Oliver
Cromwell and broke the mould, or God made John Wesley
and broke the mould. The inference is that He does not
always break the mould when He makes a man; that the
vast majority of people are run through the same mould.

Nothing of the kind! There is neither man nor woman but stands separate, alone, in the dignity of individuality, and who can say with Jesus, " To this end have I been born, and to this end am I come into the world." It is sad that so few find out the greatness of individuality, and consequently fail to discover the meaning of individuality and personality.

The Lord provided for the hungry multitude because they had been three days with Him. There is another important principle here. Jesus did not feed them in order to persuade them to listen to His teaching. When a tea-meeting is necessary to get people to listen to the Gospel there will be failure. That is not the method of Christ. To build an Institute in connection with a Church, and provide all kinds of entertainment for the young people, in order that they may come to the Bible-classes, is to be foredoomed to failure.

In the case of the Pharisees and Sadducees who demanded a sign, the Lord refused what they asked; first because their motive was wrong; and secondly because no sign would have convinced them. They had already had the signs, and were wilfully blind.

His treatment of the disciples—those disciples to whom the Lord always spoke with sympathy—was that He definitely and sternly rebuked them in a series of indignant questions. Yet observe also that He led them on until they did understand what He meant.

I gather up the impressions made upon my soul, as I have watched the Lord in these stories. The first is that of His perfect understanding of every case as it came before Him.

The second is that of His quick sympathy, the sensitiveness of His soul, that immediately responded, whatever the need by which He stood confronted.

Yet again I am impressed by His sustained loyalty to principle. He never deviated by a hair's-breadth from the pathway of His loyalty to the Kingdom of God.

I am impressed finally by the very sternness of His rebuke of the disciples who failed.

Ah! but there are two little phrases in the course of this passage that are very revealing, far more revealing than we know. When He was about to open the ears of the man, "*He sighed.*" In the presence of the demand for a sign by the Pharisees and Sadducees, "*He sighed deeply in His spirit.*" Thus twice I hear a sigh coming up from His soul. Behold, "a Man of sorrows, and acquainted with grief!" Behold a Man exercising a ministry full of healing power and elemental light; but never forget that this service was costly. The principle of the Cross ultimately to be revealed supremely on Calvary, ran through all, making Him what He was to the men of His own age, making Him what He is to the men of today.

XVI

"And He said unto them, verily I say unto you, there are some here of them that stand by, which shall in no wise taste of death, till they see the Kingdom of God come with power."—MARK 9 : I.

Mark 8 : 27–9 : 13.

THE stories which we grouped in our last meditation gave a graphic revelation of the conditions obtaining at the end of the second period of the ministry of the Servant of God, which was practically also the end of His more formal and public propaganda. The multitudes were interested, and were prepared to receive His gifts. They were prepared, moreover, to crown Him and follow Him in the establishing of a material kingdom, in which He would supply their needs. The rulers on the other hand, were definitely and desperately hostile to Him. The disciples were dull of spiritual apprehension, needing to be warned against the leaven of the Pharisees and Sadducees. At this time in the ministry of our Lord He might fittingly have employed the words of the great Servant of Jehovah, as found in the prophecy of Isaiah:

" Who hath believed our message? and to whom hath the arm of Jehovah been revealed? For He grew up before Him as a tender plant, and as a root out of a dry ground: He hath no form nor comeliness; and when we see Him, there is no beauty that we should desire Him. He was despised, and rejected of men; a Man of sorrows, and acquainted with grief: and as One from Whom men hide their face He was despised, and we esteemed Him not."

The paragraph now under consideration tells the story of a crisis in the ministry of our Lord, and of a new beginning. In the teaching ministry of Jesus there were two distinct stages. The burden of His early teaching was that of declaring His Messiahship, and of bringing men to understand that He was the Messiah, in fulfilment of prophecy. The second matter of importance in the teaching ministry of our Lord was that He should show men that Messiah must go by the way of suffering and death, to His crowning. Men who were familiar with the ancient prophecies knew full well that the two aspects had been suggested. At the time, however, they were so strangely puzzled by this fact, that there were those who declared that there would be two Messiahs, one, a suffering Messiah, and the other, one who should come in glory, and establish a Kingdom.

In this paragraph we are at the parting of the ways, at the hour of crisis, when He ended the first phase of teaching, and began to devote Himself, within the narrower circle of His disciples, to the second stage. This particular verse has been selected as text because I believe it to be central to the whole paragraph. With slight variation the statement which our Lord made upon this occasion is found in exactly the same contextual relation in Matthew, Mark, and Luke.

The statement opens chapter nine in Mark's Gospel; and of its placing there, Dr. Morison says:

"It was in a mood of mental somnolence that Hugo de Sancto Caro concluded the eighth chapter with the thirty-eighth verse, and carried forward into a new chapter the verse before us."

Here is one illustration of the unfortunate division of our Bible into chapters. By its system of paragraphing the Revised Version attempts to remedy the blunder, and yet the supreme mistake was a chapter division at all, at this point. Observe the sequence of events. Jesus journeyed north until Cæsarea Philippi was reached; and there at some one point, as Mark says, somewhere among those villages, came the sudden halt, and the challenge to

His disciples: "Who do men say that I am?" The answers were given, and then He challenged that narrower circle of His own, "Who say ye that I am?" Then came the hour toward which the Lord had been moving, the victory for which He had been working, the hour of illumination, when one man, Peter, made his great confession, "Thou art the Christ, the Son of the living God." That confession was immediately answered by our Lord with another confession, "Thou art Peter, and upon this rock I will build My Church; and the gates of Hades shall not prevail against it." Mark does not record this, but Matthew in his Gospel, which is supremely that of the Kingdom, tells the story of that word of Jesus.

Immediately following these confessions of Peter and of Jesus, a new note in the teaching of our Lord was sounded. He "began . . . to show unto His disciples, how that He must . . . suffer"; and the use of the word *began* there, and the emphasis I place upon it, are warranted. Never before had He talked of His coming Cross or suffering. Never before had He spoken of the resurrection which should crown the Cross. Never before had He spoken of the second advent. All this teaching began then. The supreme note of the teaching was that of the Cross.

This gave rise to the fear, born of love, in the heart of Peter that made him say, "Be it far from Thee, Lord"; and called forth the sudden, startling, stern answer of the Lord to the man whom He had commended for his confession: "Get thee behind Me, Satan: thou art a stumbling-block unto Me: for thou mindest not the things of God, but the things of men." Then followed the teaching of the disciples and the multitudes in the presence of the Cross, His insistence upon the necessity for the Cross; and at the end of that whole incident, the words: "I say unto you, There are some here that stand by, who shall in no wise taste of death, till they see the Kingdom of God come with power."

[181]

Then there were six days of silence, followed by the transfiguration mount; and after that the descent from the mount, and the conversation by the way.

Thus the text selected is seen as central. It gathers up and emphasizes that teaching of Jesus; first that the Kingdom is to come in power—note the confession about the Church—but supremely that the Kingdom can only come in power by the way of the Cross. "There are some here of them that stand by"—a special reference in His mind undoubtedly to His own apostles, although others would be included—"who shall in no wise taste of death, till they see the Kingdom of God come"—not in perfection, not in finality, but "in power." This was a reference undoubtedly to the fact that those who had said they were afraid, and shrank from the Cross, should yet come to understand that the Kingdom comes in power only by way of the Cross.

We are at once reminded of a paragraph in Paul's first letter to the Corinthians, which has the closest spiritual relation to this word of Jesus (1 Cor. 1: 18–25). From the paragraph we select these phrases: "The word of the Cross . . . is the power of God." "Christ crucified . . . the power of God." "Verily I say unto you, There are some here of them that stand by, who shall in no wise taste of death, till they see the Kingdom of God come with power."

Our Lord was declaring, not that these men who were round about Him could ever see the Kingdom come in its perfection in the present life. He was declaring to them, startled, amazed, mystified as they were by the strange new thing He was saying, that by that very process from which they were shrinking, and naturally so, the Kingdom of God would come with power.

Now this is still a stumbling-block, not to the Jew alone, but to many others; still foolishness, not to the Greek only, but to many others. This view of the way through which the Kingdom comes continues to baffle the philosophy of the age and the world. These are "the things of God," to which the "things of men" are opposed. This is God's way to victory. Men cannot understand it even yet. Still too often His disciples mind the things of men rather than the things of God.

In order that this meaning and value of our text may be apprehended, let us consider the ideas of the text in the light of its context; first, the idea of the Kingdom; secondly, the idea of the Kingdom coming in power; concluding with an inquiry as to how these men really saw it come in power.

The Kingdom idea runs throughout the whole of this story.

We are inclined to think, or we sometimes speak as though we were, that our Lord at this point departed from what evidently had been the master passion of His ministry, that namely, of the establishing of the Kingdom of God in the world. We seem to imagine that this reference to the Church, and to the Cross, and to a second advent were all removed from the theme of the Kingdom. It is of supreme importance that we recognize that they are closely related to the purpose of the Kingdom of God. When our Lord challenged these men, "Who do men say that the Son of man is?" it was a Kingdom passion that moved Him. With singular daring, and arresting intention, He made human opinion concerning Himself the supreme thing in His ministry. He did not ask what men thought of the things He had done. He did not ask what men thought of the things He had said. He asked, "Who do men say that I am?"

In view of all that followed, in view indeed of all that had preceded, wherein we have seen Him moving forward with singular authority and dignity, we immediately recognize that He was seeking to discover whether men would recognize Him as supreme. When the answers came He was not satisfied until He asked the inner circle, "Who say ye that I am?" and one man had confessed

Him supreme. That is the real value of the confession.
Thou art not John the Baptist, Elijah, Jeremiah, a
prophet; Thou art not one looking for Another; Thou art
the Other for whom all have looked; the last and final
One, to the brightness of Whose coming, longing eyes
have long been lifted, Messiah, anointed King, and Priest.
It was for that confession the Lord was seeking. His
question was the question of the King. All prophetic
references to Messiah looked upon Messiah as King,
through Whom should come the establishment of the
Divine Kingdom. This is the real meaning of the word.
Christ is but the Greek form of Messiah, or *anointed One.*
Messiah is not a name; *Christ* is not a name. When we
speak of the One Whom we worship as Christ, let us
remember that is a title, and not a name; marking the
eternal Son of God for one mission and one work. It
is the title of an office, the office of supremacy, of Kingship, of the One Whose business it is to ransom men,
and realize the Kingdom of God.

All this is patent also if we listen to the confession of
Jesus. "Upon this rock I will build My ecclesia, My
church." "My ecclesia." This was a word in common
use at that time, used of the Hebrew nation as constituting a theocracy, and used in every Greek city with regard to the governing body in the city. It is a word
saturated with the ideas of authority and kingship.

When our Lord said, "Upon this rock I will build My
ecclesia," He really inferred, Upon this rock I will build
My Kingdom. The reference is to the Kingdom realized,
the functions and the purpose of the Kingdom revealed
through the instrument to be known as His Ecclesia, His
Church. The master passion in the heart of Jesus here,
as always, was that of the Kingdom, and its establishment.

So also, the function of the Church is essentially revealed: "Upon this rock I will build My Church; and the
gates of Hades shall not prevail against it." The Church

[184]

is a conquering Kingdom, bringing all kingdoms into subjugation to itself. "And I will give unto thee the keys
of the Kingdom"; by the Church the moral standards of
life are erected and revealed to all kingdoms, until coming
into harmony with it, they become the one Kingdom of
our God and of His Christ. The supreme idea is that of
the Kingdom.

The Kingdom throughout all this period, was not seen
in power, but in weakness; an ideal, but not realized;
a vision, but not a victory. In the answers that they gave
to Him, reporting the things said concerning Him, is a
revelation of the failure of the Kingdom ideal. The vast
multitudes of men had not seen the Kingdom, and although here was one soul illuminated, so that he confessed Him Messiah, in his halting a moment afterwards
was a revelation that the Kingdom seen, was not yet with
power. In the "must" of the new unveiling of Jesus,
when He said that He must go to Jerusalem, was a revelation of the Kingdom in weakness, for notice with what
carefulness He named the opposition that confronted
Him in Jerusalem: elders, chief priests, scribes. That
was no careless grouping, but the naming of all the authorities within the city; elders, the civic rulers; chief
priests, the religious rulers; scribes, the moral rulers. All
the authority within the city—civil, religious, moral—was
massed against Him. The Kingdom was in weakness;
and as He Who represented it, in Whom it was brought,
Who had come for its revelation and establishment,
moved to the centre of national life, to Jerusalem, He
came into the realm of hostility and suffering, and He
must suffer, and be killed. The Kingdom in weakness, is
the picture presented to us here.

Yet once more glancing over the picture from another
standpoint, the way of the coming of the Kingdom in
power is revealed. First, this is seen in the declaration
of the Lord Himself. As I hear Him speak and interpret
the thing He said in the light of subsequent events, I

[185]

know that there is a deeper meaning in the "must" of
Jesus. When He said the Son of man must go to Jerusalem and suffer, He was not declaring that He was
hemmed in by circumstances; He was not declaring that
He was the victim of forces that were against Him.
Partially, yes, we may have admitted it; but there is a
deeper note. The "must" of Jesus is something profounder than that.

In the next book to the Gospel stories, the book of the
Acts, I find the first recorded address of this very man,
Peter, who made his confession of Christ, and then
shrank from the Cross and was so sternly rebuked. In
that first address delivered on the day of Pentecost, I
find an account of the Cross, strangely full of light.
Speaking to these men in Jerusalem, within a few minutes or hours after the illumination of Pentecost had
come to him, Peter thus spoke of the Cross: "Him, being
delivered up by the determinate counsel and foreknowledge of God, ye by the hand of lawless men did crucify
and slay." Now mark the words of Peter. That to
which he referred in the second place was that which
has been first in our consideration. Ye rulers of Israel
did crucify and slay by the hands of men without the
law; that is by Gentile hands, ye crucified Him, and slew
Him. Yes! but Peter had now seen something more
than that in the Cross, and so he declared that He was
"delivered up by the determinate counsel and foreknowledge of God." In the "must" of Jesus there was recognition not of the compulsion of circumstances, but of the
compulsion of the will of His God, and of His coöperation with God. Into the "must" of Jesus there is gathered the strange and mystic light which reveals Him even
at this juncture, not as One going as a Victim to be
murdered, but as the one Priest, proceeding as a Victor
over all circumstances including the death to which He
went, in order that He might accomplish a purpose, and
build a Kingdom, and realize the will of God.

[186]

That value of the " must " is borne out by the fact that
He interpreted His death by His resurrection. When
they presently descended from the mount of transfiguration, they inquired what this resurrection from the dead
should mean. That was the arresting thing to them.
Strangely enough they never seemed to grasp its significance, or to have been able to believe in it, as something
to come immediately. Even after He had answered their
inquiry, they were inclined to think of resurrection as
Martha did. When Jesus said to her, " Thy brother shall
rise again," she said, " I know that he shall rise again in
the resurrection at the last day." By which she meant,
Do not try to comfort me with a far-off resurrection; I
want him now! I think these disciples had the same
attitude toward the resurrection. They believed in it as
a far-off event.

We must never forget this fact, that there is no instance in these New Testament records of Jesus referring
to His Cross, but that at the same time He also referred
to His resurrection. The Son of man must go up to
Jerusalem, and suffer, and be killed, and the third day
rise again. That is not the language of a man who says:
I am beaten by circumstances; but I must be loyal to a
principle; I must go on, though I die. No! It was the
calm, strong, amazing language of One Who saw death
interpreted by resurrection; of One Who must suffer and
die and be raised again. In the mystic language of our
Lord, even though as yet we have not come to the full
realization of it, we begin to hear the thunder of His
power, and find the Kingdom coming in power.

Then in all the teaching that followed—His stern rebuke of Peter; the statement He made to the multitudes
as to the necessity for following Him by the way of the
Cross if they would be in coöperation with Him in the
building of the Kingdom; and the final and resultant
words concerning His second advent in the glory with
His Father and with the angels—in all these things, we

[187]

catch the tones of power, and see that our Lord knew and declared that the Kingdom would only become dynamic by the way of the Cross.

Then followed that wonderful event of the transfiguration. The disciples saw the Lord transfigured. It would be better, perhaps, if we changed the word "transfiguration," anglicizing the Greek word; and read it thus, They saw the Lord metamorphosed. "Transfiguration" is a perfectly accurate word, only we are apt to think of it as though they saw Him with light falling on Him. On the contrary, He Himself was metamorphosed, changed completely in some strange mystery of glorification and realization.

The disciples saw Moses and Elijah talking with Him. Mark does not tell us this; but another of the evangelists. They heard Him talking with them of the exodus that He was about to accomplish; that is, of this going to Jerusalem, and dying, and rising again. Then the disciples said, "Rabbi, it is good for us to be here: and let us make three tabernacles; one for Thee, and one for Moses, and one for Elijah." We have been forever criticizing them, and trying to say what they meant when they said that; all the while forgetting that the evangelist tells us that they did not know what they were doing; and did not know what to say, so they said that!

But now observe most carefully that they heard a voice, which said to them, "This is My beloved Son: hear ye Him." There had been six days of silence, because He had brought them face to face with the Cross, and they had shrunk from it. I think this was quite natural. Who could understand this strange mystery that One could build a Kingdom by dying, that One could gain a victory by being defeated, that One could come to crowning by the way of the Cross? Who could understand? We hardly yet believe it! It was revolutionary!

This is surely what they were thinking on the mount. Lord, not that Cross to which Thou art going; let us stay here! Let us build three tabernacles here. Let us stay in this light, in this glory, in this holy conversation. Yet the conversation was of the exodus; and if they had stayed there, the exodus had never been accomplished! The Divine voice rebuked them: "This is My beloved Son: hear ye Him." The supreme and sacramental glory of the mount of transfiguration was not that of its flashing splendour, but of the conversation concerning the Cross, and the ratification of that conversation and purpose by the Divine voice.

These men saw the Kingdom come in power in His dying, in His rising, and in that immediate spiritual coming again, which took place in their experience on the day of Pentecost.

They saw the Kingdom coming in power in His dying. Grant their terror, their sense of defeat; and yet remember what they saw. During these days they saw things that they hardly saw at the time; but they knew afterwards that they had seen them. Impressions were made upon their souls, the value of which was not immediate, but which came after. In all these last and tragic events they saw the unconquered King. In every incident from that moment of foretelling, to the final act and fact of death, they saw Him moving with authority, with power, with dignity. Take this illustration. One of their own number, Judas, was plotting and planning with the priests for the arrest of his Lord; and in the dark and terrific business we are told that the priests said to Judas, "Not during the feast." Judas took the thirty pieces of silver, the bargain being made, and went with the money, oh! ghastly thing! into the very presence of Jesus, charged by the priests not to betray Him until the feast was over. While Judas was plotting with the priests, Jesus was talking to His disciples, and He said: "After two days the passover cometh, and the Son of man is delivered up to be crucified." When Judas came into the presence of Jesus, after a little while Jesus

looked at him and said, " That thou doest, do quickly ";
and he went out, and betrayed Him at the feast. Not the
priests arranged the hour of His dying, but Jesus Himself.

This same activity in power runs all through. They
saw Him in the garden, in the intervals of their sleeping,
heard His words as He came back to them through the
hours of His agony. They were all kingly words. They
saw that strange thing happen in the garden, which we
hurry over in our reading too carelessly. When the
guard came to arrest Him, led by Judas, Jesus said,
" Whom seek ye? " They replied, " Jesus of Nazareth."
He said, " I am "; and those soldiers fell backward in
His presence. Why? I am not going to answer the
question. I have no details, but I pray you, mark it.
These disciples saw this strange sight. Something happened that made these men fall back; and then something
more wonderful happened, for they bound Him and took
Him away. Through the trial they watched Him, some
of them, and saw Him kingly, saw Him in the midst of
the mock trial solemnly affirm His Messiahship, His
Kingship; kingly to the end, until in the final act He
said, " Father, into Thy hands I commend My Spirit."
As we listen we remember words He uttered long before,
" Be not afraid of them that kill the body, and after that
have no more that they can do." The men about the
Cross had killed His body, but His spirit was commended to God, and He died as a King. We remember
once again words that He uttered: " No one taketh My
life away from Me, but I lay it down of Myself. I have
power to lay it down, and I have power to take it again."
These are the things of the Kingdom in power, strange
things, mystic things, things that raise questions, things
the full value of which the heart of man challenges, and
wonders whether they can be so. These are the things of
power; the strange mystery of a kingly dying in agony
and pain, and yet in triumph. So they saw the King-

dom of God coming in power; not in finality, but in power.

Then upon the resurrection I need not dwell. About that resurrection Paul said He " was declared the Son of God with power . . . by the resurrection of the dead"; and Peter declared: " He begat us again unto a living hope by the resurrection of Jesus Christ from the dead." In those resurrection days, in the commissions He uttered, and in other appearances, He made them see the Kingdom, no longer as an ideal outside them, but as a power operating within them; until as He had told them in the upper room, He came again, in the coming of the Paraclete.

He so came, and these men began to preach, and they saw the Kingdom without weakness, in strength prevailing amongst the men listening, who had been hostile. Then they knew that this coming of the Kingdom in power, was by the way of the Cross.

These men saw the Kingdom of God come, not in perfection. That has been our mistake in reading our text, as we have interpreted it by the transfiguration mount. Not in perfection, and not finally; but in power; with mastery and force mastering the things against it, and proceeding toward its final glory.

Thus, and thus only the Kingdom still comes in power; only by the way of the Cross; and as the Cross is borne by those who name the Name. It is not easy to believe, and it is less easy to practice. Do we not, even within the Christian Church, often need to hear the rebuke of Jesus as He says to us: " Thou mindest not the things of God but the things of men "? We are seeking to establish the Kingdom by the methods of men, by their policies, and their programmes, and their machinery. The Kingdom of God can never be so established. The Kingdom of God only comes in power by the way of the Cross.

There is one terribly solemn suggestion in this text.

[Mark 8: 27—9: 13]

Our Lord was speaking in the presence of the multitudes, yet surely with special reference to His own, and He did not say, All shall see the Kingdom of God come in power. He said, " Some here . . . shall in no wise taste of death." Judas never saw the Kingdom in power. There is an attitude of heart toward the Lord that cuts off from seeing the Kingdom come in power; and even though we may not become our own executioners in the literal sense in which Judas did, we may live our life, and yet never see anything of the power in operation. If we know what it is to come so near to Him as to be able in very deed, to share His sufferings, then through us the Kingdom may come in power.

XVII

"And He answereth them and saith, O faithless genera-tion, how long shall I be with you? How long shall I bear with you?"—MARK 9:19.

Mark 9:14–29.

THIS cry came welling up from the heart of Jesus. In it, pain and indignation merge; and the cause of each is revealed. There is evident pain in the plaintive in-quiry, "How long shall I be with you?" In it the same note is discernible as in that old-time song of the vine-yard, in which Isaiah declared that God concerning His people, asked with equal plaintiveness, "What could have been done more to My vineyard, that I have not done in it?" After about three years of public ministry, our Lord broke out into this question, "How long shall I be with you?" The plaintive inquiry was immediately followed by another, which is vibrant with the sense of wrong and indignation, How long shall I tolerate you? The question suggests most solemnly, that there is a limit to His patience.

The cause of everything is revealed in the opening exclamation, "O faithless generation." He spoke of the whole age in which His ministry was being exercised. The word was not one of rebuke to His disciples alone; though they were included. The word was not a rebuke only for the man who brought his boy; he also was numbered with those of the generation. The word was not one of rebuke for the scribes alone; though of them it was true. The whole atmosphere in the midst of which the Lord exercised His ministry, the very spirit of the age, was that of faithlessness, unbelief; "O faithless generation."

The words of this text are central to the paragraph. Before them, massed in brief sentences, we have a picture of the things that Jesus found in the valley as He left the mount of transfiguration. He found disputing scribes, a distracted father, a demon-possessed boy, and defeated disciples. After the exclamation of the text we have the story of what He did with all these. He silenced the scribes, He comforted the father, He healed the boy, He instructed the disciples. So, passing into this atmosphere of unbelief, there welled up out of His heart these words, O faithless generation, how long will it be necessary for Me to be with you, ere you will understand or consent to believe? Nay, how long will it be possible for Me to remain in such an atmosphere, and carry on My ministry; how long can I bear with you, and where shall the limit be set to this intolerable unbelief? How long shall I tolerate you?

All this was the immediate sequel of the transfiguration. Here is one of the points of singular agreement between these Gospel writers. Matthew, Mark, and Luke tell the story of these things as immediately following upon the transfiguration scene and experiences. In the reading of each Gospel, we descend swiftly and abruptly as it seems, from the height of glory and wonderful radiance, to the depth of degradation. We have stood with Him upon the holy mount, and have seen Him transfigured; and the glory has been too bright for the feebleness of a sinner's sight; so bright that even the three disciples were dazed, and said things that they themselves did not understand, so bright that we have never yet been able perfectly to understand the thing that happened on that mountain. Then in the valley we come face to face with one of the supreme illustrations of degradation that the New Testament affords, and the revelation is the more striking the more carefully we consider it. On the holy mount the voice of God had spoken concerning Jesus, and it had said, " This is My beloved

Son." On the mountain height we saw the Only-begotten Son of God in glory. Descending to the valley, we hear the father say to Jesus, This is my child, my only child; literally, This is my only-begotten son. On the mount of glory, the Only-begotten Son of the Father; in the valley, the only-begotten son of a man, demon-possessed. The Lord is seen passing down from the glory, into that atmosphere of unbelief, and meeting that boy. It is in that way we must look at the valley scene.

Therefore we pause to consider the mountain in the background; that we may more clearly and accurately observe the valley in the foreground; and both, in order that we may discover the relation between the mountain and the valley.

Going back to the paragraph which gives the account of the transfiguration, we look at that mountain scene again in comradeship with those three men; yet also in the illumination of the Holy Spirit Who came to them afterwards, and enabled them to tell the story of the mount. Peter in his Letter declared that the holy mount had meant to them the fulfilment and ratification of ancient prophecies, for there they had seen the operation of the coming power of God through Christ. Omitting the sacred title of Christ, and the supreme title, Lord, I here resolutely use the name of His humanity, the name given to Him by Divine command, and by His mother's love, the name by which He had been known, and necessarily familiar through boyhood and young manhood, the name by which these disciples, ere there broke upon them the sense of His glory, had perpetually called Him, Jesus! There on the mountain height, the perfected spirit of Jesus having gained complete mastery over all temptation, physical, spiritual, and vocational, changed the tenement of the body, and fitted it for the super-earthly life. Until we have understood that clearly, we have never seen the glory of the holy mount. The happening upon the mount was part of the private life of Jesus, rather than the public ministry. He had withdrawn Himself from the place of the crowds to Cæsarea Philippi, there to challenge His disciples as to the result of His mission. We must dismiss that old legend or opinion that Jesus was transfigured on Mount Tabor, which was not in this neighbourhood, and upon the crown of which even at that time, a city was built. He was certainly transfigured on Mount Hermon, that is on one of the heights of that mountain, a little farther to the north than Cæsarea Philippi, in a place of loneliness. He had escaped from the crowds, He had even at last left at the foot of the mountain nine of His disciples, taking only three with Him. We are impressed by the privacy of the transfiguration scene. I think personally that so far as the real value of what happened then is concerned, no disciple need have been present. It was something lonely and peculiar in the life of Jesus. There was value in the fact that they were there, for them in the after-time, and perhaps for them also at the moment. I do not share the general view that these men were taken there because they were the chief disciples and the best. More probably they were taken because they were the weakest of the twelve. Remember it is not the strongest saint who is taken to the place of special vision. The strongest saint can do without the vision. It is much easier to go to the mount, and see the glory, than to stay down in the valley, amid that crowd of scribes.

Part of what these men were privileged to see,—for they did not see everything clearly,—that glory falling there upon Jesus irradiating Him, was not the shining forth of Deity, for Deity has no shining forth that is spectacular, or that can be apprehended by the eyes of sense. The only way in which the glory of Deity can ever be seen by men, is as it is veiled, hidden within humanity. The glory of the Deity of our Lord was not manifested there, but along the quiet ways, and in the compassionate ministries, in all the little things of life.

What then happened upon the mount? In that hour of the transfiguration, Jesus of Nazareth came to the full and ultimate perfecting of His human nature. In that hour we see the true finality of human life, so far as this world is concerned, as within the original plan of God. To illustrate in the simplest way. Had Adam never wandered from the pathway of the Divine command, or sinned, or fallen, he had never died; but having come to the end of probationary life, and completed his course, he would have been metamorphosed, changed, in this same manner, and prepared for the super-earthly life that lies beyond;—that life about which we know so little, and which in anxious moments sometimes we doubt altogether, but which surely exists, infinite in its mystery. Jesus at this hour came to that point of the perfecting of His human personality. By an infinite mystery God created a new Man in the creation of Jesus. By the mystic and awful purity of the Divine Conception He was sinless in His birth. Through all the years of youth and manhood up to this moment He had faced all the temptations to which man must be subject, mastering them, being victorious over them;—physical temptation, spiritual temptation, and the last and subtlest of all, vocational temptation. The last breath of that temptation had come to Him when Peter had said, God have mercy on Thee, not this way of the Cross! With stern and resolute heroism Jesus had said, Get thee hence, Satan, thou art an offence unto Me. That was the last victory over vocational temptation.

Then, immediately passing to the mount, His life perfect, complete; every temptation having been met, and mastered; the whole citadel of His manhood held through all the prior period of years, inviolate; He was transfigured before them. The spirit of the Man, Jesus, always supreme, now that life was completed and rounded out, changed the tenement of His body, and fitted it for the super-earthly life. There ended the human life of

[Mark 9: 14–29]
Jesus, in so far as the life of Jesus was a revelation of a Divine purpose, of a Divine ideal, a pattern of humanity in itself.

What did He look like that day? How little we know. The descriptions are all graphic, and most suggestive. Of the men who wrote, Matthew, Mark, and Luke, neither was an eye-witness. They received their impressions from others, and confined their attempts at description to His features and garments. Luke simply says that the fashion of His countenance was altered. Matthew says, " His face did shine as the sun." As to His garments Matthew says they became white as the light; Mark says they were glistering and white, so that no fuller on earth could make a like whiteness; and Luke says they were white and dazzling. The metamorphosis of the Person of Jesus was so wonderful, that in subsequent days, the writers of the story could only gain from eye-witnesses these descriptions: that the fashion of His countenance was changed, His face did shine as the sun; and that the strange and mystic glory of the Presence saturated His garments with light and glory so that they were dazzling and glistering. There is nothing to be added to it; it remains a mystery. Here, however, is the fact of the Man coming to the fulfilment of His human life.

Observe in the next place, that in that hour of the ultimate victory of Jesus as within His own personality, the supreme interest of His heart was revealed; for in that hour of His perfecting He was admitted to the company of the spirits of just men made perfect. Moses and Elijah were seen there holding conversation with Him. Having passed into the condition for the super-earthly life, in His manhood He entered into fellowship with those who had gone before Him. What then was the supreme interest of His heart? In that hour when He came to a marvellous perfecting; when once in the history of the human race, there had been revealed God's meaning in humanity when it is sinless; the supreme interest of His heart was of the exodus that He was about to accomplish. His heart even then in its selflessness was weaned from the lure of the life of glory which He had gained, and was, in an infinite compassion given back to the valley, the world, and the darkness. In the moment of His own supreme victory, He saw the earth subjugated, mastered by evil, suffering as the result of that mastery; or as one of these men upon the mount, John himself did afterwards write in his Epistle, the whole world was lying in the evil one, beleaguered, imprisoned, oppressed, ruined. He talked with Moses and Elijah of the exodus. Himself, of that race, but separate from it by His own perfection, did in that hour of His ultimate crowning, assume responsibility for that race, and talk of the fact that He would break a way through, break down the prison gates, cut the bars of iron asunder, divide the sea, lead the exodus. He talked of His coming Cross and resurrection. The supreme and master passion of the heart of the perfected Man was for the perfecting of the men who suffered, and the bringing back of the Kingdom to God, its rightful King.

In that hour the voice of God was heard, and it must be interpreted by the whole atmosphere of the occasion. "This is My beloved Son," is the ratification of the perfection of His life. He, the Son, perfected by faith, was at once the File-Leader and Vindicator of the faithful; and to this witness was borne in that transfiguration light and glory. Then the command to the disciples, "Hear Him," was in order to their perfecting by faith. All authority to teach had been given to Him. He had been speaking of the exodus. "Hear Him" said the Divine voice. These men had been afraid to hear Him six days before, when He spoke of this very Cross; declined to discuss that which was now the subject of His conversation with Moses and Elijah. Thus they were brought back to that very point, and commanded to hear Him.

From that mountain height they descended to the valley; and the cry that escaped His heart in the presence of all that He saw was this: "O faithless generation, how long shall I be with you? How long shall I bear with you?"

Look then a little more particularly at what He saw of unbelief. The supreme interest of this valley scene is that of unbelief, revealed in different phases. There were the scribes, wilful and persistent unbelief; there was the father, unwilling unbelief; there was the boy, irresponsible unbelief; and there were the disciples, unconscious unbelief. The whole atmosphere was an unbelieving atmosphere.

The scribes questioned the disciples, the force of the word really being that they disputed with them. It was a most mean and paltry business, so far as these scribes were concerned. Then Jesus asked a question, "Why question ye with them?" and the father of the boy went on to tell Him the story of his boy. That was the subject of their question, of their disputing. The disciples were defeated. Here was an evidence of inability. Jesus being away, these people gathered round the disciples, laughed at them and mocked them, questioned them and disputed with them. Here was an evidence that their own unbelief was warranted! The very last scene before our Lord moved toward Cæsarea Philippi was one with these men, who had demanded a sign, which He had declined to give. Now Jesus being away, these nine disciples were left, and they were failing. Our Lord had already given sign after sign, had they had the eyes to see, the hearts to understand, or the wills to believe; but they were not willing to do so. Our Lord came back into that atmosphere of critical, wilful, persistent unbelief.

The father, aware of the efforts of the disciples and

their failure, said to Jesus, "If Thou canst do anything, have compassion on us, and help us"; and uttered that last cry, very beautiful and heroic, "I believe; help Thou mine unbelief"; all which nevertheless revealed his unbelief. He did not want not to believe; he would rather have believed; but he did not believe. He made a venture; he had the will to believe; but he did not believe. Our Lord came into that atmosphere.

Then the boy, with his irresponsible unbelief. It is admitted that the boy did not believe in Jesus; he could not, for he was under the dominion of a demon. There was incapacity for the exercise of faith. A boy, an instrument of faith and vision and hope; spoiled, blighted, blasted, ruined; unable to believe. No blame attached to the boy, but the fact is nevertheless a tragic one. Spoiled humanity! The highest function of humanity is belief, that activity of spirit that proceeds upon the pathway of reason, until it comes to some great promontory, and then spreads its wings, and upon the basis of its earlier journeying, takes eternity into its grasp.

Then there was the unbelief of the disciples. Six days had passed, and they had been six days of practical silence between these men and Jesus. If we are to thoroughly understand this scene, we must go back to the things that preceded them. Six days before, these men had passed under a cloud, when our Lord began to speak of the necessity for His suffering, His dying, His rising; His coming passion and exodus. They were not volitionally rebellious against Him, but they were unable to accept His teaching; and their inability had cut the nerve of their power. Be it remembered these men had cast out demons; when He sent forth the twelve, they came back rejoicing because they had cast out demons. Here, however, something had happened; something had come in between them and their power. They were still loyal to Him, remaining in the valley at His command; waiting there, desiring still to carry on His enterprise; but in the

presence of this boy they were paralyzed, helpless. What
had happened? All unconsciously to themselves at that
moment when faith had failed them, and they had not
followed Him even though they had not understood Him,
there had been the paralyzing of their power. That is
what our Lord meant when He told them afterwards that
the reason of their failure was that of their little faith, as
Matthew tells us; and the full secret of success was that
of prayer, as Mark declares.

Once more, and finally, as we watch our Lord in that
valley of unbelief, so cold, so chill, so disappointing, that
even out of His heart there sprang that wail, " O faithless generation, how long shall I be with you? How long
shall I tolerate you? " let us observe most carefully that
all that He did followed upon the experiences of the
mount. The choice there made, was not to enter upon
the ultimate realization of His own human life. Through
that victory in His life He turned back to the race of men
to share their burdens and carry their sorrows and their
sins, and make Himself, O wondrous Man! responsible
for all the causes of their human suffering and their pain.
When we watch Him descending from the mount of
transfiguration, let us remember that it was a new descent, within the measure of His humanity, as wonderful
as the first descent. Read again the great chapter of the
Self-emptying of the Son of God in Philippians; that
wonderful chapter in which we see Him in His eternal
right, in the form of God. Then we read, He did not
think this equality with God a prize to be snatched at, and
held, for the purpose of Self-aggrandizement, but emptied
Himself. The supreme and ultimate wonder of this fact
is a glory which blinds us whenever we try to look upon
it, this Self-emptying of Deity in some awful mystery
that we cannot fathom. Now behold Him again on the
transfiguration mount. He emptied Himself of all the
rights of His humanity, and set His face toward the
shadows and the darkness of the valley. All the activity

in the valley was inspired and energized, not by the victory of the mount, but by the Self-emptying of the mount; not by the fact that He did there come to the ultimate in His humanity, but by the fact that having come to the ultimate He took that humanity, perfected, completed, transfigured, glorified, and bore it down again to the level of the valley, and to the deeps into which humanity had fallen. Now we begin to understand His power.

He will first silence the questioning scribes by a question. "What question ye with them?" said He to the scribes, and they said no more. He then gave these men another opportunity to believe. First He wrought the wonder. If the hour ever come when He can no longer tolerate a generation, when He can no longer bear, we may rest assured it will be in the hour which is so dire and dark and awful, that God Himself can do nothing more! There is the possibility! Do not look at it in some wide area. Let us take it to our own souls. There is the awful tragic possibility in our life that wilful unbelief can be so blind, so persistent, and so rebellious that at last Christ will have to say, No longer! But He will never do it until He has given us the ultimate opportunity. These scribes were laughing at the disciples, and criticizing them because they were feeble, calling in question the power of the Lord. Into their midst He came down, and worked the wonder. It was another opportunity for them.

Is there anything more beautiful than His dealing with the father? How He called forth his faith when he was in an agony. In a method of speech that was almost rude perhaps—which method we miss in translation—he said to Jesus, "If Thou canst do anything, have compassion." Brought into the presence of the Master of the disciples who had failed, he doubted if He could do anything. Jesus looked back into his eyes and said, "If thou canst! All things are possible to him that believeth."

Bear in mind, that man had certainly heard the words of our text, " O unbelieving generation, how long shall I be with you? How long shall I tolerate you?" Now when the man said, "If Thou canst," Jesus said, "If *thou* canst! All things are possible." Then the man, never more beautiful than now—no hypocrite this, no man pretending to believe,—said, "I believe." That was the dawning of faith. He was not sure; so he added, "Help Thou mine unbelief." That is the grandest faith possible, the finest exercise of faith. Whereas faith is always crying, Lord, I believe; behind are the lurking questionings and the wondering doubts; and instead of letting faith master us, we cry out, Lord, help our unbelief! So surely as a soul is learning the lesson of this story, so rapidly results shall follow. The Lord honours the will to believe. The man believed in the best way possible; and the Lord immediately responded. He won an honest faith that day, and the man was compelled thus to tell all the truth about his mind and soul. "Lord, I believe; help Thou mine unbelief." Immediately, the Master turned to his boy, and cast the demon out.

We have seen the tragedy of a boy made for faith, unable to believe, demon-possessed. Now see the things that happened. He cast the demon out; and the boy lay there, pale, pinched, looking dead. Then Jesus took him by the hand, and lifted him up, and he arose. I think that boy believed in Jesus afterwards. The Lord gave him back his boyhood, his youth, his hope, his capacity for dreams, visions and faith; and I think to the end of time, that boy's faith was centred upon the One Who had given him his chance.

Then He patiently instructed His disciples, told them, as Matthew records, that the reason they failed was because of their little faith. The faith that faltered at Cæsarea Philippi was paralyzed in the valley, until He came back to them; and so He declared that, " This kind can come out by nothing, save by prayer "; prayer being used there, in its finest and truest sense; prayer is the activity of faith; prayer is that resting of the soul in Jesus, which rests at last in the will of God, and prompts the power of God. So these men were recalled to faith, and instructed as to its true exercise.

" O faithless generation, how long shall I be with you? How long shall I bear with you?" In that inquiry we hear the pain of Jesus. Unbelief gives Him sorrow because it harms man. Is not His pain most poignant in the presence of the little faith of His own? Not those disputing scribes outside the Christian Church to-day, who are striving to prove our incapacities, and laugh at us for our failure; but we who are inside with such little faith that we seem to work no miracles, and do no spiritual wonders; we grieve His heart most of all.

Then I should be untrue to the one thing that is searching my own soul, unless I gave attention to the last question, terrible, bitter, " How long shall I tolerate you?" There are necessary limits to His bearing with unbelief. Sometimes it seems as though He were asking that question about me; and about the Church! Then let us together say to Him: Lord, we believe. Help Thou our unbelief!

XVIII

" Have salt in yourselves, and be at peace one with another."—MARK 9 : 50b.

Mark 9 : 30–50.

IN our last meditation we considered the events which followed immediately upon the experiences of the holy mount. In the valley we saw the demonized boy, the distracted father, the defeated disciples, and the disputing scribes; and our Lord's dealing with all. He cast out the demon, gave the boy back to his father, instructed His disciples as to the secret of their failure, and silenced the disputing scribes.

The first paragraph in our present meditation tells what immediately followed. Jesus and His disciples left the neighbourhood of Cæsarea Philippi. He led them through Galilee, evidently along by-paths, and the less frequented roads, for the express purpose of giving them further teaching concerning all that lay before Him of suffering, death, and resurrection. They listened to Him, but did not understand, and were evidently afraid to ask Him.

The measure of their failure is illustrated in the story which follows. It is evident therefrom that in the intervals of His teaching they had been disputing among themselves as to their respective greatness. This is one instance of many in the Gospel stories, recording the doings of these last days in the mission of Christ, revealing the unutterably sad fact, that when their Lord attempted to draw these men into sympathy with Himself, as He walked the *via dolorosa*—His face steadfastly set toward Jerusalem, His passion baptism, and the consummation of His mission—they broke in sooner or later upon His conversation, either by asking a similar question, or by their own disputes concerning which should be counted the greatest. One can almost imagine that the fact that Peter, James, and John had been with Him on the holy mount, had given rise to the dispute. It may be that when they came back to the nine who had been left in the valley, they assumed some air of spiritual superiority, because they had been with Him on the mount. Be this as it may, we are told that they disputed amongst themselves which should be the greater; and at last, when they came to Capernaum, the Lord Himself raised the subject. All that follows in this paragraph is related with this subject, and all finds culmination in the text: "Have salt in yourselves, and be at peace one with another." In it then, we have His final words in this relation.

In order that we may better understand their value, we must take time to set this story clearly before our minds; beginning with the Lord's inquiry when they came to Capernaum. In the early days of His Galilean ministry He made Capernaum the base of His operations, and there is every reason to believe that the house where He sojourned was that of Simon Peter. When they were in the house He asked them, "What were ye reasoning on the way?" They were silent, and did not answer Him, for they had disputed one with another in the way who was the greatest. Immediately that He asked the question, they knew that their disputing had been unworthy, and so they were silent. Then, accepting the shame that was evidenced in their silence, the Lord proceeded to teach them, and first of all stated the whole fact as to respective greatness within the ranks of His disciples, and in His Kingdom in this word: "If any man would be first he shall be last of all, and minister of all." This was not a suggestion on our Lord's part that if a man were ambitious he should be relegated to some place of obscurity, but it was a revelation of the true secret of greatness in

His Kingdom. Not the man who masters others, but the man whom every one masters, and is thereby compelled to serve, is the greatest within the Kingdom.

Having so said, He gave them the beautiful illustration that we all so much admire. He took a little child and put him in the midst of them; and then taking him in His arms He continued His conversation. He took a little child—not specially prepared for the occasion, not a catechumen who was prepared for the hour—but an ordinary boy, perchance the boy of Simon Peter, and then continued, "Whosoever shall receive one of such little children in My name, receiveth Me: and whosoever receiveth Me, receiveth not Me," but God, "Him that sent Me."

In the Revised Version at this point, correctly, there is a new paragraph. The new paragraph, however, does not mean that the subject is changed. "John said unto Him, Teacher, we saw one casting out demons in Thy name: and we forbade him, because he followed not us." John was not making a boast in something he had done. He confessed to failure. John, in many regards the most wonderful of the apostles, the man of keenest insight, quickest intuition, recognized here immediately that he had been doing something wrong. If indeed it be true that to receive a little child, an ordinary everyday child, is to receive Christ, and to receive God, said John within himself, What did I do when I forbade that man who in the Name was casting out a demon? Verily the light had broken in upon him.

Our Lord first answered the confession of John: "Forbid him not: for there is no man who shall do a mighty work in My name, and be able quickly to speak evil of Me. For he that is not against us is for us. For whosoever shall give you a cup of water to drink, because ye are Christ's, verily I say unto you, he shall in no wise lose his reward." Then, resuming the discourse where it had been interrupted, He said, "And whosoever shall cause one of these little ones that believe on Me to stumble, it were better for him if a great millstone were hanged about his neck, and he were cast into the sea." Continuing in most solemn and searching teaching, He enforced this principle, until at last He reached the words, " Have salt in yourselves, and be at peace one with another."

In the light of the context then, let us consider this injunction, observing the two things: " Have salt in yourselves," and " Be at peace one with another." The instruction is the revelation of a sequence. First then, the salt that produces peace; and secondly, the peace that is produced by salt.

We recognize at once, that we are in the presence of one of the paragraphs of the New Testament which has caused difficulty and perplexity to expositors. This is specially so with regard to the previous verse to our text: " For every one shall be salted with fire. Salt is good; but if the salt have lost its saltness, wherewith will ye season it? " The injunction, " Have salt in yourselves " grows out of this declaration and this inquiry. We may get nearer the heart of our Lord's meaning as we allow the text to be interpreted by the things already said, even though at first it seems as though there was little connection. " Have salt in yourselves." A little while before He said, " Every one shall be salted with fire." That was not a new beginning, but something that followed upon words such as these, " unquenchable fire," " Gehenna."

The explanation of the meaning of our Lord's use of the figure of salt may be derived from the previous statement, " Every one shall be salted with fire." The term " fire " interprets the term " salt " for this particular occasion. There are other occasions where the term " salt " may be used with another signification, though in the last analysis I should hardly be prepared to admit that; for I believe at its heart it is always allied to the meaning it

[209]

has here. Fire destroys the perishable, and perfects that which is imperishable. Our Lord in the previous teaching had referred to Gehenna. Let us remember that He was speaking in the hearing of men to whom that connoted one particular idea. They knew perfectly well that He was using a most drastic figure of speech, one that was terrific in its suggestiveness. The valley of Gehenna, a gorge outside Jerusalem, was historic. In the valley of Tophet, Solomon had first erected an altar to the worship of Moloch. At a later and more depraved period in the history of the kingdom of Judah, Ahaz and Manasseh had offered human sacrifices to Moloch in that very valley, until the reformation period came under king Josiah. One thing which Josiah did in the course of his reformation was to defile the valley where Moloch had been worshipped, casting refuse there, making it from that time through all the successive years the place where all the evil things of the city were cast out for destruction. The purpose of Gehenna then, was the purification of the life of the city. Those smouldering fires, destroying vulgarity and obscenity, were in themselves witnesses of the necessity for the sanitation of Jerusalem.

This was a drastic figure, and our Lord was not the first who made use of it. When this began cannot be said, but Tophet, Gehenna, was the perpetual figure employed for the place of punishment beyond this life, the strange and mysterious realm in the universe of God, made necessary for the purification of that universe; hell itself, with all the old meaning of the word delivered from its base and corrupt materialism; hell, as Jesus said, where "their worm dieth not, and the fire is not quenched." That was the reference, first of all to a place geographical and actual, as a civic necessity, and secondly and consequently, to a place and state moral and spiritual, and as equally a necessity in the Divine economy. In other words, fire as our Lord used it here, was the symbol of the principle that makes no peace with evil.

The fire of Gehenna is the holiness of God. Said Jesus at last to these disciples, Have that fire burning within yourselves, and so be at peace one with another. " Every one shall be salted with fire." Fire destroys the perishable, but perfects that which is imperishable.

Change the figure to salt, and see how near we are to the thought. Salt prevents corruption and preserves soundness. Behind the word " soundness " is the thought of sanitation, and involved in the word " sanitation " is the conditon of health; and at the heart of the word " health " is the principle of holiness. Salt prevents disintegration, and corruption, and preserves soundness and health. Salt is also of the fire nature; a subtle, penetrative, permeative flame that searches out every element of destruction, and holds it in check, and annihilates it; in order that there may be opportunity for the growth and development and enlargement of that which makes for health. " Have salt in yourselves."

To come nearer to the Lord's meaning when He laid this charge upon His disciples, we must recognize that the moral and spiritual values are revealed in the previous teaching. There is first that which is relative, and then that which lies behind it and is personal, apart from which the relative is impossible of realization.

Notice first the relative teaching. " Whosoever shall cause one of these little ones that believe on Me to stumble, it were better for him if a great millstone were hanged about his neck, and he were cast into the sea." Christ was here calling for such passion for service in order to the perfecting of others, that sudden and violent extinction is counted preferable to causing a little one to stumble. He was holding up before the eyes of His astonished disciples an ideal, that seemed for the moment to have very little application to their disputing by the way. I think as He talked, the boy was still in His arms, and that though spiritually here He may have come to the consideration of the life of the little ones who had but

[211]

recently believed in Him, He was not far away from
the child, nor the child from Him. With that ordinary
boy, suddenly arrested, apprehended, caught up in His
arms, He said: Rather than make this little child stumble,
it were better for a man if a great millstone were hanged
about his neck, and he were cast into the sea.

Then He immediately passed from that description of
relative passion for service to the individual condition
that makes it possible. He declared in effect that such
passion is generated by the personal intolerance of evil
which prefers maiming, to deflection from the way of
truth. The hand, the actual deed; the foot, the approach
or direction toward evil; the eye, the sight or desire that
inspires the approach, and issues in the deed; all must be
dealt with. Our Lord here calls for such passion for
purity within the soul, that if necessary it shall be maintained by maiming and mutilation. The supreme thought
running through all the teaching is that of the necessity
for purity, at all costs. " Have salt in yourselves "; let
there be burning within you the very fire which makes
conflict with sin and with evil. It is as though the Lord
had said: Unless this awful fire of Divine holiness burn
within you as a passion that destroys within your lives all
evil things, there will be no escape from the ultimate
Gehenna, in which that fire is forever consuming. It is
as though our Lord had said to those first disciples: The
only way to escape the ultimate Gehenna of fire, is for
that fire to burn within you, of your own volition, thus
purifying the soul. It is Christ's call to resolute and
sacrificial purity. When the writer of the letter to the
Hebrews wrote, " Ye have not yet resisted unto blood,
striving against sin," he did not mean a resistance that
makes the blood flow through blows implanted by an
enemy. The reference was surely to Gethsemane, when
" His sweat became as it were great drops of blood ";
the mental pressure and agony being so terrific that all
the functions of nature were arrested and revolutionized.

Salt! Not some light sentimental word is this, suggesting an application that is merely invigorating and refreshing in some moral sense; but the salt that is fire, of the very fire of hell itself against sin; so that the right hand, the right foot, must be cut off, the right eye be gouged out, in order that the soul may be clean and pure.

Peace among ourselves then is not something that may be arranged for, by taking counsel with one another, in order that we may abandon some conviction that we hold dear. Strong lasting peace, that knows no ultimate disturbance, must be based upon a purity that is produced by salt which is fire; "first pure, then peaceable." Our Lord by this apparently strange teaching, flashed back upon the disputing by the way the light of the Divine estimation of it, and revealed the fact that all such disputing sprang out of the toleration of evil within the soul in some form or another; and that wherever those who name His name, and profess to follow Him, and are walking after Him, dispute among themselves as to greatness, they are revealing some malady far deeper than the symptom would suggest to the casual observer. They are revealing the fact that down beneath the disputation is disease, spiritual and moral, which cannot be treated with rose-water, and needs the fire of salt, terrific in its burning, and destructive of all that is capable of destruction; fire which destroys the perishable, but thank God, gives the soundness of health every opportunity.

Now, glancing back from this word of Jesus to the original cause of the story, to the fact of their disputing, and then to John's confession, and all that it meant, we gather what the peace is, which salt produces. I shall make two suggestions only.

The action of such salt first produces the transmutation of ambition. Wherever there is the action of this salt there is the death of the absorbing passion for greatness, and the birth of the edifying passion for service. Mark the difference between these things. The passion for

[213]

personal greatness is always a disrupting element anywhere and everywhere, in all human life and society.
Wherever that passion burns there is the destruction of
peace, and of a true order. These men were troubled
about who was the greatest. In the place of that absorbing passion for greatness was born, what for lack of a
more striking word I have described as the edifying passion for service. He who would be greatest, let him be
least of all, minister of all. When this salt is in the
life, when this fire burns within the soul, it indeed

> " Burns up the dross of base desire,
>   And makes the mountains flow."

Wherever this salt is active in the life, there is born a
passion not for the exercise of authority, but for the
rendering of service. Surely no one can read this carefully without being ashamed. No congregation of Christian souls can consider these ideals, and this teaching
of Jesus, without coming to the almost appalling recognition of the fact of how little we know of this experimentally. Yet, thank God there have been and still are
multitudes of those in whom this salt burns, producing
God's own purity; and in every such case they are those
whose one mastering eagerness is to serve; and where
there is eagerness to serve, then the little one is received;
and where there is eagerness to serve, disputes about
greatness finally end. Where there is eagerness to serve
there is peace.

But not only does this salt produce the transmutation
of ambition. It produces also the enlargement of fellowship. Everywhere this salt operates, there is the death of
the sense of the dignity of official privilege. Now this
was the trouble in the case of John. John told the Lord
—and the grace of his heart is revealed in the fact that
he made confession—that " We saw one," not attempting
to cast out demons, but doing it. " We saw one casting
out demons "; not by any of the incantations of the

heathen, but " in Thy name; and we forbade him, because
he followed not us "! He was irregular, he was not in
the true order, he was not in the appointed succession,
he was outside! Oh! the devilishness of it—I am not
going to withdraw that word—the devilishness of this
sense of official privilege and dignity. Quick and sharp
and stern, like a crack of thunder following a blaze of
lightning, came the Lord's word, " Forbid him not: for
there is no man which shall do a mighty work in My
name, and be able quickly to speak evil of Me. For he
that is not against us is for us." Yet I wonder if I have
misinterpreted the tone and temper of Jesus by suggesting
that He spoke in any such harsh accents! I do not know,
for it seems to me after all that if this were a word of
thunder, behind the thunder was all the refreshment and
coolness and beauty of a high conception of fellowship.
" He followed not us." No, but " he . . . is for us."
Jesus here used the plural, putting the twelve back into
fellowship with Himself; He is for us, not against us.

Wherever this salt burns in the life, there is not only
the enlargement of fellowship that results from the death
of the sense of the dignity of official privilege; there is
also the birth of the recognition of the supremacy of the
name. " He that receiveth one such little child *in My
name.*" That is what arrested John, and made him say,
" Teacher, we saw one casting out demons *in Thy name;*
and we forbade him." So our Lord immediately responded, taking up exactly the same thought as He said,
" No man can do a mighty work *in My name,* and be able
quickly to speak evil of Me." Presently He said another thing, which we have rather lost by our translation.
" Whosoever shall give you a cup of water to drink, *in
the name that ye are Christ's.*" That is quite literal. We
have translated actually as to sense, " Because ye are
Christ's "; but we have lost something of the impact.
" Shall give you a cup of cold water to drink in the
name that ye are Christ's, Verily I say unto you! "

The dignity and the supremacy of the name was revealed. That man does not follow Me, but if he, in the name, cast out a demon, then that man is included in the fellowship. So the borders of fellowship are flung back, and the company of the comrades of the Crusade is enlarged; but we shall never be willing to admit that, until this salt, this fire, permeates the life and purifies it.

In conclusion note again the command. "Have salt in yourselves"; that is the personal note. "Be at peace one with another"; that is the relative note. The first is superlative, the second is sequential. If we would have true peace one with another, our first business must be to obey the earlier injunction, "Have salt in yourselves."

Yet look back once more to the statement and question preceding the text, which gives a wider view of the meaning of the experience, on which we can only enter as we go back to the narrowness of the injunction. What then is this statement and this inquiry? "Salt is good; but if the salt have lost its saltness, wherewith will ye season it?" This is a larger word, having a wider application. This is a word that is true to the music of that which Jesus had already said in His manifesto, on an earlier occasion. "Ye are the salt of the earth." In that word of Jesus all the world was taken into account. Then immediately we are reminded that men having salt in themselves, exert an influence of salt in the world; and only as we have salt in ourselves and are at peace one with another can we exert the influence of salt in the world, or become peacemakers.

What do we know of this salt, which is a fire, and oftentimes a pain and an agony, burning with a passion for purity that will make no terms with evil in our lives? It is only upon the basis of such purity, resulting from such action of the fire of salt and the salt of fire, that we can ever be at peace.

XIX

" From the beginning of the creation, male and female made He them. For this cause shall a man leave his father and mother, and shall cleave to his wife; and the two shall become one flesh: so that they are no more two, but one flesh. . . . Suffer the little children to come unto me; forbid them not: for to such belongeth the Kingdom of God."—MARK 10:6–8, and 14.

Mark 10: 1–16.

IN this paragraph we have two stories. The first is that of the coming to Jesus of certain Pharisees, who questioned Him on the subject of divorce; and of the answers He gave them. The second is that of the bringing of children to Him; and of the manner of His reception of them.

Both Matthew and Mark put these stories thus in close relation to each other as to the time of their taking place. This is interesting, in that the teaching of Jesus in the two events constitutes a revelation of the Christian ideal of the family.

Before attempting to consider that ideal as revealed in the paragraphs there are two things which we ought to do. First we should note, with some care, the hour in the life of our Lord in which these things happened. Secondly, we must disentangle the essential from the accidental, in these stories.

As to the first. Between that teaching of His disciples in the house in Capernaum, and the things recorded in these paragraphs, much had transpired in the ministry of Jesus, which Mark passes over in silence. Jesus had probably twice visited Jerusalem in the interval. He had sent out the seventy upon their mission. After they returned, He had Himself been in Peræa, accompanied by His apostles. Here we see Him leaving Galilee for Judæa, for the last time prior to His crucifixion. He was now definitely and finally on His way to the Cross. This was the beginning of the last journey. The bearing of this on our subject is that we see the Servant of God bent on redeeming work, but insisting on that ethic of life which is founded on the binding nature of the Divine thought and purpose for humanity, and revealing its true value to society. His face was set toward the Cross; His heart was filled with the passion for redeeming men; but not for a moment did He lower the standard of Divine requirements.

As to the second of these preliminary matters. We must disentangle the accidental from the essential. The whole question of divorce was accidental. The disciples' mistake about the children was accidental. The essential things in these stories were; first our Lord's teaching on the subject of marriage; and secondly, our Lord's inclusive declaration of truth concerning all children. When I use the word "accidental," I do not mean that these things are unimportant. They were things occurring by the way. Incidental things, perhaps, would be a more accurate description. Here, as ever, our Lord brought to bear upon these things, accidental or incidental, the light of essential and eternal truth. The distinction is important, because when the accidental things are once set in the light of the essential, we see them in their true value and proportion.

To those then, which we have described as accidental, we will return in conclusion, giving ourselves first to the essential things.

Here then we find Christ's revelation of the true ideal of the family, as He dealt first of all with the nature of marriage, and secondly with the inclusive truth about children.

His teaching concerning the nature of marriage is

found in these words: " From the beginning of the creation, male and female made He them. For this cause
shall a man leave his father and mother, and shall cleave
to his wife; and the two shall become one flesh: so that
they are no more two, but one flesh." This is essential
truth, and in the light of it He immediately dealt with
the accidental: " What therefore God hath joined together, let not man put asunder."

The inclusive truth about the children is contained in
the words: " Of such is the Kingdom of God." That inclusive and essential truth being recognized, all the accidental things are dealt with by the preliminary words,
" Suffer the little children to come unto Me; forbid them
not." So He corrected the accidental mistake of the
disciples, in the light of essential truth concerning children.

First then, our Lord's teaching here concerning the
nature of marriage. The words were carefully chosen.
Here, as so constantly in the teaching of our Lord, He
said nothing new; but took these men of His day back to
their own sacred Writings, and quoted from them. In
these words then, we have a threefold revelation of the
truth concerning marriage, according to the Biblical revelation, according to Christ's teaching; and consequently,
according to the Christian standard. He first declared
the fundamental truth, " From the beginning of the creation, male and female made He them." He then uttered
the experimental truth concerning marriage, " For this
cause shall a man leave his father and mother, and shall
cleave unto his wife." Finally, He spoke words which
we may speak of as constituting the functional truth concerning marriage, " The two shall become one flesh."

In answer to the questions of the Pharisees, our Lord
directed their thinking from their own view, or from
their interpretation of the law of Moses, back to the
original intention. There was arresting dignity and authority in the method of Jesus. Moses allowed a bill of

divorcement to be written, said they. Said Jesus, This he did for the hardness of your heart; and immediately sweeping back, behind their interpretation, and even behind the word of Moses himself, and the whole Hebrew economy, He took them to original and fundamental things, Divine intentions, and purposes, " From the beginning of the creation." Before that state of society in which they were then living; before that word of Moses which was born of the hardness of man's heart; before that sterner word of Moses which was embodied within the Decalogue; before all the habits of the men of the past; He took them back to the very beginning of things: " From the beginning of the creation."

We turn back with Him to the beginning, and to the story of the beginning with which these men were familiar, and from which story He quoted for their sakes.

"And God said, Let Us make man in Our image, after Our likeness: and let them have dominion. . . . And God created man in His own image, in the image of God created He him: male and female created He them."

Such is the declaration of the Hebrew Scriptures, from which Jesus made His selection and quotation.

Quite apart from this accidental subject of divorce, tragic as it was in the hour in which the question was put to Jesus, tragic as it is to-day, let us consider the subject of marriage. Mark with great care what Jesus did. He emphasized the teaching of the old economy on this one point. That teaching is that man is a unity, and not a unit; that man is dual, but not two; that the full ideal of humanity is the union of fatherhood and motherhood; that spiritually and in the last analysis, humanity is not represented in man, or in woman, but in their union. Man is in the Divine likeness and the Divine image partially; woman is in the Divine likeness and the Divine image partially. Not in man is a full and perfect representation of the Divine likeness and the Divine image; not in woman is a full and perfect representation of the Divine likeness and the Divine image. In each there are elements of the Divine likeness and the Divine image; but in the mystic union is the full unveiling of the truth concerning God. God is not Father alone, He is Mother also. In the essential mystery of the Divine Being, there are not only all those quantities and qualities which we associate with man; there are those quantities and qualities which we associate with woman. Consequently, thinking in each case upon the very highest level, in the union of man and woman there is the expression of truth concerning God as there cannot be in the loneliness of the one, or the isolation of the other. When to-day questions are asked about divorce, men do not usually begin here; but this is where Christ began. If the question of divorce is to be discussed, said Jesus in effect, let us get back to the beginning of things, and see what God meant in the creation of humanity. From the beginning of the creation He created them male and female.

In the complexity of modern circumstances this is not always possible of realization. The words of Jesus as recorded by Matthew in this very connection are significant. Do not let us forget, moreover, that Jesus said ere He uttered them: " Not all men can receive this saying, but they to whom it is given." Knowing the difficulty, I quote the words of Jesus: " There are eunuchs which were so born from their mother's womb: and there are eunuchs that were made eunuchs by men: and there are eunuchs that made themselves eunuchs for the kingdom of heaven's sake." In that verse Christ recognized the fact that in the complexity of human conditions into the midst of which He came, there might be celibacy through natural causes, or through force of circumstances; or there might be voluntary celibacy in the interest of the Kingdom of God, which is high and holy. Nevertheless in the original purpose of God, humanity is completed in man and in woman. When I hear of woman's sphere,

I am always inclined to remind those who speak of it, that she has no sphere! I will immediately add to that, neither has man a sphere! The sphere of Divine expression is the unity of man and woman, in which she is a hemisphere, and he a hemisphere. " Male and female created He them." That is the eternal purpose underlying the Divine thought and conception.

Our Lord then proceeded again to quote: " For this cause shall a man leave his father and his mother, and shall cleave unto his wife." " For this cause." For what cause? We go back again to Genesis, from which Jesus was quoting: "And the man said, This is now bone of my bones, and flesh of my flesh; she shall be called Woman, because she was taken out of Man. *Therefore* shall a man leave his father and his mother, and shall cleave unto his wife." Let us also turn to the apostolic exposition, as it is found in the Ephesian letter: " Even so ought husbands also to love their own wives as their own bodies. He that loveth his own wife loveth himself; for no man ever hateth his own flesh, but nourisheth and cherisheth it. . . . *For this cause* shall a man leave his father and mother, and shall cleave to his wife, and the two shall become one flesh."

By this teaching of the context of the words which Jesus quoted, and by the teaching of the apostolic interpretation of our Lord's meaning, we find that the cause is that of the fundamental unity. Involved, is the great spiritual declaration, that when God created man, He created male and female, and the two aspects of Deity are to be represented in the two. They make the unity of humanity. Because then the woman is the complement of the man; that part of him, apart from which he lacks, and is imperfect as an instrument; he shall leave father and mother and cleave to his wife. The holy apostle in the paragraph in Ephesians says exactly the same thing; the cause is that of fundamental unity.

What then is the experience in itself? Mark the super-

lativeness of the ancient word endorsed by Jesus, and endorsed by apostolic interpretation. He shall leave the
nearest and the dearest he has ever known, father and
mother, for the nearer and the dearer than they. In other
words, the experience upon which marriage is to be based
according to this Divine ideal, is that of supreme recip-
rocal affection. I have simply put into other words that
master utterance of Joseph Cook of Boston, in which he
declared that the only true foundation for marriage is
that of a supreme affection between two. The basis of
experience in marriage is the outgoing of love to love
consummating a union which is indissoluble. Behind
such outgoing of love to love, is the fundamental Divine
conception and fact of creation, " Male and female created He them."

Finally our Lord quoted the words, " The two shall become one flesh." In that unity of the flesh there is the
sacramental symbol of the spiritual unity which, if it be
non-existent, marriage is a disaster, a sham, and the occasion of all misery.

Observe the sanctity of this ideal. The Roman and
Greek Churches count marriage a sacrament. I wonder
whether they are not right. The Roman Church calls it
a sacrament, the Greek Church calls it a mystery. I pray
you remember that Paul also called it " a mystery."
What is a sacrament? That may raise a great controversial question, and there is nothing further from my
mind than a desire for controversy; but if indeed a sacrament be an outward and visible sign of an inward and
spiritual grace, then I affirm that marriage is supreme
among the sacraments.

Marriage is a condition of Divine expression and activity, therefore where its fundamental significances are
forgotten, and its fundamental laws are disobeyed, it becomes the most tragic of all experiences. Any nation
which forgets the Divine ordinance of marriage, and
what it means, will become a ruin, in spite of all its

strength in other things! It is for the Church of God to come back to Christ's teaching on this subject, understand it, and stand by it, in face of obloquy if need be. By so doing she will act in the interest of the race.

While Jesus was talking thus to His disciples, people outside were bringing children to Him.

Without dealing with the story, which is so familiar, let us listen to the final words which Jesus uttered about these children: " Of such is the Kingdom of God."

Carefully observe in the first place that this is an inclusive statement, the reference being to children as children, quite apart from privilege or disability. The statement of Christ in the case of a child is not made more true, if the child has been privileged. The statement of Christ in the case of a child is not made less true, if the child has suffered disability. That was a promiscuous gathering; those crowds that came after Jesus everywhere were made up of all sorts and conditions of people; and they brought their children. They were not carefully selected children, but those of the common folk. Of these children He said, " To such belongeth the Kingdom of God."

Mark then the statement, " To such belongeth the Kingdom of God." They were all included, and our Lord further emphasized that declaration by expository words: " Forbid them not "; and " Whosoever shall not receive the Kingdom of God as a little child, he shall in no wise enter therein." Our Lord thus declared, not only that all the children are included in His Kingdom; but that, in order to be included, all older people must become children. John Ruskin once said that what man needs is not so much to graduate, as to backslide; not to go forward into new cleverness, but to backslide into the simplicity of childhood. Our Lord was thus declaring essential truth.

As I look in wonder and amazement,—being influenced as were the apostles by the thought that children must not go to Him, because He was engaged on such important business that He could not be interrupted,—I see that He gathered them to Himself, and said, These are in the Kingdom, and if you, apostles, disciples, desire to enter, you must join the children.

All this has many applications. I want to make one. These children, find them where we will, in the tenement house or in your own home, are all spiritual, they are of God in the deepest fact of their being. We have had fathers of our flesh who disciplined us. Shall we not much rather obey the Father of spirits? God is the Father of spirits. In an almost amazing and tremendous mystery, God has united Himself to humanity in the propagation of the race, so that wherever children are conceived and begotten, God coöperates and creates eternal spirits.

When of these little children He said, "To such belongeth the Kingdom," He did not mean that they were perfect, but that they were potential, and plastic; each one separate, no two alike. Out of the ancient Scriptures comes back to us the old word so often misunderstood: "Train up a child in his own way, and even when he is old he will not depart from it." Not, Train up a child in the way it should go, but in the way God meant it should go; in its own way, according to its personal capacity and lonely dignity. There is no boy nor girl, in privileged home or in slumdom, but in that boy, that girl, are resident individual, lonely, magnificent capacities, which belong alone to that boy or girl. I sometimes think in these days when the passion for collectivism is so great,—a perfectly accurate passion,—we need to return to the emphasis of this individual note, lest we become merely a nation of numbers. Let us remember that if God gives a little child its essential spirit life, in that life there are potentialities that are peculiar to it.

Let us also remember, a little child is plastic, capable of realization.

" A child's face is the window of its soul,
That yet untrammelled by the world's control,
Like some still pool upon a summer's day,
Ruffles to every wind that blows that way.

" And it is like a yet wide open door,
That every year Life shuts a little more,
It stands wide-thrown, and to and fro pass free
Of its fresh thoughts the white-robed company.

" And it is like a harp that silent stands,
Waiting the touch of any passing hands
That chance to pluck the clear obedient strings,
Giving the hidden melodies their wings.

" A little pool that ruffles to the winds,
An open door where each one entry finds,
A stringèd harp to answer song or hymn,
So is a child's face to his every whim."

That is the Kingdom of God, the plastic possibility.
Oh! the tragedy of it, if that child should live in a home
where the winds that sweep, are such as nip and blast and
destroy, where the guests that enter through the door, are
such as harm and defile; where the hand that sweeps is
such as does not make music but destroys it. I pray
you, look on the sanctity of this ideal, for where it is
realized, home is heaven, and the nursery is God's work-
shop.

We may now return to the accidental or incidental
things. First as to the question of divorce. Where the
ideal of marriage which our Lord revealed, is realized,
divorce is unthinkable and unnameable. The question as
it was asked, revealed the laxity of the age in which Jesus
lived. He was asked to decide between rival schools on
this subject which then existed; the school of Shammai,
the strict, and the school of Hillel, the liberal. The latter
was the most popular at the moment. Hillel had advo-
cated divorce for trifling causes. When these men asked

their question, there was in the background of their thinking, the dark and sinister figure of Herod. In answer
Christ first appealed to Moses, and gave interpretation of
his permission. Then He gave His inclusive answer,
"What God hath joined together, let not man put
asunder." Presently, when they were alone, the disciples were so perplexed, that they asked Him further
concerning the matter, and He gave them His answer,
recorded in Mark, which answer must be interpreted by
His manifesto. There is one, and only one reason for
divorce. There, I affirm again, the Church of God must
stand, for the glory of God, and in the interest of humanity.

As to the incidental things in the second story. What
is more natural than that those who are of the Kingdom,
should find their way to the King? Mark the mistake of
the disciples. We may think we should never make that
mistake. I think that we are in danger of making it even
yet. We still too often relegate work among children in
our corporate thinking within the Church, to some secondary place. We still imagine that our Lord has business on hand too important, to give very much time and
attention to children.

This is one of the very few occasions upon which our
Gospel story tells us that Jesus was angry. "He was
moved with indignation." When next we recite these
words that constitute the magna charta of childhood,
"Suffer the children to come unto Me," never let us
forget that if they are tremulous with the tenderness of
His love, they are vibrant with the thunder of His wrath
against the men who hindered the children in their coming.

It is as though our Lord said, If you will only let these
children alone, they will come; if they do not come, it will
not be their fault, it will be yours! I maintain that this
is true. If the children do not find their way to Christ,
it is always our fault, either that we did not reveal Him

at all; or that revealing Him, we libelled Him. Oh! let the children see Him, and they will be after Him. "Suffer them; forbid them not!"

Then He took them in His arms, and put His hands upon them, and blessed them. From the hour in which He did this, Christianity has become preëminently the religion of the child. There the Church must keep them; for the satisfying of His heart, and for her own wellbeing. Dr. Noah K. Davis of Virginia University some time ago said this remarkable thing, which I leave you to challenge, to agree with, or to correct. "Classical literature knows nothing of children. Christian literature is full of children."

Oh! the glory of the Christian family where this ideal of marriage is realized and where this truth concerning children is accepted. May God multiply such families.

XX

*"Why callest thou Me good? None is good save one,
God."*—MARK 10: 18.

Mark 10: 17–31.

THE selection of the text is intended as an indication
of the purpose of the meditation. It is that of fastening
attention upon the Lord Himself, rather than upon the
young ruler. Of course we must see him also, and indeed, observe the whole movement of this story; but we
shall do that in order to consider as carefully as possible
these arresting and remarkable words of Jesus.

It is almost certain that this incident occurred immediately after those in which the Lord revealed the true
ideal of marriage and uttered the word of inclusive truth
concerning the children. As we saw in our last meditation, Matthew and Mark place these two incidents in
close connection. Luke omits the story of the enquiry of
the Pharisees, also the teaching of Jesus on the subject of
marriage in that particular connection. Matthew, Mark,
and Luke place this story of the young ruler in immediate connection with the reception of the children by our
Lord. This connection is at least interesting and suggestive, as it may help us to understand what this young
man heard Jesus say, and saw Him do, which made him
come to Christ in the way he did.

His coming was due to a noble impulse, resulting from
a true passion, and a deep sense of lack. Witness his
quest, as expressed in his enquiry, " Good Teacher, what
shall I do that I may inherit eternal life?" Witness
also his manner. He, a young ruler, wealthy withal, did
nevertheless in the presence of the Galilean peasant, kneel
and address Him with profound respect; and by that
very attitude and speech he showed the fineness of his
natural spirit.

The words of our text constitute the first part of the answer of Jesus to the question: "Good Teacher, what shall I do that I may inherit age-abiding life?" This answer has caused very much trouble to expositors. The words have created serious difficulty in the minds of some who, believing in the Deity of our Lord, have understood them as constituting a repudiation of personal goodness on His part. On the other hand, there have been those who, at once accepting that interpretation and meaning of the words, have used them as evidence that our Lord laid no claim to Deity. In his weird article in the "Encyclopædia Biblica," dealing with the person of Jesus Christ, Schmiedel admitted the authenticity of five fragments of the four Gospels, because in those fragments Jesus seemed to renounce all which we now associate with His name. Among the five, this was one of the passages that Schmiedel allowed to remain as genuine. Let us at once admit that if Jesus did here mean to repudiate goodness, the deduction is inevitable, that He also repudiated Deity.

Let us then consider His statement, endeavouring to discover what our Lord really meant, when He spoke to the young ruler; and that, not merely for the purpose of intellectual illumination, but in order that we may consider in the second place, the bearing of the statement on this great quest for eternal life.

First, then, the statement itself. "Why callest thou Me good? None is good save one, God." The plain meaning of the passage is that which we first attempt to gather. There are three records of the event in the Gospels. Matthew's record of the first words of Jesus differs from those found in Mark and Luke. Jesus is recorded in Matthew's account as having said to the young man, "Why askest thou Me concerning that which is good? One there is that is good." The words in Mark and Luke are identical.

These two statements are not alike, and they do not

mean the same thing. The statement as found in Matthew: " Why askest thou Me concerning that which is good? One there is Who is good "; is not the same as, " Why callest thou Me good? There is one that is good, even God." The change in Matthew's record in the Revised Version is unquestionably justified, and we need not now enter into the discussion as to the reason of the change. This fact, however, does not call in question the record of Mark or Luke; neither does it mean that Matthew is inaccurate. Here, as so often in the case of these Gospel narratives, the two are needed in order to understand all that Jesus said. Matthew recorded one part of our Lord's reply to the man, Mark and Luke another part of that same reply. As to the order of statement, I shall assume that He first said that which is found in the text, and then added that which is recorded in Matthew, granting that the reverse may be equally correct, and that it would make no material alteration to the deduction which I propose to make, whichever order were followed.

Hear then the answer of Jesus on this wise; first the words recorded in my text, and then the words recorded in Matthew. Said the young man: " Good Teacher, what shall I do that I may inherit eternal life? " Said Jesus, " Why callest thou Me good? None is good save one, even God. Why askest thou Me concerning that which is good? One there is Who is good." It will immediately be seen that there is no contradiction, and indeed, Matthew's addition makes the other question the more emphatic. First, " Why dost thou call Me good? "; secondly, and therefore, " Why dost thou ask Me concerning goodness? " and each of the questions ending with the affirmation that, " One only is good, that is, God."

When we read this word of Jesus we are driven to one of two conclusions. In that word our Lord either repudiated goodness and Godhead; or else He claimed goodness and Godhead. Simply take the words of Jesus, and listen to them with the fearlessness of a child, and there can be no escape from this alternative. To the young man He said, " Why callest thou Me good? One is good, even God." Did He mean that He was not God? Then He meant that He was not good. Did He mean that He was good? Then He meant that He was God. There is no escape from the alternative, and it is a question of vital importance, as to which He really meant.

I unhesitatingly accept the second interpretation; first of all calling to bear upon the enquiry, the witness of the rest of the record of the life and teaching of Jesus. If there is one thing more noticeable than another in the revelation of this Person in the four Gospels, it is His quiet, insistent, and unhesitating claim to sinlessness. From the beginning to the end, never did there pass His lips, so far as may be gathered from the recorded words, a single sentence in which He seemed to admit sin. He did most definitely and positively challenge those who were His critics, " Which of you convicteth Me of sin? " He did most continuously and insistently claim that in His own life He was not merely attempting to please God, but that He actually pleased God; as in such sentences as these, " I do always the things that are pleasing to Him," " My meat is to do the will of Him that sent Me," " I can of Myself do nothing," " As the Father gave Me commandment, even so I do," " My teaching is not Mine, but His that sent Me." Quietly, without apparent argument, and yet with persistent definiteness, He claimed sinlessness. To my mind it is unbelievable that upon one occasion He should make a contrary declaration. If the writings recording all the rest of the years, and all the witness of His life, attest His sinlessness, we are driven to the conclusion, that He was not repudiating goodness; but in the form of an enquiry, arresting the attention of a man, He fastened it upon the fact of His goodness.

We must carefully consider the witness of the context, as to what Jesus meant. Here are two lines for us to follow: first, the things that followed in His dealing with this man will help us to understand what He meant by the first thing He said to him; and secondly, the things that followed in His exposition of the incident to His puzzled disciples subsequently, will help us to understand what He meant by these words.

First then, the things that followed in His dealing with the man. Immediately after the words of Jesus, the measurement of certain standards of life was placed upon him. Jesus employed the second table of the Decalogue. There were two tables. On one, four commandments were engraved; and on the other, six. Our Lord made no reference at all to the first four. In abbreviated form He used the six, not in the order in which they are found in the Decalogue, but nevertheless including the whole. " Do not kill. Do not commit adultery. Do not steal. Do not bear false witness. Do not defraud," thus adopting an inclusive statement of the last commandment, " Honour thy father and mother." The standard of measurement which Jesus placed upon this man for the moment, was that of human inter-relationships, the laws which govern the life of man as to his relationships with his fellow-men.

The answer of the young man was immediate, "All these things have I observed from my youth." This was no empty boast; but the plain statement of honest truth. He was modest and upright, when measured by that standard. Let us emphasize for a moment the standard which Jesus did not employ at first, the standard which measures a man's relationship to God. Call back to mind these first four commandments in their spiritual intention. The first commands that to men there shall be one God, and that He shall be as God: " No other gods before Me," which does not mean having precedence, but, Before My face, in sight, in view anywhere. It is the command for the realization by man, of God directly, immediately; that God shall be to him as God. In the second command man is forbidden to help himself, in the worship of the true God, by creating anything which he supposes is in the likeness of the true God. The second command sweeps out from between the soul of man and God, all intermediaries of every kind. While the first command calls man into direct relationship with God; the second insists upon it that he shall not aid himself to direct communication, by putting anything between his own soul and God. The third command indicates that which will be the necessary outcome of obedience to the first two; the hallowing of the Name. The name of God is to be held as sacred. Finally and inclusively, the result of such hallowing of the name is revealed in the hallowing of time. The fourth commandment is not one that deals with the Sabbath only; it deals with seven days out of seven days; the requirement, On six days thou shalt work, is as definite as the commandment, On the seventh day thou shalt rest. It is the hallowing of time in work and worship; work and worship alike being related to Him.

Our Lord did not at first apply that test to the young man. When he said to Him: "All these things have I observed from my youth, Jesus looking upon him, loved him, and said unto him, One thing thou lackest; go, sell whatsoever thou hast, and give to the poor, and thou shalt have treasure in heaven: and come, follow Me."

With all care, consider that word of Jesus. Jesus called that young man to an abandonment so complete, that obedience must be the equivalent of worship. We so often quote these tender and gracious words of Jesus, and what wonder that we do! Yet we are in danger of quoting them as though they were simple and gentle; whereas they are imperial, kingly, absolute, autocratic. If Jesus Christ were not a good man, and were not more than man, when He asked the young ruler to do that, He asked him to break the second commandment of the first four. If He be not a good man, and if He be not more than man, then when He asks any man to submit

[234]

himself so completely to His authority, and to His will, He is asking that man to break the law of God. This is always true. It is true of all men. By the rights of my manhood, by the rights of my soul, by the rights of that spirit-life which is of God, I will submit my soul, my spirit, my will, to no man, if he be man alone. I will call no man master; I will call no man father in that spiritual sense; I will consent to submit my judgment to none. Yet Christ said to this young ruler, " Follow Me." It was an imperial, autocratic demand that he should yield the whole of his manhood to Himself.

What then is this? Christ is seen putting Himself in the place of God to the soul of a man. There are devout souls to-day, who say that they cannot say to Christ, " My God," but that they can say, He is in the place of God to my soul. I am prepared to begin there; only I would remind you that to put any one in the place of God to the soul, who is not God, is to put the soul in the direst peril possible. In that moment Jesus did put Himself in the place of God to the soul of that man. Sell all that thou hast, all that binds thee to the old masteries and sanctions of life, and come to Me, with the endowments of thy glorious manhood. Jesus, beholding him, loved him, saw the splendour of his manhood, and said, Wouldst thou find that for which thou art asking, life? Follow the good, which is to follow God; and to do it, follow Me.

Let us next look at the exposition He gave of the incident to His disciples, and we shall have further ratification of this interpretation. " Jesus looked round about," and He said, " How hardly," that is, " With what difficulty shall they that have riches enter into the Kingdom of God!" They were amazed. Then He said: " Children, how difficult is it for them that trust in riches to enter into the Kingdom of God! It is easier for a camel to go through a needle's eye, than for a rich man to enter into the Kingdom of God."

From these sentences let us simply take the thrice repeated phrase, "Enter into the Kingdom of God." That was the subject under consideration. It is as though He had said to His disciples: What was that man's difficulty? What did he refuse to do? He refused to enter into the Kingdom of God, when he refused to follow Me. Jesus had set before him, as the door into the Kingdom, Himself, the God of the Kingdom; and when a man will not respond to the call of God, he refuses to enter into the Kingdom of God.

"Then who can be saved?" said they. Mark His response. With God all things are possible; with man it is impossible. I know the danger oftentimes of attempting to build a doctrine upon a preposition, but there is vast significance in this preposition. Jesus did not say, All things are possible *to* God, as though He had meant, God can do anything. He said, All things are possible *with* God, as though He meant that a man with God can do the impossible thing. It is not that God is able to do impossible things, but that man is able to do impossible things with God. With men it is impossible. That young ruler, coming from men, judging life by their ideals, responding to their ordinary sanctions of life, went away sorrowful; he could not enter in. But, it is as though Christ had said: I stood before him, and if he had but obeyed Me, followed Me, then with Me he would have entered into My Kingdom. With God, he would have been enabled to do the impossible thing, and enter into My Kingdom.

The light then broke anew upon Peter as he said, " Lo, we have left all, and have followed Thee "; and Christ said in effect: That is perfectly true; you have left all to follow Me; and having left all to follow Me, you have by that process entered into the Kingdom of God, wherein you have found far more wealth than you left behind when you entered in. There is here a suggestive line of teaching which is often challenged. Do men who give up

wealth, and brothers and sisters, for Christ, receive a
hundredfold in this time? Yes! How little we know of
giving up for Christ, how very little! Yet the measure
in which we have known anything of it is the measure in
which we have known what it is to possess all things
through Christ. One house gone; but a hundred doors
are open! One brother in the flesh lost; but a thousand
brethren in the spirit, whose love is deeper and whose
kinship is profounder, gained. If this is not the final line
of application, I believe it is a true one. No man who
really enters into the Kingdom, abandoning everything
for Christ's sake, but finds within the Kingdom things far
more precious and wonderful, in the actualities of present
experience, than those he has left.

What then, in the light of this whole story, is the bearing of the statement of Jesus on the quest for eternal
life? There is a quest for eternal life far more widespread than we sometimes imagine. We remember the
words of the preacher in the book of Ecclesiastes, " He
hath set eternity in their heart." What a significant declaration, and yet how true! " He hath set eternity in
their heart." It is true of all the sons of men. The
passion for eternal life is present in all human hearts. It
may find a thousand means of expression, some of them
entirely and absolutely unworthy; but it is there. May I
describe it as the panting necessity of the human soul;
the great underlying consciousness that the soul belongs
not to the limited and the localized and the near and the
dust, but to the vast and the eternal. " He hath set eternity in their heart." When that passion rises to its
noblest form of expression, it employs the very words
of this young man, " What shall I do that I may inherit
eternal life?" Mark him well, a man of fine, natural
temperament, a man of wealth and position, and yet conscious when he came to Christ of the very thing Jesus
Christ expressed to him in another form and guise, that
he lacked something. Life, eternal life, is a quality

rather than a quantity, is infinitely more than life without end. It takes in the whole sum of things, and knows
within itself that it is master of them all; and the passion for that is everywhere present in the human heart.

But observe another thing. The quest for eternal life
when it is followed upon the level of human life alone,
and without relation to the larger things, is always hopeless and helpless. If I have quoted from the preacher,
the declaration " He hath set eternity in their heart," let
me complete the quotation. It is a wail of despair: " He
hath set eternity in their heart, yet so that man cannot
find out the work that God hath done from the beginning
even to the end." There, in a sentence, is at once the
passion and the paralysis of the human heart; eternity
within the heart, creating a desire to know whence we
are, and to interpret the strange mysteries of life; and
yet, as the preacher, with his pessimistic soul said, God
has put eternity in the heart, but so that men cannot find
it, so that men cannot be at rest. Even in the noblest,
that consciousness abides. This young man knew his
lack.

Now take the teaching of Jesus in the whole story, and
put it in relationship with that quest. What is eternal
life? I leave the story that I may use the words of Jesus
in another connection. " This is life eternal, that they
should know Thee, the only true God." How can they?
" And Him Whom Thou didst send, even Jesus Christ."
Our Lord's declaration is that eternal life consists in the
proper relation of the soul to God; that a man lives the
age-abiding life, when he lives in right relationship with
God. In that self-same word, moreover, our Lord revealed the fact that the way of God's approach to the
man who is seeking eternal life is through His Son Whom
He had sent. Come the Son wheresoever He may; He,
the Only Son of the Father, confronts the human soul,
standing before that soul in the place of God; and God
contracted, focussed, veiled for unveiling, hidden for

revelation, is brought within the compass of the finite mind, that men through the revelation, may encompass that which is infinite. The philosophy becomes the grace of God, as we see Jesus confronting the young ruler, and saying: " Follow Me "; and,—sweep out everything that hinders that following!

The experience of the soul finding and following is the experience of life; so that in the midst of death, man begins to live; in the midst of dirges he begins to sing; and while all the mists and the darkness are round about him, he sees the light, and is able to say:

> " I stand upon the mount of God,
>   With sunlight in my soul;
> I hear the storms in vales beneath,
>   I hear the thunders roll;
>
> " But I am calm with Thee, my God,
>   Beneath these glorious skies;
> And to the height on which I stand
>   Nor storms, nor clouds can rise."

That is eternal life; and it is found when the soul comes to God through Jesus Christ.

XXI

" For the Son of man also came not to be ministered unto, but to minister, and to give His life a ransom for many."—MARK 10 : 45.

Mark 10 : 32–52.

OF the revelation of the Lord Jesus Christ in the Gospel according to Mark this verse constitutes the central statement. Like a perfect gem it flashes with radiant glory and beauty, but unlike a gem, it does not reflect light. Its wondrous lustre is that of the truth it declares ; its light is within itself. One of our poets has reminded us that

> " Full many a gem of rarest ray serene
> The dark, unfathomed caves of ocean bear."

But the gems in these dark unfathomed caves bring no light there. This verse flashes from within, in the darkest abyss of human sin and need.

Nevertheless in our study of it we find that its internal light is interpreted by its setting. Its final setting is the whole of this Gospel. All the story of Jesus, the Servant of God,—from His introduction in the briefest words, to the last picture of Him passing back into the heavens, and from that exalted height working with His own ;— all the light is focussed in the text, and enables us to study its meaning. Its immediate setting is the whole of the paragraph, verses thirty-two to fifty-two.

After the solemn hour in which, dealing with the young ruler, Jesus definitely placed Himself in the place of God to the life of man, He resumed His journey to Jerusalem. Here Mark, with brevity and yet with remarkable clearness, gives a description of that journey as it was thus resumed. First Jesus went resolutely forward, alone ;

then following Him at some distance, were the twelve apostles, amazed; and then beyond them, came the crowds, afraid. The solemn atmosphere takes possession of the soul as the brief description is carefully read. We see the Lord, the Man of sorrows and acquainted with grief, none being able to understand Him, none of the twelve in close companionship with Him, as He resolutely trod the *via dolorosa* which was to find its consummation in His passion. We see the twelve men, loyal-hearted, but stupefied, amazed at the more recent tones of His teaching, at the things He had now been saying and doing. Finally we see the crowds with that mystic sense, so often found in a crowd if there is anything strange, weird, supernatural in the atmosphere, afraid, filled with awe, and filled with reverence.

After a while He gathered the twelve about Him in secrecy from the crowd, telling them in greater detail even than before, the story of all that to which He was going. While they were in that atmosphere, James and John preferred their request, and with infinite grace and tenderness He replied, though all the rest of the twelve were angry with the two, for the request they had preferred. The Lord then rebuked the ten with great patience, making that rebuke the occasion of uttering these central words: "The Son of man also came not to be ministered unto, but to minister, and to give His life a ransom for many." Then they passed on to, and through, Jericho, and as they went, Bartimæus was given his sight.

Let us consider the statement, first in itself; and secondly, in the light of these incidents.

First, the statement in itself. The music is so perfect, so final, that it carries its own message. Its notes are revolutionary and hope-begetting. It is revolutionary; the Son of man, Messiah, anointed to Kingship and to mastery, and to government, the One upon Whose shoulders the final government must rest; came not to be served, but to serve. Two millenniums have run their course, and the world has not yet understood that. Even the Church has hardly begun to apprehend the profound significance of the startling declaration. Yet again, the note is hope-begetting. "To give His life a ransom for many." Behind the great and gracious word, lurk the dark shadows of slaveries, oppressions, and tyrannies, all the things that blight and blast humanity. The Son of man came to give His life a ransom for the many. The finest possible exposition of the text is that of silent meditation. I propose emphasis only, rather than anything in the nature of detailed interpretation.

I lay emphasis first upon the Person speaking, and then upon the declaration made. "The Son of man." That was our Lord's favourite description of Himself. It is at least worthy of notice that in the Gospel records no one spoke of Him as the Son of man save upon one occasion; and that was when He had so often used it that His enemies said, "Who is this Son of Man?" Remember also its Messianic suggestiveness to the men who heard it. All its associations were Messianic to the religious men of His own age. When they heard Him speak of Himself, not as "*a* Son of man," but "*the* Son of man," they would immediately associate the title with their apocalyptic and prophetic writings, and know that by the assumption of the title He was at least suggesting His Messianic mission. The very fact that "Son of man" was the title of the Messiah, and that the Lord evidently loved it, and constantly used it, fastens attention upon the human note. Messiah! Yea, verily, but Son of man; Lord and Master of all the universe, but kin to all those who are to be ruled; and over whom He will reign; infinitely removed from man in His authority which is final and perfect, and from which there can be no appeal; but in all points tempted like as we are; a Man of sorrows acquainted with grief, knowing our hungers, our wearinesses, and our tears; the Son of man!

Remember in the next place, when our Lord used that

title here, that it was a declaration in close connection
with that He had but recently said to the young ruler.
To that man, He had suggested essential things concerning Himself, had put Himself in front of him as in the
very place of God, commanding him to a following which
included unequivocal and unrestrained surrender. Now,
He referred to Himself by a title which suggested the
method of manifestation of the essential truth. There is
no contradiction. He had not ceased to speak as within
the realm of His absolute authority as Son of God, but
mark the statement: "The Son of man *came*"; and the
employment of the verb in that connection suggested existence ere He came, and dignities and glories and mysteries which men could not understand, as all being centred in His person. He came; and He came for a purpose; and the purpose existed before the coming.

> " Through the veil
> Of His flesh divine,
> Shines forth the light,
> That were else too bright,
> For the feebleness of a sinner's sight."

So we listen to a voice that came out of the eternities,
deep calling unto deep; the voice of " the Son of Man."
Now with equal brevity and for emphasis only, let us
hear the declaration, He " came not to be ministered
unto." I prefer a much simpler rendering, " not to be
served." He came as the Self-emptied One, as to ambition, and as to His own well-being. According to this
declaration in the heart of Jesus,—reverently using the
merely human name for the moment,—there was no ambition for Himself; there was no carefulness as to His
own well-being. Not to be ministered unto, not to compel men to gather about Him, to serve Him, and lift Him,
and honour Him; not to secure His own immunity from
suffering or sorrow, or to make sure of His own joy and
His own pleasure. But " to serve." Self-emptied, He

was God-centred; and that first as to ambition. When our Lord said that He came not to be ministered unto but to minister, He did not refer to the fact that He came to serve men, but that He came to serve God. He came not to be ministered unto, having no ambition of His own, no care for His own well-being; but He came with one ambition; ambition for the glory of God, and the good pleasure of God, and the accomplishment of the purposes of God.

So we have this wonderful unveiling of a Person in human history, self-less as to ambitions, with no care for His own personal well-being; and God-centred, having one supreme, burning, overmastering passion, conditioning all thought and speech and action, that God's name should be glorified, that His Kingdom should come; not to be ministered unto, but to minister; not to be served, but to serve.

Had the great statement ended at that point, we should have stood in awe in the presence of this Self-emptying of Jesus, but we should have heard no Gospel. In the final words of the declaration we hear the Gospel, and the music of the evangel breaks upon the soul. This is not something additional; but the unveiling of the inner heart of that self-same Servant of God: " To give His life a ransom for many " is to seek the glory of God, in the well-being of man. God is revealed through Jesus, as One Whose glory is realized in man's ransom, redemption, healing, restoration.

Let us attempt to look at this great statement again in the light of its setting. Here general impressions will help us better than detailed examination, especially in view of our familiarity with the stories contained in this whole paragraph. " The Son of man came not to be ministered unto, but to minister, and to give His life a ransom for many." In the first part of the paragraph we see the pathway of His service, as He told His disciples that He must go to Jerusalem and suffer, and be killed, but rise again. Then as James and John came to Him with special request, and the ten were about Him, we see the comrades of His service, and mark His method with them. Finally, in that which at first blush seems to be separated from the great line of thought, but which is really closely connected with it, we have an incident of His service immediately following, as the cry of the blind beggar broke upon His ears.

With regard to the first paragraph revealing the pathway of service, note its definiteness, the particular care with which Jesus at this point attempted to arrest the thought of His disciples, and fasten that thought upon the actuality of the sufferings to which He was going, and the triumph which should result therefrom. Taking the paragraph as a whole, let us attempt to see what Christ said as to the pathway of His service. First, He declared that the pathway of His service was advance on His part to the place where all that was opposed to God, and so destructive of man, was for the moment centralized—Jerusalem. Those familiar with the history of the time, will remember the three great world-powers then existing; the power of a military despotism and government as centred in Rome; the power of decadent intellectualism and commercial prosperity as centred in Greece; and the power of a degenerate religion as centred in Jerusalem. Jerusalem was the very centre of these forces in certain senses, having to do with that which is fundamental to human life,—religion. This Son of man set His face toward Jerusalem, the place where all that was opposed to God was at the moment centralized, and consequently the place where everything that was destructive of humanity was centralized. He had often been in the city before. How He loved it! He must go again; knowing that all the world forces were there, and waiting with the one definite and specific intention of silencing His voice, and destroying Him.

Notice in the second place,—and here is the mystery—

He went to that place to gather the whole onslaught of
those evil forces upon Himself. He went deliberately, as
God, to feel its opposition utterly and finally. He went
deliberately, as Man, to bend to its destruction. The
forces were those in opposition to the way and the will
of God. The forces consequently were those that made
for the destruction of humanity. As God, He went to
gather them into His own personality; historically and
visibly as Man, He went, that upon Him the destruction
might fall.

Yet once more; the pathway of service was not merely
that He advanced to the place where opposition was
centralized, was not merely in order that He might gather
its onslaught upon Himself; the pathway of His service
was one which He trod in powers which were invulnerable, and which all opposition could not overcome. Consequently, He went not merely to the Cross, but to the
crowning; not merely to death, but to resurrection; not
merely to the clouds and darkness which were about the
Throne, but to coöperation with the righteousness and
judgment which are the foundation thereof. He could
say to this little group of men that on the third day He
would rise again. His pathway to the passion was one
trodden in the strength of invulnerable powers; the power
of perfect acceptance of the will of God, the power of
complete coöperation with the activities of God; the
power that was the more powerful, in that it depended
upon none other power than itself.

So we see this Son of man moving toward the scene
of the things that blight and spoil humanity, because they
are against God. We see Him moving thereto, in order
that He may gather all the onslaught into the experiences
of His own soul; but we look into His eyes and there is a
light that tells of victory. All moral forces were against
Him. There was no escape; He must be beaten, He must
be crushed, He must be killed! No! There are moral
values sustaining His soul, and spiritual forces renewing

Him. When they have killed the body they have nothing more that they can do; and He will be the Leader of those moral values and spiritual forces out into new power and life. This was the pathway of the service of the Son of man.

Then look quite briefly at this old and familiar, and yet beautiful picture of the comrades of His service. It is significant that they are divided into two groups, the two, James and John; and the ten. Look at the two, and listen to what they said that day. I separate myself immediately and resolutely from all expositors who discredit them. I do not believe that this was the cry of men hungry for personal ambition. " Teacher, we would that Thou shouldest do for us whatsoever we shall ask." And Jesus said, " What would ye that I should do for you? " They said this, " Grant unto us that we may sit, one on Thy right hand, and one on Thy left hand, in Thy glory." Before we criticize them, let us remember the atmosphere. " In Thy glory! " But He was going to be spit upon, He was going to be scourged, He was going to be mocked, He was going to be killed! Yes, they knew it all; but they knew Him, and that He was coming into His glory, and they wanted to be associated with Him in the power of that glory. Oh! great men were these; not wholly intelligent, ignorant of the very things to which He was going, the processes through which He must pass; not knowing the bitterness of the cup, or the abysmal agony of the baptism; but believing that somehow He must come into His glory.

Then notice His grace. He admitted them to the fellowship of His sufferings. He told them, in effect, that positions of honour did not at all matter. He said He could not give these spiritual positions to any except to those for whom they were prepared; but because these men had seen His glory, even though they were ignorant, and could not understand; because faith had risen in that dark hour of foretelling to ask for association with Him,

[247]

He said: Yes, you shall drink of My cup, you shall be
baptized of My baptism!

We had better leave that story where the Gospel leaves
it. If we cannot, then we join the ten, and the ten were
angry with the two! The rebukes of Jesus were reserved
for the ten; and even there, they were very gracious and
beautiful. He called the ten and said to them, You do
not understand this matter, you do not understand
these men. "Ye know that they who are accounted
to rule over the Gentiles lord it over them." The
request of these men is not for the kind of authority
of service which expresses itself in sacrifice! Then He
left the ten and the two; and the last word was this:
The Son of man did not come to gain a kingly crown in
the way men usually seek to do so. The Son of man did
not come to raise His voice and clamour amid men, as to
who is to be the principal power in the world. The Son
of man came to divest Himself of dignities, and strip
Himself of royalties and bind upon Himself the yoke of
slavery and service, that He might lift others, and so win
the ultimate throne of empire by the love and loyalty of
those whom He thus lifts. He said in effect, to the ten
and the two, to the twelve, and to all their successors
through the ages; if you would know anything of authority and power with Me, you must come this way with Me.

Then came the incident of the healing of Bartimæus,
the incident taking place in that very atmosphere and
connection. First we hear the beggar crying out for help,
and see him rebuked by the disciples. We will not be
angry with them, but will try and understand them. Unless I misinterpret this story altogether, the disciples were
saying within their own souls, We do not quite understand what Jesus is trying to teach us, but these are big
things. His mind is occupied with supreme things. We
cannot attend to that man. A blind beggar must not be
allowed to interrupt Him now! But Jesus stood still, and
said, Call him! Then He healed him!

The great is always operative in the little, and all the vastness of Christ in His outlook and intention as revealed supremely in His declaration of the text, is illustrated in the fact that on the way to Jerusalem He could stay to answer the cry of one blind beggar. I go further, and say this. To have refused would have been to deny His teaching about service. Nay! to have refused the cry of a man in his agony would have been to deny His Cross, for not lightly did He heal. " Himself took our infirmities, and bare our diseases "; and behind the strength that went out as a healing power, there was ever the unfathomable mystery of His atonement.

The King is coming into His Kingdom! Oh, yes! the heathen are saying to us to-day, Where is your God? There never was a darker hour, judged by human standards, in the history of the world, than that hour when they nailed the Prince of life and glory to the Roman gibbet on Calvary. Have we the vision of James and John? Do we still rest in the confidence that the King is coming into His glory; that

> " . . . After last, returns the First,
> Though a wide compass round be fetched;
> That what began best, can't end worst ";

that though, in the march of the movements of the ages, humanity must suffer long, and the innocent with the guilty; though we seem to see

> Truth for ever on the scaffold, Wrong for ever on the throne,—
> Yet that scaffold sways the future, and, behind the dim unknown,
> Standeth God within the shadow, keeping watch above His own? "

It behooves men who are of the Christian faith to rise to the heights and to take large outlooks. The King is coming into His Kingdom!

> " The darkness is deepest before the dawn;
> When the pain is sorest the child is born."

That is the Christian attitude.

Fellowship in the greatness of His Kingdom is conditional upon fellowship in His cup, in His baptism, in sacrifice. How little do we know of this experimentally, how little have we ever known! Where can we begin to have real fellowship with our King? The first blind beggar we meet is our opportunity. The first local, and apparently unimportant case of necessity that cries out, is our chance. If Jesus should have passed that blind beggar and refused to help him, because His thoughts were so great, He would have cut the nerve of His coming passion. He could not pass that man by, because He was mastered by the passion that took Him to the Cross. So God help us to go forth, seeing the coming of His glory, sharing the travail of His soul, and doing it with the next who asks our help.

XXII

"And on the morrow, when they were come out from Bethany, He hungered. And seeing a fig tree afar off having leaves, He came, if haply He might find anything thereon: and when He came to it, He found nothing but leaves; for it was not the season of figs. And He answered and said unto it, No man eat fruit from thee henceforward forever. And His disciples heard it. . . . And as they passed by in the morning, they saw the fig tree withered away from the roots."—MARK 11: 12–14, 20.

Mark 11: 1–25.

THIS is admittedly a strange story, strange that is, in the sense of being unusual. Any one reading this Gospel for the first time, who was really and intelligently interested in it as a record of the life and work of Jesus, would inevitably be arrested and surprised. Moreover there are elements in it which have persistently caused difficulties to expositors, and that quite naturally. Cursing and destruction were not the usual methods of Jesus. Let it be at once said that therein is one of the chief values of the story. When Isaiah was denouncing the politicians of his day for their secret intrigues, and foretelling the Divine judgment which must fall upon the nation, amongst other things he said: " Jehovah will rise up as in Mount Perazim, He will be wroth as in the valley of Gibeon; that He may do His work, His strange work, and bring to pass His act, His strange act." When in the Divine economy judgment becomes punishment, chastisement, and necessarily so; it is nevertheless God's strange work, His strange act. So this action of Jesus was undoubtedly strange; yet it is clearly central to this particular paragraph.

Before proceeding to a consideration of the story in its

relation to the larger whole of the paragraph; and so to its true value and teaching; there are one or two things to observe about the story in itself.

This is the only account of an exercise of power, on the part of our Lord, which was wholly destructive. There is the story of His destruction of the swine, but that act was linked to the deliverance of a man. Here however is a story, and the only one, of our Lord definitely destroying.

There is no more warrant for criticizing our Lord for destroying a tree for the purpose of teaching, than there is for objecting to a Christmas tree for our children, or the plucking of the petals from a flower in a lesson on botany.

But further, there is no ground for supposing that our Lord did this. I recognize the difficulty of the passage, and suggest that sometimes the simplest and most obvious meaning is the true. Upon this fig tree there ought to have been no leaves. There was such a thing as " the first ripe fig before the summer "; but whenever that appeared, it appeared before the time of leaves. I turn over the page in the Gospel, and find that our Lord Himself used the figure later: " Now from the fig tree learn her parable: when her branch is now become tender, and putteth forth its leaves, ye know that the summer is nigh " (13:28). This happened undoubtedly in the earliest spring time, before the summer was nigh, before the time of leaves. But seeing that there were leaves, there should have been that first ripe fruit. The Lord came and found that there was no fruit. The tree was precocious, and its precocity in leaves demonstrated the fact that there was no possibility of fruit. It was a tree that had failed in itself, and so became a perfectly just illustration of that which our Lord desired at the moment to teach. Beyond that I shall not go, as to the controversial aspects of the story.

First, it is well that we should remember the time in

the ministry of our Lord at which this occurred. Here begins the story of the last week in His earthly life. In this paragraph we have in view three days of that last week. On the first day He entered into the city in triumph, looked at the Temple, and retired at eventide to Bethany. On the second day He journeyed in the morning back again to the city with His own disciples, and on that journey destroyed the fig tree; then having entered into the city and Temple, He cleansed the Temple, and at eventide left the city. On the third day He returned to Jerusalem, and on the way the disciples saw the fig tree withered from the roots, and our present study halts with our Lord's instruction to them in the presence of the withered tree.

Let us bear in mind that this last visit to Jerusalem was official, solemn, condemnatory. Necessarily when we come to this passion week in the life of our Lord, we are almost overwhelmed by such thoughts as those which are suggested by the words of John, " He came unto His own, and they that were His own received Him not." We think of it as the hour of His rejection, as the hour in which the men of His own nation and people finally said, " We will not have this Man to reign over us." All that is true; but it is equally true that this was not merely the hour when His nation rejected Him; it was the hour when He finally rejected that nation. With great solemnity and gravity of manner and method, He arraigned the rulers before Him, compelling them to find verdicts concerning themselves, and pass sentences upon themselves; until in solemn denunciation He actually came to the hour in which He said,—and mark the words now most carefully:—" The Kingdom of God shall be taken away from you, and shall be given to a nation bringing forth the fruits thereof." It was the last, solemn, and awful word of Jesus. We shall come next to the account of how He dealt with the rulers; but in this story we are in the presence of preliminary things.

[253]

First there was our Lord's definite provocation of demonstration. That also was an unusual method. How often we read that He hid Himself, or escaped from the multitudes. Multitudes thronged and pressed Him wherever He went, attracted by His teaching and the wonders He wrought. He was never hostile to these crowds; and yet He was always turning from them, escaping or sifting them, making it still more difficult, as it would seem, for them to come to Him. He had never definitely provoked anything in the nature of demonstration, but there can be no escape from the conviction that this was exactly what He did at this time. Crowds were there; He might have passed, as He had passed upon other occasions, almost unnoticed into Jerusalem; quietly and meekly walking in the midst of His own. Here He made definite arrangements, the actual carrying out of which must inevitably draw attention to Him, and centre it upon Him. So we see Him, in what we sometimes speak of, and in some senses correctly, as the triumphal entry, drawing attention to Himself, compelling the whole city to know the hour of His arrival.

Then we have this symbolic miracle, wrought in the presence of His own in the hours of the early morning, when by a word He destroyed the fruitless tree; and immediately following it, the instruction to His disciples, when on the following morning Peter drew His attention to the withered tree, and our Lord replied, " Have faith in God," and proceeded with His teaching.

The whole movement here is national; and to the paragraph, this destruction of the fig tree is central and symbolic, as I have no doubt our Lord intended it to be.

Without giving attention to the details of these stories, that are all so familiar, let us glance at the contextual revelations of the whole scene, in the centre of which this miracle of destruction occurs; in order that we may gather for ourselves the central teaching of this act of Jesus.

We see Him first coming into the city as King. This again is something new, almost unusual in this Gospel. He has been presented to us here as the Servant of God, stripped of His royalties, divested of His dignities, the whole truth concerning His mission crystallized into that wonderful declaration which we have considered, " The Son of man came not to be served, but to serve." Here we are introduced to this same Person, still the Servant of God, but the Servant of God in such a way as to draw attention to Himself as King, and acting with a definite authority. As the crowds declared, He came in the name of the Lord, the Representative of Jehovah, the Representative of the God of this people. He came now in national aspect, doing that which He had done individually in the case of the young ruler, putting Himself in the place of God toward these men and toward this nation, drawing attention to Himself by the method of His advent, until there came from those Galilean crowds that quotation of their own ancient psalm, in which they declared the supreme truth, " Hosanna ; Blessed is He that cometh in the name of the Lord."

Here He was seen, the Servant of Jehovah, coming to establish His Kingdom ; the Kingdom described by Himself when He said He came not to be ministered unto, but to minister ; the Kingdom of service, in which positions of greatness were those won by lowliness of service rendered ; the Kingdom which was to be founded upon that to which He did in mystery refer, the giving of His own life as a ransom.

So we see Him coming nigh, coming in the majesty of meekness, stripped of all those things which men usually associate with royalty ; riding upon an ass. We are often told that this was a royal thing to do ; but let it be remembered that there was a clear distinction between animals upon which kings rode, even in the East, and the animal usually described as " a beast of burden " upon which our

Lord rode as He came into the city. I suggest one
method by which the meekness, the lowliness, the poverty,
the absurdity, of this entrance may be understood. In
imagination think, not as a Hebrew, but as a Roman; and
think of the triumphal entry of a Roman emperor into
his city; and then look at this pageant of poverty, lacking
all the things usually associated with royalty and greatness. A procession of poverty, the scattering of the
clothes the people wore, the broken branches of the trees,
and the shouting of the Galilean mob! So He rode in the
dignity of a great meekness, divested of all the things that
humanity had for so long associated with Kingship, and
still associates with Kingship. It was a pageant of poverty.

He came for investigation. In that first day toward
eventide, entering into the Temple, Mark records that
"He . . . looked round about upon all things." It
was the look of investigation, the look of inquisition, the
look of One Who had the right so to look, the look of
the supreme and final authority; it was also the look of
the heart of an infinite compassion, the look of the eyes
bedewed with tears. "He . . . looked round about
upon all things."

What were the conditions that He found? I take His
own word spoken on the next day; the Temple "a den
of robbers"; its intention violated, and its shelter sought
by vice masking under the garb of religion; the precincts
of the Temple invaded by money-changers who, contem-
porary writers tell us, were so nefarious in their practices,
that their witness was refused in the courts of law; and
all in the name of religion; the Gentile courts desecrated
by the presence there of animals for sacrifice; these
things apparently in the interest of religion, the making
of religion easy; which is always a perilous thing, contrary to Divine intention, and an evidence of a degenerate
people.

He found the spiritual and moral rulers antagonistic to

Him, His ideals refused, His interference resented; and
preëminently and supremely, the death of faith, the true
principle of national life. That is what I think He meant
when He said to His disciples, " Have faith in God." He
was not giving them the secret for destroying fig trees;
but the secret for so living that they should not be destroyed as the fig tree had been destroyed. When the
Son of man came to Jerusalem for His final investigation, He found faith missing, He found leaves without
fruit.

Now in that atmosphere we turn to this central act of
judgment, and without any further dealing with the details, we enquire the meaning of this act, and what our
Lord intended to teach His disciples, and His Church for
all time.

He meant first to teach that the fruitless must inevitably be destroyed; that life is God-given, and always for
the purpose of fruit-bearing. For simplest illustration I
turn back to the commencement of my Bible, and find
that He made trees, each bearing seed after its kind, for
the production of fruit. It is but a figure, a symbol, but
it runs down through all Biblical teaching, and especially
with regard to this ancient people Israel. The national
life was a God-given and God-sustained life, but its purpose was the bearing of fruit. We read that great wail of
the psalmist concerning the vine that was planted and
broken down, because it failed to bear fruit (Ps. 80).
We hear in that lament sung by Isaiah in the fifth chapter
the plaintive cry of Jehovah because His people had
failed: " He looked that it should bring forth grapes, and
it brought forth wild grapes;" and of this, the prophet
gave his own interpretation and explanation: " He looked
for justice, but behold, oppression; for righteousness,
but, behold a cry." Because the nation created and sustained by God, had failed to produce the fruit which was
the natural outcome of the life which He had thus created and sustained, the decree went forth: " I will tell you

what I will do to My vineyard: I will take away the
hedge thereof, and it shall be eaten up; I will break down
the wall thereof, and it shall be trodden down."

All these things of the past were brought home to this
little group of disciples by our Lord in the cursing of
the fig tree. If for any reason fruit is not forthcoming,
the instrument provided for the bearing of fruit must be
destroyed. The tree was the symbol, but the nation was
in His mind. He came after the long centuries, to His
own, but His own received Him not; and therefore by
their refusal to receive Him, and His Kingdom; by the
absence of fruit, the necessity was created for the destruction of the instrument. With the morning the disciples saw—mark the significant words, and how the simple and sacred symbol applies,—the tree withered from
the roots.

When attention was drawn to this, our Lord gave His
disciples the interpretation. The central value of that
interpretation is that faith is the principle of fruitfulness.
They wondered at His power to destroy, or so it would
seem from the simple reading of the story. " Rabbi, behold, the fig tree which Thou cursedst is withered away!"
He immediately replied, " Have faith in God." He gave
them the secret of making destruction unnecessary; and
therefore the secret of removing obstacles to the Kingdom, as He continued, if you have faith, then you shall
say to a mountain, Be removed, and cast into the sea.
In the life of the nation, when faith perishes, the principle of life perishes, and the possibility of fruitfulness
passes away. Even so, for these men—to whom He was
about to commit the great responsibilities of the Kingdom
of God, taking them from the ancient people,—if they
were not also to perish, here was the supreme and abiding necessity, " Have faith in God." Fruit was not found
in the nation, because life had departed; and life had
departed, because faith in God had departed.

He then charged them to pray; for prayer is the expression of faith. He showed them also that the prayer which is the expression of faith, must be the expression of life, mastered by compassion, forgiving, as well as seeking for forgiveness. Prayer love-purified, is the true exercise of faith. So He brought these men—representatives of those who were to follow them, the whole Church of God, to which this great responsibilty of the Kingdom of God was to be committed—face to face with this central secret of life. Faith in God is the secret of the life of fruitfulness.

The teaching of this story is for all time, and the application is not merely to the Church. It is specifically a national teaching. It may be well for us as members of the Church of God, and of this nation, to face the simple and yet searching lesson which this act of Jesus reveals. The life which we live as a nation is a life which God has given. All that we are as a nation in all its essential greatness, we owe to Him. By His compassions we have come to be what we are; by His deliverances we have lived in peace and in liberty; by His illumination we have proceeded from strength to strength of understanding and of experience. It would be a work of supererogation to trace the history of this country, but the whole secret may be summarized in a verse from the ancient psalms, "The opening of Thy Word giveth light." Changing the form of rendering in harmony with the real significance of the passage: The going forth, or the letting loose of Thy word giveth light. If in one rapid act, the history of England, and of her most illustrious daughter, the United States of America, be reviewed, it will be seen that anything that has been noble and upward has been the result of the illumination of the people by the going forth of the Word of God. From the moment when our literature was born in the paraphrases of Cædmon, on down through every century, as the light Divine was given, so the people have risen. Oh! how slowly; because how disobediently we have received the Word.

Yet let us remember that everything in our national life
that is really great, that has in it the true element of
beauty and nobility, is the result of God's compassion and
God's deliverance and God's illumination. Our national
life, British and American, is verily a Divine creation, and
has been sustained by God as surely as was that of Israel
of old.

Are we producing fruit after our kind, fruit that is
true to the life which God Himself has created and sustained? Surely it is good for us to-day; that in the darkness we may have faith, that under the clouds we may
consider, that in the midst of perplexities we may turn
ourselves back again to the history of our life and its
true significance, and ask ourselves quite solemnly,
Does the Son of man, as He comes to us to-day, find
fruit?

I thank God that there are other teachings in this same
symbolical realm in the New Testament. There is the
parable of the barren fig tree, with its last terrible note:
If it bear no fruit cut it down. But between the sentence
of the proprietor, and that consent of the intercessor,
came intercession and work: " Let it alone this year also,
till I shall dig about it, and dung it." In the intimate
teaching by our Lord of His disciples, speaking within
the Church, He referred to pruning and purging in order
to the bearing of fruit. In the light of this other teaching
upon this solemn act of Jesus, I declare that unless we
are responsive to the life which He has created; unless
we are responsive to His chastisements, learning to submit ourselves to them unreservedly, we also as nations
shall wither from the roots.

XXIII

" This poor widow cast in more than all they that are casting into the treasury."—MARK 12:43b.

Mark 11:27-12.

THE paragraph from which the text is taken gives a condensed account of the events following upon the discovery by the disciples that the fig tree which Jesus had cursed, had withered away from the roots. Matthew gives the story of these events with more fulness. We shall now only glance at them in their relation to the incident in the treasury, which Matthew omits.

That story gains much from the fact that it constitutes a picture of light and beauty, in the midst of a time of great darkness in the ministry of our Lord. In this hour, when the Son of man was the object of intense hostility, and when He was exercising His authority in the solemn and awful work of denouncing and rejecting a fruitless nation, there appeared one poor lonely widow woman, in whom faith in God was active and powerful. She stands in striking contrast to the men who were seeking to destroy the Son of man.

Let us first glance at this dark background of hostility, then observe the nameless woman; and finally consider our Lord's attitude toward her. The lines of consideration are: first, the Son of man and His foes; secondly, the woman worshipper; and finally, the Son of man and His friend, that one woman.

Throughout the whole of this survey, the Son of man is seen acting in judgment. The word judgment is full, gracious, significant. Judgment becomes condemnation and punishment, or commendation and reward, according to the attitude of the human soul in the presence of its inexorable exercise. Here, from beginning to end, from the moment when Jesus was challenged, first as to His authority, to this last scene in the temple, our Lord is seen as the Son of man, sitting in judgment, and exercising the right thereof.

First then, let us look at Him in the midst of His foes. The stories in this paragraph are all well known. We will mass them for the sake of the impression of the Lord which they convey in these last days of His earthly ministry. Four questions were asked of Jesus on this day when He went back into the city and to the temple, after the disciples had discovered the fig tree was withered away from the roots. There was first the question of unbelief: "By what authority doest Thou these things? or Who gave Thee this authority?" There was then a question of sinister intent, formed, fashioned, and framed in order to bring Him within the grasp of His foes: "Is it lawful to give tribute unto Cæsar, or not?" There was then a question of flippant rationalism; the cynical and brutal question of the Sadducees, who, supposing a case, enquired who should be the wife of a man in the resurrection. Finally there was a question of pure casuistry, the question of a lawyer, about the relative values of laws. Throughout the whole scene Jesus is seen, not caught, trapped, or beaten; but sitting in judgment, and with quiet, calm dignity silencing His opponents; until at last it is finally declared, "No man after that durst ask Him any question." The whole scene ended with our Lord's asking a question, and uttering a denunciation of hypocrisy.

The first was the question of unbelief asked by the men who were in authority in the temple. They recognized the things He had done, but raised the question of His right to do them. They knew He had wrought things that were superlatively wonderful. Probably it is true that their enquiry related to the cleansing of the temple on the previous day. While they were compelled to

admit that His action was something out of the common,
for which they could not account, that some mysterious
power had been at work under His control, which made
money-changers flee, cleansing the temple for a brief
hour from all its defilement; they nevertheless raised the
question of His authority. Our Lord's method with them
was twofold. He first revealed their unfitness to receive
an answer, by showing that they had already been dis-
honest in the case of the ministry of His forerunner;
and then He answered the very question He had declined to answer; answered it inferentially, as He gave
them the parable of the vineyard, and of the sending of
messengers by the proprietor, until at last the son was
sent. At the close of the parable they discovered that He
was speaking of them, and describing their national condition; and therefore that involved in His answer was an
answer to their enquiry; His authority was that He was
the Son of God.

Then perchance, in some pause, there came to Him
that iniquitous and unholy coalition of opposing political
parties in Jerusalem, of Pharisees and Herodians; the
Herodians claiming that the Jewish nation at that time
must be subservient to Rome, for Herod was a vassal
of Rome; the Pharisees protesting against the yoke of
Rome being laid upon the shoulders of God's ancient
people. These two parties were always at war, always at
strife. They now formed a coalition, and asked a question with sinister intent; so that if He should say it was
lawful to pay tribute to Cæsar, He would abrogate His
own claim of Messiahship which He had made so patent
by the provocation of demonstration on His arrival in
the city but yesterday; or if perchance He should say it
was not lawful to give tribute to Cæsar, then He could
be arrested for treason against the State. Mark the
subtlety of the question, and the supremacy and finality
of the answer as a philosophy of life: "Render unto
Cæsar the things that are Cæsar's, and unto God the

things that are God's." It was a condemnation of both
the parties that stood confronting Him; first of the men
who were against the domination of Rome, but who were
not rendering to God the things that were God's, the men
who were tithing mint and anise and cummin, and neglecting the weightier things of man's soul; the condemnation also of the Herodians who claimed that it was
lawful to give tribute to Cæsar, and in their deepest
hearts were with Herod prepared to rebel against Cæsar,
if they might but have escaped from his tyranny. They
were both silenced.

Then, perhaps again after some interval, there came
the Sadducees with the question of their flippant rationalism. The grotesqueness of their illustration constitutes
its brutality. To read these stories with all naturalness
is to be impressed by the unholy levity that linked the
great questions of immortality, the resurrection, and the
spiritual life, to such an illustration as they supposed.
Our Lord answered first by sweeping away the possibility
they suggested, as He declared that in heaven they neither
marry, nor are given in marriage. Then immediately
passing behind the illustration to the Sadducean philosophy that caused it, which denied the immortality of man
the fact of resurrection, the existence of the spirit, and
the very being of angels; He reminded them that in their
own scriptures God declared Himself to be the God of
Abraham, Isaac, and Jacob; and settled the question
when He said that God " is not the God of the dead, but
of the living"; and thus in one word, assured men that
they limit their vision if they forget that those " loved
long since, and lost a while," are still living. The Sadducees had no more to say.

Then one man amid the crowd, having observed that
Jesus had well answered these questioners, came to Him
with his own peculiar question: Which is the greatest of
the commandments? He did not ask Him to put commandment into comparison with commandment, but to

reveal the principle of real greatness in law. It was an honest question, a sincere question. Our Lord immediately replied with nothing of sternness in His answer, with nothing of rebuke. Selecting, not from the Decalogue, but from other of the ancient laws of the Hebrew people, He showed the central principle of law, the true inspiration of the law, and of obedience to it: " Thou shalt love the Lord thy God with all thy heart, and with all thy soul, and with all thy mind, and with all thy strength. . . . Thou shalt love thy neighbour as thyself." The man was arrested and amazed. He admitted that the answer was final. Then from amid all the hostility, there came from the lips of Jesus the tender words, " Thou art not far from the Kingdom of God." The questions of His foes were over.

Then our Lord propounded one question, and we have no account of any answer made to Him. It was a question that suggested thought on their part concerning Himself in view of His Messianic claims. How is it, He asked, that David speaking by the Spirit, described his son as his Lord? There the question remains—Christ's one arresting question—waiting for the answer of all such as are perplexed in the presence of His personality, and demanding at least either that we declare that David was mistaken, and that Jesus was of our kith and kin alone; or that we recognize that David, as Jesus said, was inspired; and that while according to the flesh He was of the seed of David, according to the deeper mystery of His Being, He was the Son of the Eternal God. With the question He left them, warning those who listened, against the hypocrisy of the scribes.

That is a hurried survey, but it will bring us into the atmosphere of this last scene in the life of Jesus, in which He was present in the temple. How often He had been there. Remember the scenes that we have surveyed in our study of His life; those recent happenings, that marvellous hour when He cleansed the temple; the electric atmosphere of hostility, the awful impulses of hatred that were brooding, waiting to arrest and slay Him.

Now observe the last thing that Jesus did. Passing from those inner courts of the temple He came to the outer court, known as the court of the women, where the great chests stood to receive the offerings for the priests and the poor. There He sat down, lingering in temple precincts, gazing with longing and love-lit eyes upon the desolate wilderness in the midst of which He found Himself, looking for some flower, some fruit, something that would satisfy His heart. The last stern and terrific word of denunciation uttered, He waited, in the treasury, in the place where people were bringing gifts, in which though man was constantly forgetting it, there was a sacramental symbolism. Where the heart is, there the treasure will go. That is not the quotation, I know. But the change is implicated. Where the treasure is, there will the heart be also; and, therefore, where the heart is, there the treasure will go. Upon all giving, there rests the light of a Divine scrutiny and appraisement.

So waiting and watching with the Son of man, we see what we should not perhaps have noticed, had He not drawn the attention of His disciples to it;—a woman amid the crowd, a poor, lonely widow, dropping into the treasury two mites, a farthing. In the light of what happened He declared that when she dropped in those two mites, she dropped in " all her living." Do not be persuaded to doubt that. There have been many attempts made to prove that she did not give all her living, and that our Lord did not really mean that. For the moment, however, forget that final word, and look at her gift; two mites, equal to a farthing; two of the smallest current coin. We should never have seen it if attention had not been drawn to it. If a list of subscriptions that day had been published, these two mites would have been included in the final item, of amounts below a certain value! Yet out of the midst of all the gifts, the Son of man selected these two mites; and lifted them into the light of the centuries.

Looking at those two mites, those little coins, and speaking of them in the singular number, as one gift, I see here first a gift of faith; secondly, a gift of sacrifice; thirdly, a gift of spiritual life; and finally a gift law-fulfilling. I see one lonely widow woman doing a thing out of the passion and inclination of her inner life, un-observed so far as she knew by any eyes, in all probability attempting to hide from everybody the thing she did. Yet I see this one lonely woman in the midst of that crowd that day, standing in contrast to all the men who had harassed the Lord. All the hostility massed in the questions that we have tried hurriedly to survey is ranked on one side; and over against it is the simple act of a woman who put two mites into the treasury.

It was a gift of faith. The temple was the house of God to that woman. Her gift was the sacramental sym-bol of her loyalty to God. She, as surely as the great law-giver of her nation, " endured as seeing Him Who is in-visible." We would never have seen those coins, if Jesus had not pointed them out, but what are they? A sacra-mental evidence of a woman's belief in God. When He cursed the fig tree, and the day came when it withered from the roots so that the disciples were amazed by the swift withering, He told them the secret of how the na-tion might escape a like withering as He said, " Have faith in God." He had just been in the temple, and the rulers of the temple who were the rulers of the city, had challenged Him as to His authority, and thereby had re-vealed their lack of faith in God. But behold, one woman among the crowds, the sacramental symbol of whose faith in God are the two mites which she drops into the treasury.

Again, it was a gift of sacrifice; " all her living," a tremendous dedication. I go back to the scene before it, and I see a coalition of Pharisees and Herodians who came to ask Jesus a question about tribute, about the things they were to give in recognition of right, authority, and benefit received. That is what taxation really is. We may object to it and quarrel with it, and may be perfectly right in our objection with regard to some of its methods. But in the payment of taxes we are making our personal gift to the well-being of the State, our acknowledgment of the benefits of the government under which we live. That matter lay behind this question whether they should pay to Rome, or whether they should not. They were in the region of gifts. Remember also, their question was one of selfishness. It was one of expedience, dealing with the whole relation of a man to his fellow-men in the State; and the relation of a man to his fellow-men was degraded by the question they asked. Here, however, was a woman, probably knowing little about these Pharisees, or of the discussion of principles, of difference between Herodians and Pharisees, but recognizing her immediate relation to her God. Hers was a gift of sacrifice. She cast into the treasury " all her living."

Again, and this is the deeper note: it was a gift of spiritual life. It was the result of vision, and it was the expression of feeling. There are moments when one wishes one could draw aside the veil and know more. We would like to know where that woman lived, and how she lived, and how she suffered, and what her poverty meant; a lonely widow woman in the great metropolis, and she only had those two mites that day. They constituted "all her living." What made her find her way through those women's courts, and drop the whole of her living into the treasury? Vision! She saw finely, and her heart responded to what she saw. That act was a demonstration of the spiritual life, an argument against rationalism, a refusal to accept a Sadducean philosophy that asked men to be content with the dust, and to live in the realm of the material. By that act, unknowingly, her whole soul responded with holy love, to the vision; and in the dedication of her living was her recognition of the vision which her eyes beheld.

Yet once again, it was a gift law-fulfilling. Hear the question: "What commandment is the first of all?" Hear the answer of Jesus: "Thou shalt love the Lord thy God, . . . thou shalt love thy neighbour." What relation had that to the gifts that were placed in the treasury in the temple? All gifts placed in those chests in the treasury of the temple were divided between the priests and the poor. Now, however much the priests were degraded, let us never forget that to the simple heart of this woman they stood as the representatives of God, they stood for relationship to God. And the poor? She was of the poorest of the poor, but they were her neighbours; and when she dropped her gifts into the treasury she was keeping the whole law. She was expressing her love to her God, and her love to her neighbour. So I repeat, that while Jesus waited and watched, He saw in that dark and desolate hour, one woman in whose life, all unconsciously, Divine requirements were being fulfilled. The sacramental symbol of the beauty and glory of her life, in her gift of two mites, contradicted and corrected the atmosphere which was hostile to sacramental symbols.

Look finally, not at the foes of the Son of man, not at the woman worshipping alone, but at the Son of man Himself. He had claimed but recently to be the Son sent to the vineyard for fruit, when the husbandmen had illtreated and murdered all that had preceded Him; but He knew that their fate would be His, for the husbandmen were saying ere He came, "Let us kill Him."

In His final question there was a further revelation concerning Himself. He was David's Lord. Offspring of David, yes; but Root of David also; the One from Whom David had come, the One Who after the flesh had come from David.

Here then, are three things to be observed. First let us observe His observing. Then let us hear His appraisement of the things that He saw that day; and remind ourselves how He was, and is for ever vindicated in that appraisement.

Observe first, His observing. Here Mark is very particular: " He sat down over against the treasury, and beheld *how* the multitude cast money into the treasury." He did not behold the multitude casting in. He was not watching them. He beheld *how* they did it. In the very simple and artless declaration of Mark something is revealed concerning Him that was peculiar to Him; in which He stood, and stands for ever differentiated from all others. What was He watching? Oh! not the trick of the hand, or the poise of the head, although all these things may very often be suggestive. Christ was looking deeper. He was looking at the motive behind, the reason for the giving, the impulse of the donation, the inspiration of the offering. That is what He is always doing. He beheld *how* they gave.

In the Old Testament, in the dim twilight of that earlier dispensation, there is a great psalm. It is the song of a woman, Hannah. In the midst of her song, celebrating the government of God, she said, " By Him, actions are weighed." Here the Lord is seen weighing gifts, and when the gift is to be weighed, the important thing is the weight He puts in the other side of the balance. He was observing *how* they gave. That is what He always watches. The Lord of pity and compassion is watching to-day *how* this nation is giving. We see in our newspapers a list of names connected with large amounts. Then presently there is that remarkable group at the last, "Amounts Under——"! All the poetry is in the last item, and not in the first. The compassion of the human heart is finest and purest among the gifts where there is no record of a name. He is still observing *how!*

But He was observing, unobserved. We have no hint

in the Gospel story that the woman knew she was watched, or that she was told. She is seen in her gift, and her passing. He called His disciples privately, and drew their attention to that which had happened; but He did not tell her. I do not think she ever knew. I think that she lived all her days, and never knew, until there came one sweet morning of the light that never fades, when He met her on the other side; and then she found that He had kissed the poor copper of her gift into the gold of the eternities.

Then note His appraisement of that offering. Drawing the special attention of His disciples to it, He said this to them, " This poor widow cast in more than all." It is an amazing thing, this! He did not say, This poor woman hath done splendidly. He did not say, This poor woman hath cast in very much. He did not say, She hath cast in as much as any one. He did not say, She hath cast in as much as the whole of them. He said, " More than all "! Presiding over the temple coffers that day, the Lord of the temple took the gifts and sifted them. On the one hand He put the gifts of wealth, and the gifts of ostentation; and on the other, two mites—" more than all "! That we may not misunderstand it, He gave the reason: " They . . . of their superfluity "! Oh! how the thing scorches, how it burns. Superfluity!

A little girl, during the war, wrote a letter to the Prince of Wales, a sweet letter, which was printed in all the papers at the time. She sent, I think it was sevenpence-halfpenny, and ended her letter by saying, " I am so glad I am an English girl, but I am sorry for those German children." That was an unveiling of the glory of the Christian heart in a little girl! I think that day Jesus took the sevenpence-halfpenny, and said, More than all! And why? Because His standard is quality; and the quality is life. When a gift has that quality, that gift is God's currency. God can do much more with small amounts that have that quality, than with all the gifts that come from superfluity.

The gift that is not easy, that comes out of blood, out of penury, is current in the spiritual realm, and God can do infinitely more with it than with the gifts that come out of superfluity.

The last thing concerns the vindication of our Lord. Was He right? Business men will forgive me if I am commercial here. Those two mites, given in that way, so that He was able to commend the giving, have produced more for the Kingdom of God in two millenniums, than all the other gifts that day. Oh! the inspiration of this story! How it has helped lonely, poor, and sorrowing hearts to give. Running on, and running ever, these two mites are rolling up their dividends, and their results are great and mighty, inspired by what that lonely woman did. May God help us to give to Him in the light of this story; and may He grant that the glory of it, and the beauty of it may be a transfiguring power upon our giving. I do not think a collection is ever taken but that somewhere He finds a copper coin, and kisses it into gold. Of course this is two-edged. He still writes across many a gift, *superfluity!*

It is not for me to measure the gifts to God, I cannot; but it is for us ever to remember that religion, politics, ethics, were all included in that gift, and are always included in our giving. Giving is still a sacramental symbol. The giving which is true is the outcome of vital religion, high politics, true philosophy, perfect ethics.

XXIV

" *Watch.*"—Mark 13 : 37.

Mark 13.

Thus in one arresting and ringing word of command, the Son of man summarized the duty of His followers, in view of a prophecy which He had uttered of a most solemn and imperative nature. The interpretation of this command to watch must be sought in a consideration of the prophecy. Therefore, without any further preliminary words, let me indicate the scheme of the meditation, and proceed therewith.

I propose first to survey this prophecy of Jesus; secondly, to attempt to indicate its teaching in its bearing upon our present situation; in order that I may finally emphasize the command to watch.

First then let us survey this prophecy of Jesus. It is at least a noticeable fact not to be forgotten, that Matthew, Mark, and Luke record this Olivet prophecy. Moreover, they all place it in the same relation to the ministry of Jesus; at its very close, in that last shadowed week. Matthew gives the prophecy with greatest fulness. Mark and Luke give the same sections of the prophecy.

Two matters demand our attention, preliminary even to this survey of the prophecy as a whole. They are those of the occasion upon which our Lord uttered it, and that of its full content.

Jesus had come to Jerusalem, departing from His usual method, and provoking demonstration. Having done so, and looked round about upon all things on that first day, He passed out to the quietness and the seclusion of Bethany. On His way back to Jerusalem in the morning He had destroyed the fig tree. Then moving into the temple He had cleansed it by the exercise of a most re-

markable power, and had then entered into conflict with
the rulers. This was followed by that last act of judgment in Jerusalem, when He sat and watched the givers
in the treasury, and appraised the value of the gift of the
lonely woman.

Immediately following these things, His disciples drew
His attention to the temple itself, as Mark tells, to the
stones of the building, as Luke declares, to the precious
stones and the glory and beauty of the building. It was
a significant action. He had been there with them before.
Why did they at that moment draw His attention to this
temple? Surely, we see in their action the result of their
own attitude of mind. He had cleansed the temple; He
had denounced the temple; finally uttering its doom,
"Your house is left unto you desolate." Now they drew
His attention to the temple itself; and immediately with
swiftness and inclusiveness, He predicted its complete
destruction, telling them that not one stone should be left
upon another that should not be flung down.

Then leaving the temple and the city, they climbed
Olivet, until they came to a place which the evangelist
describes as " over against the temple "; that is, a place
on the mountain side from which they could look back on
the temple. These men, strangely moved by the things
He had been saying, came to Him with their question.
Four men are named by Mark as coming to Him. They
asked Him, " When shall these things be? What shall be
the sign of Thy coming, and of the consummation of the
age?" The prophecy constitutes our Lord's answer to
that threefold enquiry.

To glance at the prophecy as a whole, I return to the
record in Matthew's Gospel. There we discover that in
it there are three distinct sections. In answer to their enquiry, our Lord first spoke to these men purely from the
standpoint of the Hebrew Messiah (Matt. 24:4-44).
These are predictions that have in them the note of
things concerning Israel, the Hebrew people, the Messiah

of the Hebrew people, and the theocracy of God, according to their ancient economy. At the forty-fifth verse in that chapter is a break in the discourse, with this question: "Who then is the faithful and wise servant?" In the next section (24:45–25:30) there is a new outlook, no longer upon the Hebrew nation, but upon the Christian Church, and the responsibility of that Church. At verse thirty-one in chapter 25 is another beginning: "But when the Son of man shall come in His glory." The outlook is thence no longer upon the Hebrew nation, no longer exclusively upon the Christian Church; it is world-wide, upon the nations. In the central section He never spoke of Himself as the Son of man. He closed the first section with that descriptive title. He resumed it in the third section.

He was evidently looking with clear eyes while the clouds were gathering about Him, and He walked the *via dolorosa*, and knew His death was imminent. His disciples had asked Him, "When shall these things be?" this casting down of the temple. "What shall be the sign of Thy coming, and of the consummation of the age?" Here we see the Lord, never more wondrously, looking quietly on, and viewing the coming centuries from the standpoint of His ancient people Israel; from the standpoint of His new people, the Church; and at last from the standpoint of the nations of the world.

Looking at one age from the three standpoints, the perspective is not always clear. Our Lord was describing, not so much the whole course of the age, as the crises, the mountain tops. As standing upon some height we look out upon the mountains and see one great mountain peak before us, and shining in glory behind it another, which seems near enough to the first peak to kiss it; but when we have travelled to the first we discover that between us and the other, there are whole stretches of valleys; so here, things seem to be near together which are really as far apart as the first advent and the second.

Therefore, we need most carefully to remember the necessity for the sense of perspective as we study a prophecy
like this.

In the thirteenth chapter of his Gospel, Mark has no
record of that second section where the outlook is upon
the Church; and no record of that final section where all
the nations are gathered together before the Lord. He
only gives the first section, but with much more of detail
than that recorded by Matthew. Let us, therefore, simply
move through this thirteenth chapter, in order to the discovery of its movement, in the answer of our Lord to the
enquiry.

His answer to the enquiry commenced at verse five;
and in the paragraph (verses 5–8) is a record of introductory warnings, the value of which is not exhausted in the
following paragraphs, but runs through the whole of what
our Lord subsequently said. He called His disciples first
to take heed as to their loyalty to Himself. He definitely
told them that when they heard of wars and rumours of
wars they were not to be troubled, for wars and rumours
of wars were not the sign of the end. He told them
finally, that whenever they should hear of such things
they were to know that they were the beginning, the
birth-pangs of travail, a travail that proceeded toward re-
birth and new life.

Having said so much He began to speak immediately
to the men who were round about Him, giving them
personal instructions (verses 9–13). In that paragraph
He told those immediate disciples of a period of persecution that was imminent. We know to-day how literally
that word was fulfilled in their particular history, and
how in that particular period of persecution, the strength,
the comfort—in all the true sense of that great word
comfort—that sustained them, was that of the presence
with them of the Holy Spirit.

Then He proceeded in the next section (verses 14–32)
to describe the crises, of which there are two. In verses

14–23 He first foretold distinctly all that was fulfilled at the fall of Jerusalem within a generation. Continuing, He said, " But in those days, after that tribulation "; and we may be inclined to think that " those days " of verse 24 must be close to the end He had already described in verses 14–23. As a matter of fact, here we have two mountain peaks, but between the first and the second there are great valleys.

Luke makes this fact a little more clear: "And they shall fall by the edge of the sword, and shall be led captive into all the nations; and Jerusalem shall be trodden down of the Gentiles, until the times of the Gentiles be fulfilled " (Luke 21 : 24). That little verse covers a period from the fall of Jerusalem until to-day. Jerusalem is still trodden down of the Gentiles, because the times of the Gentiles have not yet been fulfilled. Yet notice, with that illuminative declaration, Luke resumes exactly as Mark does. "And there shall be signs in sun and moon and stars." To return to Mark, in verses 24–32, He speaks of another crisis after the fall of Jerusalem, the crisis of His own definite and positive second advent in judgment; and all ends with instructions in verses 33–37. " Take ye heed "; and thus we are brought back to the key-note, as at the commencement.

In attempting to gather the teaching of Jesus, notice first that the prophecy contains a clear revelation of the fact that according to the conception of the Master Himself, the age from the Cross to His personal advent would be one of perpetual conflict and turmoil. Our Lord's outlook upon this age was not that of one in which there should be a gradual cessation of strife between the nations, by the victory of the preaching of His Gospel, until the whole earth should be reduced by that preaching to a condition of peace. I am told that these prophecies were compiled after the events. If so, I can only suggest that if a man had been compiling these records after the events, he could have written far more clearly. Our Lord had no expectation that in this particular age war or turmoil would cease. He distinctly revealed the fact that right through the age there would be conflict and turmoil to its very end. Indeed He foretold upon this occasion—in harmony with all the great prophets of the Hebrew economy—that the consummation of this strange and mystic age, the meaning of which was never perfectly known by the ancient Hebrew seers, would be in carnage and bloodshed, clash and strife.

Observe in the second place that in this prophecy we have the definite declaration that wars and rumours of wars are not the sign of the end of the age. They are neither the sign that the end of the age is near, nor that the end of the age is distant. In order to our peace of heart, and to the clarity of our testimony to-day, Christian people need to be reminded of the fact that Armageddon is not yet. Armageddon in principle, is often repeated but not yet in finality. Josiah the king was killed at Armageddon. Zechariah the prophet saw Armageddon in his own age. Har-Magedon is yet to be; but wars and rumours of wars are not the sign of it. Wars and rumours of wars are part of that perpetual process in which God, overruling the forces of the world, makes the wrath of man express itself to His ultimate praise, and girds the remainder upon His thigh, restraining it as within His own will.

Observe in the next place how in this prophecy our Lord uttered the most solemn warning against false Christs and false prophets, declaring that in hours of stress and strain, of wars and rumours of wars, of pestilences and famines and earthquakes, such would arise. From that hour until this, in all the history of the Christian Church, it will be seen that times of strong emotional distress have been times of grave peril concerning the person of the Lord Himself, and there have continually arisen false Christs and false prophets. The warnings of our Lord are most clear, that in such times we

need to take heed that we are not lured from our loyalty
to Him by any voice that claims to be His, or by any that
shall tell us, Lo! here is Christ, or there is Christ!

If this language of our Lord, as recorded by Mark,
Luke, and Matthew, means anything, we have an explicit
declaration that the approach of the final manifestation
will be heralded by supernatural signs, stars falling, sun
darkening, moon refusing her light, the powers in the
heavens shaken; and that the Son of man will be clearly
manifested.

It was in connection with such foretelling that our
Lord gave the authoritative assurance that these things
must be. "Heaven and earth shall pass away; but My
words shall not pass away." This is a great text. An
application of its declaration may be made to the whole
teaching of Jesus; but its first application is to this apocalyptic utterance, this prophetic foretelling, this clear declaration concerning the end.

Still further observe that in this prophecy of Jesus
there is an arresting insistence upon the fact that the
time is not known. It was here He Himself did say,
"Of that day or that hour knoweth no one, not even the
angels in heaven, neither the Son, but the Father." Immediately afterwards He added, "Take ye heed . . .
ye know not when the time is"; and repeated it, "Watch,
therefore: for ye know not when the lord of the house
cometh." In those words He solemnly warned His disciples, and us, and the whole age, that we know not when.
Not in this prophecy, nor anywhere else in the teaching
of Jesus, nor in the whole New Testament is there a
single declaration that can help us to fix, even approxi-
mately within the limits of a human almanac or calendar,
the hour of the advent. Nothing could be plainer than
this: "Ye know not."

All that brings us to the final and commanding declaration as to the duty of His followers, more than once repeated in this final paragraph, and summarized in the

last word, "Watch." What our Lord meant by that is indeed focussed in the very word itself. Readers of the Greek New Testament will remember that two words are both translated in our English Version, "Watch." They are not contradictory, but complementary to each other. "Take ye heed, watch and pray: for ye know not when the time is"; and then presently, "Watch, therefore"; and finally, "What I say unto you I say unto all, Watch." I take the second word, twice repeated, "Watch," literally, Be wide awake; the positive word. I take this word, and feel my way into it, to see where it came from, and how it came to pass that men used this particular word in this connection. At the heart of it I find the thought of the market-place. Probably, therefore, the thought of watching comes from the idea of the market-place as a place of purposeful and alert gathering together. There is a passage in the New Testament where that same figure of the market-place is discovered. When Paul was writing to the Ephesian Christians he said, "Buying up the opportunity," "redeeming the time" as the old translation rendered it; and the figure again is that of the market-place; a merchant man, eager and alert; a company of such merchants, all eager and alert, with their hearts all set upon their business.

These values are all in this word "Watch." Take the word in its application to the individual soul. It means the faculties gathered together, alert, wide awake. That is what Jesus said to these men. He did not charge them to climb some mountain height, and watch the east for the flush of dawn; but He charged them to be watchful. He would put them in Jerusalem and Samaria, send them on journeyings toward the uttermost part of the earth; but He charged them that wherever they should find themselves, they were to be wide awake, all their faculties gathered together, alert, coöperative.

The word, and the meaning of our Lord in the use of the word, is interpreted by all the injunctions. They may be summarized thus. He charged them first to be careful, supremely careful in the matter of their loyalty to Him. Take heed!—twice repeated—lest ye be led away by voices which claim to be My voice, and prophets which claim to speak in My name.

The second note of injunction is that in which He enjoined them to the attitude of courage. Be not troubled when ye hear of wars, and rumours of wars. Be not even anxious when the tide of hostility focusses itself upon you, and you become persecuted, suffering. Be not anxious.

Then immediately He linked the watching with prayer. "Take ye heed, watch and pray." "Watch." This is the other word. It has exactly the same meaning, but from the other standpoint. It is the negative word. It means, be sleepless. Do not fall on sleep in this one particular matter of prayer.

Once again we are arrested by a Greek word. It is the peculiar word that describes the attitude of the soul in worship, including asking for something, but not necessarily so. There can be praying, without a petition in it, and the thought is never exhausted by the idea of asking. We may ask for something perpetually, and yet never pray in the sense of this word. Praying here is the prostration of soul in the presence of God; praying here is the wishing of the desiring soul forward toward God. We may be unable to ask for anything; and so I feel on many a day, that I do not know what to pray for. But I can pray in the sense of this word; the soul desiring itself out to God. There is a great word in an ancient psalm when the soul of a man found expression: "My soul followeth hard after Thee." That is prayer. What shall we pray for to-day? There are things we cannot ask for lest we cut across some Divine purpose; but our souls can go out to God. Watching is the sleepless vigil of the God-desiring soul.

And once more—I put it last because He put it last,

[281]

not that it is least in importance—watching is working; definite work appointed by the absent Lord; personal work, to each one his work; work in which the small becomes glorious in its relation to the whole.

Our watching is first, the solemn and resolute maintenance of our loyalty to our Lord and Master. It is secondly, that of courage of heart that is not troubled by wars and rumours of wars, and is not anxious even in the hour of suffering. It is thirdly, that prayer-life which is not for ever seeking for the second coming of the Lord, in order that we may escape from something; but that is for ever seeking His Kingdom, His glory, the accomplishment of His purpose.

Finally, watching is working. The attitude of the stargazer with regard to the advent was rebuked at the very beginning of the Christian era when the angel said: "Ye men of Galilee, why stand ye looking into heaven? this same Jesus . . . shall so come." There need be no anxiety. Our business is to fulfil His command. "To each one his work."

My last word is personal. None of the things happening in the world which surprise and startle me, surprise or startle God. None of these things—which I confess I am less able to explain to-day than yesterday, for the puzzle and the wonder grow—were unknown to my Lord so long ago. He saw the age into which He had come. He knew the measure of the forces that were against His Kingdom, which is righteousness, peace, and joy. That is the order in His Kingdom; first righteousness, then peace, and joy is never worth while until it comes out of the peace that follows upon righteousness.

XXV

Mark 14:1–26.

THE dominant note of this paragraph is emotional. As we read it we are conscious of emotional suspense, suppression, expression, caution, courage. The atmosphere is surcharged with feeling. As we attempt to visualize the scenes, we observe the personalities:—the chief priests, scribes, Simon the leper, Mary, Judas, the disciples; and central to them all, Jesus. Watching the faces, and listening to the speech of all, we detect tones which express intense and conflicting feelings; anger and affection, devotion and antagonism, evil gladness and beneficent sorrow. Gathered around the Son of man are foes and friends, all strangely moved.

While the introductory statements give us a glimpse of the avowed enemies of the Lord plotting for His death, the principal interest centres around two suppers; at the first of which Jesus was a Guest, while at the second He was Host. The gatherings were separated by six days. John tells us that the supper at Bethany was six days before the Passover. The definite time note in our story refers to the plotting of the priests and scribes two days before the Passover. The second supper was that of the Passover itself. The end was at hand, and with more or less intelligence, all were conscious of the fact. Hence the emotional activity. Let this then be the subject of our meditation. Here we see evil emotions in the foes of Jesus; mixed emotions in the friends of Jesus; and pure emotions in Jesus Himself.

Let us look at the foes of Jesus; a group, and a man; the chief priests and scribes, and Judas. As we observe the first group, the chief priests and scribes from this standpoint, watching them in order to understand the emotions that were moving them, we see that they were filled with hatred, that they were conscious of fear, and that they were glad. These three things are clearly manifest in this story.

They were filled with hatred for Jesus. This fact need not be dwelt upon, save as it is important to remember that they did hate Him with a profound hatred, an intense hatred. But there was an element that restrained them, they were afraid. They were determined to do an evil deed, and yet for a moment they were held in check. Suddenly into this consciousness of hatred and fear there came a new and unholy gladness.

For what reason were these men conscious of hatred of Jesus? He had rebuked their ideals through the whole course of His public ministry. Ideals are always closely related to conduct; consequently the whole tenor of His teaching had been to rebuke their conduct.

During the latter days of His ministry He had rebuked their failures as shepherds of the people. Functional failure is always related to organic failure. Sometimes the physicians tell us that there is a functional trouble, and not an organic one, and we are always comforted. Yet the physician would admit that functional failure is at least an organic peril. Where functional failure is as pronounced as it was in the case of these men, it is demonstration of organic failure. These men had been compelled, in the whole course of the ministry of Jesus Christ, and superlatively in these closing days, to stand disclosed; unwillingly, but definitely self-confessed as corrupt, as having failed. Their hatred of Jesus was consequently of One Who had revealed their failure.

Mark the high tribute to Jesus which this hatred created. There is no greater compliment that can be paid to a man than to be hated by certain men. The greatness of a man is revealed, not only by his friends, but by his

[284]

foes. These men who are seen acting with hatred against
Christ, by their very hatred were weaving another chap-
let wherewith to deck His brow.

They were strangely moved by fear, afraid to do the
thing that was in their heart. Read again the statement:
" Not during the feast, lest haply there shall be a tumult
of the people." Why should they fear a tumult among
the people? They were perfectly acquainted with the
fact that the great human conscience, as expressed in the
life of the multitude, agreed with the ideals of Jesus,
agreed with His condemnation of their own failure.
They feared a tumult. And why should there not be a
tumult? What is there necessarily evil in a tumult of
the people? Their fear was purely selfish; behind their
fear of the people in tumult, there lurked a craven fear
of Rome, and of the possible loss of favour, and position.
Again, what a high tribute to Jesus, that these men in
this hour were afraid of a tumult, which would be inspired by popular love of, and belief in, all that for which
He had stood.

The last note of the emotion of these evil men is that
they were glad when one of His own number, one of the
apostles, told them a way by which they could wreak their
vengeance upon Him, and kill Him. It was a gladness
born of treachery, gladness in the heart of men who
were supposed to stand for the moral instruction and
spiritual inspiration of the people. Morality was counted
as nothing, in order that their evil purposes might be
fulfilled.

Let us now turn to the emotional life of this man,
Judas, as it is here revealed. The first note—not perhaps quite clearly apparent in the paragraph, but made
clear by the paragraph as it is interpreted by statements
of the other evangelists, and especially by one illuminative word of John—is that of a man whose whole emotional nature was mastered by covetousness. John gives
us a revealing word about Judas. Having recorded his

[285]

enquiry, "Why was not this ointment sold for three hundred shillings, and given to the poor?" he adds, "This he said, not because he cared for the poor, but because he was a thief, and having the bag took away what was put therein." There is revealed the master motive in the emotional life of Judas. The word covetousness does not startle the human heart. At its mention none blushes, or blanches. Yet it is the deadliest of all deadly sins. The only word in the Decalogue that brought Saul of Tarsus to conviction of sin, as he himself confessed in the Roman letter, was the word, "Thou shalt not covet." He who could stand erect in the presence of every other commandment, bowed his head, and knew his guilt when he reached that word. Covetousness is the subtlest sin of all!

Mark the fact concerning Judas. "He was a thief, and he had the bag." Was he given the bag because he was a thief? No, but because of his capacity in business matters. Undoubtedly everything was orderly in that little company of apostles. It may seem a small thing to say about Jesus, but He is the Author of order. The weakness of Judas lay in the realm of his power. His capacity was the reason of his appointment to the treasurership of the little band; and right at the heart of his power, or capacity, lay his weakness. This is always so. When the apostle declared in one of his letters, "When I am weak then am I strong," he declared a great truth which may be expressed in another way, *Where I am strong there I am weak*. Temptation always lies within the realm of capacity. Financial ability is fraudulent possibility—not fraudulent necessity! It is not necessary for a man with financial ability to be fraudulent, but the capacity creates the possibility. Here, in spite of the brilliant essayists of the past, and the no less brilliant novelists of modern time, Judas stands confronting us, a man mastered emotionally by covetousness, the weakness of his own power and capacity.

Yet as we look at his emotional nature again, the more amazing thing is not that of the covetousness which was the inspiration of his treachery, but that of the callousness which enabled him to so act. Mark the hardening of the nature, the petrifying of the heart! The marvel of it, that any man could have lived and walked with Jesus, and yet have done this deed!

I am impressed, moreover, by the craftiness of the action of this man; cunningly choosing a moment, waiting for an opportunity. An emotional nature, hating; yes, strongly moved, wickedly unrestrained, covetous, callous, crafty. The picture is almost too dark to tarry at the looking.

So we look at the page again, to see this same emotional unveiling, in the case of the friends of Jesus. Here again we have a group and a person; the group of the disciples, and Mary.

Glance at the group of the disciples at that first supper, in the house of Simon the leper; undoubtedly the home also of Martha, Mary, and Lazarus, to whom Simon was himself surely related. The first thing we observe as we look at them is that they were angry—exceedingly, and as they thought, righteously so—with Mary. Misled by the speciousness of Judas, misunderstanding entirely the action of the woman, they were angry, that in the presence of human poverty and need, there should be this waste. Judas it was who suggested this. In his case the suggestion came out of the thieving instinct of his own heart. He was a thief, and he had the bag. It was a specious suggestion. In the case of the other disciples, the anger did not arise from covetousness. They thought that theirs was most righteous anger, they were angry with a woman for wasting what might have been given to the poor.

Look at this same group of men once again, at the second supper; no longer glad, but sorrowful, with that poignant sorrow that came out of a great dread. Jesus had

startled them by a word, " One of you shall betray Me."
In a moment every man was afraid and sorrowful; and
each in turn asked the question, " Lord is it I?" It was
a great moment of emotion; it was a moment of splendid
honesty. When Jesus made His statement He forced
them as individual men to come face to face with Himself; and the question they asked Him was not, Is it my
neighbour? but " Is it I?" It was a moment when every
man suddenly woke to the fact that there was within
himself—howsoever he hated it—something of the capacity for treachery. We see them there, strangely stirred
with sorrowful emotion and fear.

Now let us return to the first supper, and look at Mary.
Again the whole picture is one of the emotions. First observe the understandingness of this woman; how she saw
and knew, that day, what no apostle saw or knew. She
had had previous experiences of very close fellowship
with Jesus. Luke records one, John another. The first,
recorded by Luke, was in the day of sunshine and prosperity. He tells the gracious and wonderful story of how,
having rendered her share of help in the work of the
home, she *also* sat at His feet to hear His word. In the
day of joy this woman had made time for quietness and
discipleship, for adoration and listening. She had then
found her way to His feet. On a later occasion, as John
tells us, when the heaven was black with sorrow, when
Lazarus was dead, and in his grave, she found her way
to His feet in her desolate anguish, and the sequel is
known. Now this was the hour of His anguish, this was
the hour of His desolation; and this one woman, of all the
group, discovered it. The keen intuition of her heart
understood better than any other, all that He was passing
through. Mary, coming with that cruse of precious spike-
nard, approached nearer the sacred sorrow of the Son of
man, than did any other soul, at any period in His ministry. Such understandingness is a rare thing. How
few possess it! I sometimes think that the highest thing

that can ever be said of man or woman is that he or she is an understanding person.

Again, she was impulsive. There may be those who think that to be a sign of weakness. Nay, it is a thing of strength! Of course it matters what the impulse is, it may be evil, but it may be good. For a long while we have been suffering from an unholy horror of anything impulsive or emotional. This was an impulsive act, unconventional, uncalculating, imprudent if you will, on Mary's part. Of course Judas could not understand this. Even the apostles could not understand it. It was an act born of the prodigality of love, daring not to calculate. No careful, mathematical, mechanical, consideration of how much or how little was this; but the bringing of the most costly gift available, and the pouring of it out upon His head and feet.

This was magnificent impulse; emotion, without reserve; and the deepest value of it was that it brought her into true fellowship with Him, not merely in the sense of understandingness, but in the sense of coöperation. Not idly or carelessly did our Lord utter His words of commendation. Not idly or carelessly did He say to those disciples, "Wheresoever the Gospel shall be preached throughout the whole world, that also which this woman hath done shall be spoken for a memorial of her." In those words He was revealing a wonderful truth concerning the thing that Mary did. Notice how He brought together, "The Gospel" and "That . . . which this woman hath done." But six days away from that scene was Golgotha, the unfathomable darkness and mystery of the Cross; and beyond it the light of the Resurrection, and out of these came the Gospel. "The Gospel," and "That" stand side by side with each other for ever. That keen intuition of love, that uncalculating outpouring of love was Godlike, and an act in fellowship with the act of God, by which a world is to be redeemed. Mary is here to be measured, not by the inspiration of intellectual apprehension, but by the inspiration of a great heart.

Finally, and that with all reverence, let us look at the picture of Jesus presented here. It is purely emotional. In some senses there seem to be no very great things intellectually. There are however three things emotional, which impress me, as I read the story. First, His appreciation of love in the case of Mary; secondly, His reprehension of treachery in the case of Judas; and finally, His preparation for emotional communion between Himself and His disciples in all the coming days, for that is what the institution of the Supper really meant.

First, as I look at my Lord, I am impressed by His appreciation of love. Do not spoil this story by trying to explain away this attitude of Jesus toward Mary. Be simple about it, graphic and childlike, and look at the scene as it really was. They were feasting in the house of Simon the leper. A wonderful hour was that; Martha still serving; Lazarus, risen from the dead, sitting at the board, and the disciples round about the Master, blinded intellectually by the mystery of His recent teaching. Then it was that this woman came with the alabaster cruse. Note the whispering among the apostles, and the sudden, swift, almost angry protest of Jesus against their whispering. "Let her alone; why trouble ye her?" Do not be afraid to interpret the words of Jesus so. I think His very protest was a revelation of His appreciation of her love. It is very difficult for us to do; but let us try and understand what that action meant to Him. There He was, humanly speaking hemmed in by blind hate; and here was one action of understanding love! There He was, amid the hindering of His activity; and here was one act of help! There was He, in a dark and desolate land; and lo! out of the heart of a woman, a spring of fresh water sprung for the thirsty Christ! He valued it.

Look at Him again on that second occasion; and again do not rob the story of its force. He knew what treach-

ery lurked in the heart of Judas, and of his arrangements
made for His arrest; and He resented it! Try and
enter into His feelings here again, so much as may be.
Remember His purpose of love, and then see standing in
the way of it, this act of hate. Remember His power to
help, and then think of this as an attempt to hinder His
exercising that very power. Endeavour to apprehend
the world-sphere of His benevolence, and then mark how
in the highway of its operation, He saw this malevolent
action. Then we shall not be surprised at the solemnity
of His words, and the emotional anger of His soul,
against the act of the traitor.

When the traitor was excluded from the paschal board,
He instituted the sacred new feast. The supreme value
of the Supper of the Lord is emotional, not intellectual.
These symbols reveal no secrets, but they remind us of
mystery. Although Mark does not give the full account
of the words spoken at this time, we may remember them
in this connection. Our Lord said, " This do in remembrance of Me." The activity of memory produces the
renewal of feeling, the reawakening of thanksgiving. The
Holy Table is the place of the Eucharist. The Eucharist
simply means the thanksgiving. Christian men and
women who gather around the board, are priests of
thanksgiving, offering the sacrifice of praise. Our Lord
instituted the Supper with that end in view. Such pro-
vision was inspired by emotion. Jesus was making arrangements for the perpetual recurrence of an hour of
tryst between Himself and His lovers, in which they
should remember Him.

What is the value of that portrait that hangs upon the
wall, dear mother, of your son, or of your daughter away
in a distant land? It is something that reminds you of
him, of her; when you look upon the face, your heart is
moved anew. The portrait is not there to instruct your
intellect; it is there to touch your emotion. So in this
final hour, our Lord instituted this simple Feast, and es-

tablished a ritual which, whenever it be truly observed, brings Him back to the memory more vividly, and causes an emotional outgoing toward Himself.

How did the Feast end? With twelve men singing, Jesus, and the eleven. "When they had sung a hymn, they went out." Take the book of Psalms, and read from the one hundred and thirteenth, to the one hundred and eighteenth. They constitute the great Hallel, and from these Jesus undoubtedly sang with His disciples. What is singing but emotional expression?

Oh! the value and the power of emotion. Evil emotion slays the Lord of life and glory! Pure emotion makes possible the saving of the slayers.

Then let us guard our emotions. What masters them? What inspires them? Is it self? Or is it the Christ? If it be the Christ, then let us trust them, and let us obey them. Let us decline for evermore to listen to the mechanical, arithmetical, accurate, prudent, and devilish calculation, that prevents waste! Let us dare to pour out our hearts and ourselves in emotional adoration!

We may say if only He were here to-day to sit with us at the board, we could do it, and we would! Ah He is here to-day, in the person of all who are in distress. Do not let us be afraid of our hearts. Have you found out that you have one? Count this a gain indeed, and follow its dictates.

"And Jesus saith unto them, All ye shall be offended: for it is written, I will smite the shepherd, and the sheep shall be scattered abroad. Howbeit, after I am raised up, I will go before you into Galilee."—MARK 14:27, 28.

Mark 14:27–52.

IN this paragraph we have the record of a series of incidents following each other in close succession. The story is characteristic of the method of Mark in that these incidents are given with great brevity, many details being omitted; and yet with great clarity, in that the central things are made perfectly plain. Jesus and His disciples had joined in singing together the hymn appointed for that Passover feast; the great Hallel, found in our Psalter in Psalms 113–118. We can easily imagine how the last cadences of this song were still in their memory as they left the upper room, and the city, and went to Olivet. Very significant are the final sentences:

" Jehovah is God, and He hath given us light;
    Bind the sacrifice with cords, even unto the horns of
        the altar.
    Thou art my God, and I will give thanks unto Thee;
    Thou art my God, I will exalt Thee.
    O give thanks unto Jehovah; for He is good;
    For His lovingkindness endureth for ever."

They passed from the upper room, and from the city, to the quietude of Olivet. There Jesus told them of His smiting, and of their scattering. They immediately and vehemently protested, Peter being the principal spokesman of their common conviction and intention. Then they went to Gethsemane, and its overwhelmingly solemn events transpired.

[293]

The next incident was that of the arrival of Judas, and the arrest of Jesus. This was immediately followed by the action of Peter, in the use of the sword. Jesus protested against the method of the mob, and yet consented to His own arrest. Then the whole company of the disciples forsook Him and fled. Mark adds one incident. A certain young man, probably not of the company of the disciples, but aroused from sleep in some cottage by the way, as the mob moved along the road back to the city, rushed out after Jesus, covered only with the garment of the night, was seized by the mob, and fled naked.

Here then are seven incidents grouped, massed together; many details found in other Gospels are omitted, but seven incidents constituting a sequence and a unity are given. The key-note of the study is found in the word of Jesus: " I will smite the shepherd, and the sheep shall be scattered." The final note is found in the tragic declaration, " They all left Him, and fled."

The dominant note in this particular paragraph is volitional. In our last meditation we considered a section in which the emotional was clearly supreme. Here the Son of man is seen in perfect relation to the will of God, understanding it so clearly that He told His disciples exactly what was about to happen. The Shepherd was to be smitten. He was in such perfect harmony with the Divine Will, that we see Him in communion with God, daring to speak in the holy Presence of His own shrinking from the hour of darkness which He had already declared to be inevitable. We see Him finally in co-operation with that very Will, as He yielded Himself to the people against whose method of arrest He made His strong and urgent protest. The disciples are seen yielding, retreating, fleeing, because in their case, will was mastered by sight, rather than by faith. Yet once again, the enemies of Jesus are seen working out their choices, following the line of their own will. Finally the will of God is seen triumphing in spite of them, and through them, making their very wrath to praise Him, while the remainder He restrains.

Taking the words of Jesus at the beginning as the keynote, let us consider first, the smiting of the Shepherd; secondly, the scattering of the sheep; and finally, the way of the smitten Shepherd with the scattered sheep.

First then, let us consider the smiting of the Shepherd. Our Lord told these men distinctly what was about to happen: "All ye shall be offended,"—or to carry over the Greek word into the Anglicized form,—"All ye shall be *scandalized,*" that is "All ye shall be *made to stumble* in Me." Our Revisers have omitted the words " in Me," perhaps with good reason; the fact remains however that even if they are not warranted by the text, the thought is present. Our Lord was not rebuking these men; He was telling them a fact. "All ye shall be made to stumble "; not, "All of you will stumble," as though blame were attached to them. Here was the fact; before the darkness of that night should be dissipated by the dawning of a new day, the whole of them would be scandalized in Him, made to stumble in Him.

Having said so much, He gave the explanation: " For it is written, I will smite the Shepherd, and the sheep shall be scattered abroad." Jesus was quoting from Zechariah: "Awake, O sword, against My Shepherd, and against the Man that is My Fellow, saith Jehovah of Hosts: smite the Shepherd, and the sheep shall be scattered; and I will turn My hand upon the little ones." After His perpetual habit, and that of all New Testament writers, He did not quote the actual words of the Old Testament Scriptures; but the spiritual truth was contained in the quotation. He said then, that they would be offended, because " It is written, I will smite the Shepherd "; the smiting of the Shepherd would be the cause of the scattering of the sheep.

He here referred to all that was coming in His own experience, and the experience of His disciples, by the citation of a prophecy, which distinctly declared that the Shepherd of the people should be smitten by the stroke of Jehovah Himself. By that solemn quotation we are admitted to the inner working of the mind of the Lord at that moment. He knew full well, as we have seen in previous studies, that Judas was absent on the nefarious business of bargaining away His life. He saw distinctly, what He had been telling His disciples now for some time, that the end of all must be the Roman gibbet, the Cross. Yet now, in this dark hour, after singing the great Hallel, when His voice had joined the voices of His disciples in the words, " Bind the sacrifice with cords, even unto . . . the altar," His reference to His coming death declared that He was going, not to the buffeting of humanity's malice, but to the stroke of God upon His soul, the stroke of Jehovah. As one of the quaintest of old hymn writers expressed it:

" Many hands were raised to wound Him,
    None would interpose to save;
  But the awful stroke that found Him,
    Was the stroke that Justice gave."

However great and profound the mystery, that is what our Lord said as He approached the darkness of Gethsemane. "All ye shall be offended." Why? " For it is written, I will smite the Shepherd." Where is that written? In the ancient prophecy. What is the context? "Awake, O sword, against My Shepherd, and against the Man that is My Fellow, saith Jehovah of hosts." We are thus admitted to the inner consciousness of the Lord, and see Him going, not as a Victim, mastered by human brutality and malice; but as One, walking along the pathway where the severest mystery of pain would be the smiting of the Shepherd, by Jehovah Himself.

Yet, as we thus return to ancient prophecy for the interpretation of our Lord's teaching, we must include an-

other thing. Hear again this word of Zechariah. "The
Man that is My Fellow." Our Lord then was taking His
way toward a smiting which was to be endured in fellowship with Jehovah. Here we are at once reminded of the
fact that according to His own thinking, He was not
proceeding to an hour in which He would come into conflict with God. He was not proceeding to some mystery
of pain whereby He would persuade God to some new
attitude of mind and heart and will toward humanity.
He was proceeding to an hour in which there would be a
strange smiting and mystery of pain, all of which would
be in fellowship with God, and would be the outcome of
the effect of God's unchanged and unaltering attitude of
love and compassion toward men. "It is written, I will
smite the Shepherd, and the sheep shall be scattered.
Howbeit." Here immediately our Lord did that which
He never failed to do; He linked the mystery of His
passion with the mystery of the power which should immediately result therefrom; He illuminated all the darkness of the coming Cross, by the radiant light of the assured resurrection. There is not one single occasion
when our Lord made a reference to His coming Cross,
but that He linked with it a reference to His coming
resurrection. Although He faced this strange and dark
mystery of pain, outside which we must ever stand in
worship and wonder, even though He had to say that He
was going to a smiting which should issue for the moment
in the scattering of the sheep; yet He immediately said:
"Howbeit, after I am raised up I will go before you into
Galilee." The smiting was to be the way toward an appointment and a crowning and a victory. The smiting
and the dark hour would be the prelude to, and the
preparation for, a new gathering, in which He would go
before them, and lead.

If indeed therefore it be true that at this moment we
are admitted to the inner secret of the mind of Christ, we
see Him resolutely facing the smiting, understanding that

it was a smiting of Jehovah; and yet seeing clearly that
by that way He would pass out to a larger ministry, to
the ultimate victory upon which His heart was ever set.
The most reverent thing we may do is to think of Gethsemane almost in silence, for it was there in that garden
that the stroke fell upon Him; it was there that the
Shepherd was smitten.

Observe Him reverently, leaving eight of the disciples
at the entrance to the garden; taking three of them a little
further with Him; and then leaving the three, and going
into absolute loneliness. Let us observe two things; His
communion with His Father; and His coöperation with
Him.

This story of Gethsemane is one of perfect communion.
Much has been said of it in criticism by unbelievers, and
sometimes by believers themselves. It has been averred
by unbelievers, brilliant with the brilliance of mere human
intellect, in speaking of this hour, that our Lord here
shrank from suffering in a way in which many martyrs
have not done.

Is it not rather a picture of perfect communion? Is there
any evidence of perfect communion between a soul and
God so great, as the fact that the soul says everything to
God, of its own shrinking, of its own pain, of its own
agony; providing always, that the speech is united with
the saying of the one thing that is supreme: Father, Thy
will, not mine be done? There is a simple hymn that we
sometimes sing.

" I tell Him all my doubts and griefs and fears."

That is perfect communion. If there is one thing God
hates, it is to hear a song about resignation, when the
heart is hot and rebellious. In such hours, He would far
rather hear about our doubts and our fears. Here the
supreme picture is that of the Son of man telling God of
the shrinking of His own soul, and of His acquiescence in

the Divine Will. "Father . . . remove this cup from Me: howbeit not what I will, but what Thou wilt." That is communion with God!

There was coöperation with God in that very surrender of the will. This is not the picture of a vacillating soul, but that of the soul of the Shepherd, yielded to God, knowing the pain that lay ahead, the mystery, and the darkness; feeling the weight of the stroke as it fell upon Him; resolutely declaring the sense of shrinking; and yet pressing closer, into fellowship with God, and coöperation with Him.

Personally I can go no nearer. The light is

". . . Too bright,
For the feebleness of a sinner's sight."

It is dark with the darkness of essential light, upon which my eyes cannot gaze. But this I know, according to His own account thereof; in that moment the sword awoke against the Shepherd, and against the Man Who was the Fellow of God.

So we turn from a most incomplete, and yet I trust a reverent glance at the mystery of the smiting of the Shepherd, to look at this scattering of the sheep.

The first evidence of the scattering came when our Lord pointed out the false security which they felt. Peter said, If I must die with Thee, I will not deny Thee; and he meant it; he was perfectly sincere. He never said a finer thing in all his discipleship. When Jesus said to him: Before daybreak thou shalt deny Me thrice; he vehemently denied. When we are inclined to criticize him, and be angry with him, let us never forget that Jesus was not angry, and that no rebuke came from Him. Then bear in mind that these men all said the same thing. We have here, then, personal devotion to Jesus, and confidence in the power of their own will to carry out their devotion to the end. False security was the first evidence of their coming scattering.

The second evidence is found in the Garden itself, when they fell asleep while Jesus prayed. The physical failure resulted from mental dulness, and spiritual weakness. Said the Lord to them, " The spirit is willing," but He did not say strong. Turn from all the more hallowed and sacred surroundings of this story, and think of it purely upon the human level; then it will immediately be seen that if these men could sleep upon such an occasion, it was due to the fact that they had no adequate conception of that through which their Lord was passing. Their mental dulness was due to spiritual weakness. A woman will watch, not one hour, or one night, but day after day, and night after night; never shutting her eyes, in the presence of some peril threatening her child, tossed with fever; or her loved one in the place of danger. Yet these men here slept! I do not blame them. I do not think that they could help their mental dulness; I do not think they were responsible for their spiritual weakness; but the fact is patent. That was the second evidence of a coming scattering.

There was a third evidence that flamed out after they had been awakened, having its first manifestation in Peter. His was zeal without knowledge. He made use of the sword in that hour, as our Lord distinctly said, because he did not know the Scripture, and therefore had no true understanding of what his Lord was actually doing. In the moment when Peter used that sword which was intended to be a sign of his own constancy, and an expression of courage; it was really the last proof of his fear. He had not entered into that spiritual realm that is unconquerable, in which his Lord was now abiding, in the full strength of His Messianic and saving work; and he was therefore filled with fear.

Then came at last the flight: " They all left Him, and fled." If in thinking of the story we are tempted to imagine that Peter led the flight; let us look again more carefully, and we shall find that he was one of the few who did not go altogether. He did follow afar off. That flight of the disciples was inevitable. It was not blameworthy. There was no sin in it, there was no wrong in it. They could not help it, and our Lord knew that, and had told them so; you will all be scandalized in Me. The only mistake they made, if they made a mistake at all, was that they did not trust His judgment and knowledge of them. It is always easier to bear the Cross when the resurrection light falls upon it. If there were nothing in this Christianity other than the Cross, then men would flee it to the end. There came a day a little later on, when Peter was writing a letter, and he said this: " God . . . begat us again unto a living hope by the resurrection of Jesus Christ from the dead." A living hope! There was no hope in their hearts on that night. It was the darkest hour that ever came to human souls, the hour in which Jesus was arrested to be crucified. It was inevitable that these men should go. The human heart, the human intellect, cannot understand the Cross until it is seen in the transfigured light of the resurrection.

Again let us look at the Shepherd Who was smitten, and the sheep who were scattered. There is nothing more beautiful in the study than to observe His method with them.

Notice first, how He prepared them. He did not expect their fellowship in that garden. He told them so. It was not a telling, born of a sense of superiority, but of an infinite compassion, and a perfect knowledge of their capacity. He prepared them. What a strange thing to prepare men for running away, to prepare men for denial! Not strange at all, if we know Him. He told them, so that presently, when the inevitable thing took place, they should remember that He had told them. In that hour, coupled with His foretelling of failure, He uttered the prophecy of coming victory. To know all the beauty of this story, read John's account. Begin in the thirteenth chapter. It is the same story of these events in the upper room. Peter said, "Lord, whither goest Thou?" Jesus replied, "Whither I go, thou canst not follow Me now; but thou shalt follow afterwards." Peter said, "Why cannot I follow Thee even now? I will lay down my life for Thee." Said Jesus, "Wilt thou lay down thy life for Me? Verily, verily I say unto thee, the cock shall not crow, till thou hast denied Me thrice. Let not your heart be troubled; ye believe in God, believe also in Me." You ask Me where I am going. "I go to prepare a place for you. And if I go . . . I come again, and will receive you unto Myself"; in spite of the feebleness that lurks within you, the weakness that will make you deny Me. So the story runs on; the Shepherd with the sheep, preparing them, and linking His declaration of their failure with indications of His power; so that presently, in the depth of the agony of failure, they should have something to which they could hold, and be brought back.

> "Was there ever kindest Shepherd,
> Half so gentle, half so sweet?"

All this shines out yet again and again in ever increasing beauty as we observe His patience with them. Listen to the gentle reminder to Peter when He found him asleep. "Couldest thou not watch one hour?" That was no rebuke, but a reminder, a reminder of the fact that He had told him so, and that he had vehemently protested against the accuracy of his Lord. "Couldest thou not watch?"

Mark the generous recognition of our Lord in that hour. "The spirit indeed is willing, but the flesh is weak." Then consider one of the most beautiful things of all: "And He cometh the third time, and saith unto them, Sleep on now, and take your rest: it is enough; the hour is come; behold, the Son of man is betrayed into the hands of sinners. Arise, let us be going: behold, he that betrayeth Me is at hand."

If it be read so, what an infinite muddle it is. What

difficulties expositors have been put to with this passage. They have said that the Lord came to the disciples the last time, and said satirically, Sleep on! Nothing of the kind! He told them to " Sleep on now "; and they slept; and He watched them while they slept. Between the permission to sleep and the awaking, how long passed we do not know; but certainly some period. He said, " Sleep on now, and take your rest: it is enough." He meant, The hour is not come. Judas is not here yet! Sleep on now and get a rest. Then there was a waiting time. Presently He said: " The hour is come; Behold, the Son of man is betrayed into the hands of sinners. Arise, let us be going." Between the permission to rest, and the awaking, there was something which if I were an artist, I would try to paint. They could not watch with Him. They were too sleepy. Ah! well, He said in effect: Go and have your sleep out; I can watch; and He watched them while they slept. The smitten Shepherd, the Cross ahead; and yet so patient with the men who could not watch with Him that He let them take their sleep, and watched them! In the face of the Son of God, there was all anguish as He bent in prayer; and the infinite tenderness of motherhood at its best as He watched them. There is nothing more beautiful in all the dark hours than to see Him in Gethsemane watching, while those three were asleep. Then they left Him, but He did not leave them. So they were never parted from Him. " No one is able to snatch them out of the Father's hand," said He.

The great value of this meditation to us is its revelation of the good Shepherd.

Oh! Shepherd true, I may be weak, I shall deny Thee! But let me follow. He will bring me through; for He is the good Shepherd, the great Shepherd, the chief Shepherd.

XXVII

"And they led Jesus away. . . ."—MARK 14:53a.

Mark 14:53-72.

IN our previous meditation we heard the last cadences of the Hallel sung by the Lord and His disciples; and then passed out with them to the silence of Olivet. We heard His prediction of their imminent scattering; and listened to their vehement protests. Reverently we followed Him into the garden of Gethsemane, leaving eight disciples at the entrance; and three further on, but still far removed from the place of His loneliness. We saw Him in communion and coöperation with His Father, in an experience of unfathomable mystery. We watched as Judas came, and the Son of man was arrested. We saw the flight of the eleven, and of the unnamed young man. Throughout that consideration we were impressed with the grace and glory of the Shepherd.

We are now to consider the last events of that dark betrayal night. The paragraph pulsates with pain, and throbs with fever and unrest.

We see first, the swift gathering together of an illegal assembly. The high priest, the chief priests, the elders, the rulers, and, as a subsequent verse says, the whole council assembled. In other words, the Sanhedrim came together. This was an illegal assembly. The law declared that the Sanhedrim must not meet at night under any circumstances.

The law, moreover, provided that whenever the Sanhedrim met for the purpose of trying a prisoner, they should never pass sentence on the day of trial, but defer it. In spite of this they at once came to a decision that He was worthy of death.

They were evidently ready, waiting, and expecting His coming. They had entered into unholy compact with one of His own disciples to betray Him unto them. They knew full well that Judas had gone with an armed mob to arrest Him. Therefore when He was arrested, they swiftly gathered together in the darkness of the night, in the house of the high priest.

We hear the indistinct, and yet noisy clamour of the witnesses. We do not know whether these witnesses were heard singly, or whether they were all present at the same time. If singly, then the story told by one was contradicted by the next. The picture is more likely one of an irregular session of the court, in which witnesses listened to each other, contradicted each other, and quarrelled.

There was a solemn interval of tense silence in which the high priest addressed himself immediately to the Prisoner, and, according to Matthew's record, put Him on oath. Mark simply says that he asked Him: "Art Thou the Christ, the Son of the Blessed?" Matthew gives us the form of his asking: "I adjure Thee by the living God, that Thou tell us whether Thou art the Christ, the Son of God." This was the legal form of administering the oath. Jesus answered; affirming solemnly on oath, that He was the Messiah, and the Son of the Blessed.

Then immediately followed a scene of confusion. The high priest in his wrath again committed an illegal act, in the rending of his garments. A reference to the Levitical law will show that the high priest was explicitly charged under no circumstances of emotion to adopt the heathen practice of the rending of clothes. This act of the High Priest was followed by an outbreak of brutal passion on the part of the members of the Sanhedrim. They spit upon Him, and flung a garment over His face, the symbol of the death penalty; they struck Him, through the garment, and said, "Prophesy . . . who is he that struck

[305]

Thee?" "And the officers received Him with blows of their hands."

In the meantime, in the court beneath, perchance in the outer court, some few steps down from where these events were transpiring, there was taking place the busy gossip of the officers; the soldiers, and the serving maids; and there, in the midst of them, was Peter, warming himself by the fire. There follows the account of his perturbation, of his profanity, and of his denial.

Through all the story, so full of restlessness, fever, and pain, there is one element of strength. It is centralized and glorious in the Prisoner, Jesus. Strength was manifested first in His august and dignified silence; and then in His profound and pregnant speech.

Thus, as we consider the whole paragraph, we feel how full it is of the essential things of human life. Emotion is here, acute and intense; volition is here, fixed and determined. The supreme note, however, is neither emotional, nor volitional; it is intellectual. The question suggested by the paragraph is a question that concerns the inspirations of conduct; the story unveils the reasons of those conceptions of the mind, which express themselves in actual deeds. The matter of vital interest here is that of viewpoint, conception, outlook. As we look into the inner life of the personalities that pass rapidly before us, while we are conscious of the intensity of emotion, and of the fixity of volition, the most arresting element is that of the revelation of the secret motives and conceptions which produced these effects.

As from that standpoint we look at the paragraph, and at the things that it records, we are inclined at first to say in very deed: "Truth is fallen in the street." Here the intellect of the age is seen utterly at fault. To quote the words of Paul, written long afterwards to the Corinthian Christians, here the rulers of this world lacked wisdom: "Which none of the rulers of this world hath known: for had they known it, they would not have cru-

cified the Lord of glory." Here also we see light and
love, overshadowed and eclipsed, in the person of the
cursing disciple.

The first impression that the paragraph makes is that
of truth wounded, beaten down, trampled under foot,
violated. Yet we look again, and discover that Truth
was never more erect. Behold It first; silent, declining
speech, refusing a word, and most eloquent in Its silence.
Then hear It, speaking at last; in terms so simple and so
definite that there can be no misunderstanding of Its
meaning; so, speaking that every lie falls back into
shadow, and men are compelled at last to do in the clear
daylight, the nefarious deeds they had been trying to per-
form in the darkness.

From that standpoint of intellect or wisdom, looking at
these scenes, we have a revelation first, of debased intelligence in the case of the rulers; secondly, of insulted
and wounded intelligence in the case of Peter; thirdly,
of victorious and triumphant intelligence, in the case of
the Lord Himself.

The fundamental wrong, so far as the rulers were concerned was that the whole case was prejudged. That is
perfectly patent. " The chief priests and the whole council sought witness against Jesus,"—by no means to discover the truth concerning Him—but "to put Him to
death." The revelation of some intellectual obscurity or
wickedness is obvious. They were gathered together os-
tensibly for the purpose of investigation; but really they
were mastered by one determination; the death of the
Man Who was arraigned before them. The inevitable
issue of such a gathering would be that of ignorance.
Light could not penetrate their minds. They were pre-
determined to encompass, at all costs, the destruction of
the Prisoner at the bar. Ignorance must be the result of
that attitude of mind. There was no room for light.
What was said by one and another was contorted,
twisted, to the one purpose of putting Him to death.

[307]

Let us watch the proceedings, for they reveal some
striking facts. These men, mastered by this unholy passion, set upon realizing and encompassing the death of
this Prisoner at the bar, were nevertheless compelled to
a recognition of the rights of truth. Else why should
they look for witnesses at all? Why not dispense with a
trial, and at once lay violent hands upon Him? No, that
even they dare not do. They must seek some accusation
which will appear to be true. They must find witnesses;
they must have some reason for the thing they do. This
was the unconscious compliment which devilish falsehood paid to the ascendancy of truth.

True, there was a ghastly readiness to compromise, to
accept as true the basest falsehood, if only it might be
made to serve their purpose of having an appearance of
truth. Oh! it was an unholy business; it is a terrible
picture. Yet it is a wonderful illustration of that marvellous and inherent consciousness of right and wrong,
from which humanity never has, and never can escape.
Whenever humanity forgets to make its bow to truth,
then humanity is entirely and absolutely hopeless.

Only one witness borne against Him has been preserved for us. We do not know what the other witness
said. Doubtless the one witness preserved for us is an
illustration of their whole attitude of mind. "And there
stood up certain, and bare false witness against Him,
saying, We heard Him say, I will destroy this temple that
is made with hands, and in three days I will build another
made without hands." This is the most diabolical form
of untruth, because it is an untruth in which there is an
element of truth. We remember Tennyson's words:

" A lie that is all a lie, may be met with and fought out-
        right;
  But a lie that is partly the truth, is a harder matter to
        fight."

There is a sense in which there was not a word of truth

in this statement. There is a sense, however, in which it
was based upon something actually true. Notice in passing, how His words were treasured, not only by those
who loved Him, but by those who hated Him. He had
in the early days of His ministry, when first He cleansed
the temple, said to the men who asked Him by what
authority He proceeded: "Destroy this temple, and in
three days I will raise it up." It was a mysterious saying,
not understood by those who heard Him; not understood
until after His resurrection even by His own disciples.
It was so little understood by the men who heard Him,
that they laughed at Him, and said: " Forty and six years
was this temple in building, and wilt Thou raise it up in
three days? " Now even if, as they supposed, He had
referred to the temple in Jerusalem, notice what He said:
" Destroy this temple." There was no suggestion in His
word, that He would destroy it. He was speaking of
what they would do, not of what He would do. Over
against their destructive capacities, He placed His con-
structive ability, " In three days I will raise it up." The
reference, as we now know, was to the temple of His
body. They did not know that. But on the ground of
their own understanding, mark their remembrance of His
words after three years have passed; and observe their
distortion of them.

Mark twice records the fact that these witnesses failed,
and for one reason. Their witness did not agree. There
is no harmony in falsehood. A lie must always be covered by a lie.

> " Ah! what a tangled web we weave,
>   When first we practise to deceive."

The men who had been observant of Jesus during the
days of His public ministry—not His disciples, but His
watchers—had heard His words, and seen His works,
and perfectly understood His claim. That is made evident by the form of the high priest's question: "Art Thou

the Christ, the Son of the Blessed?" Why ask that question if they did not understand His claim? Nevertheless, in spite of every word spoken, and every work wrought, they were set upon His murder. Whatever intellectual conviction they might have had concerning the beauty of His words, or the beneficence of His works, such conviction must be debased and refused. Yet, in that ghastly attitude of mind, they made a false appeal to truth; and then with a lie sought to slay the Lord of truth.

Let us take next that which is last in the story, the picture of Peter. We see in Peter a man whose intelligence had been singularly illuminated, and a man who had wonderfully responded to the illumination of his intelligence. What brought Peter to that outer Court? It was the light in his own soul that took him there; and that light was shining with a great brightness. He knew his Master. He knew the insight of his Lord. That had been his first revelation of Jesus when at the first his brother Andrew had brought him face to face with Christ, and Christ had said, "Thou art Simon, the son of John: Thou shalt be called Rock." In that moment Peter had discovered in Jesus One Who knew his deepest nature; and ever after He had been patient with him, and had realized the latent capacities of his soul. Peter had not forgotten these things. He knew how for three years the Master had with infinite tenderness borne with him, led him, instructed him, and brought him nearer and yet ever nearer to Himself in love and adoration. Love and adoration in Peter, were the outcome of clear understanding.

We must not forget, nor undervalue the fact, that six months before, Peter at Cæsarea Philippi had said exactly what the high priest now asked Him. "Thou art the Christ, the Son of the Blessed." That light was still shining in the soul of Peter; and he loved his Lord with a love that was the outcome thereof. It was his love for his Lord that took him into the courts of the high priest.

Peter had followed Him afar off, yet he had followed Him! No other disciple had done this, except John; but John went at no risk, because he was related to the high priest. Peter took great risk when he went.

Neither let us forget that Peter had drawn the sword, and smitten Malchus. The impulse was a right one. Wrong things are done from a right impulse sometimes. Moses was shut out of the promised land because he did a wrong thing with a right impulse. The more clearly we see all this, the more shall we understand the sorrowful thing that took place that day. When Peter denied his Lord, he was insulting his own intelligence. Yet descending to profanity, he took his oath that he did not know Jesus at all.

Let us try to put the doings of these two places side by side. Probably the court, where Jesus stood in the midst of the priests and elders was somewhat elevated, by a few steps perhaps, from " the court beneath," as Mark says, where the officers and the maid-servants were, and Peter also. In the first false witness after false witness arose; the high priest put Jesus on oath; Jesus took the oath that the confession that Peter made several months ago was true. In the second, there was the clamour of the gossip of the officers, the saucy laugh of a servant maid, as she said to Peter, You belong to them. The great soul of Peter stumbled and fell at the laugh of that serving-maid, and presently he took an oath that he did not know Jesus; Jesus on oath, within; Peter on oath, without. Peter outside, taking his oath that he did not know Him; Jesus inside, taking His oath that what Peter had said in the better hour of his life, was true. The contrast is vivid.

Peter was lying about his faith. He did know Him; more, he wonderfully understood Him. He was also violating his own love. Here was an instance of the contradiction of sinners against themselves. He was wounding his own soul. This must be borne in mind. Peter's love for Jesus never failed; his faith in Jesus never failed. Christ had said to him, "I have prayed for thee that thy faith fail not," and his faith never failed. His hope failed, the light of hope went out; his courage failed; but never his faith, nor his love. Here then, was a man who believed in Jesus, who loved Him with a great heart, or he never had followed Him to that court; denying his faith, and the denial was a lie; denying his love, and the denial was a lie. His own intelligence was insulted; the truth that was in him, and never really destroyed, was flung in the mire.

Yet look again; and mark how that light which was the inspiration of his going to the court, though insulted when he lied, persisted; and at last mastered him. The final thing is not the denial, but the tears. The last phase of the picture is not that of a cursing, profane man; a man made into a coward by the taunt of a servant maid. The last picture is that of a man gathering his garment about him, and hurrying from the first into the darkness of the night; a strong man in tears. Another evangelist tells us that Jesus looked at him. Probably between these two courts, the higher where were the priests, and the lower where were the servants, there was only a curtain which may have been drawn aside, and from within, Jesus looked at Peter. In the course of a sermon I once heard Father Stanton say something about this very scene, which was very suggestive. Said he: "Never forget that the look of Jesus would have been wasted on Peter, if it had not been that Peter was looking at Jesus." The look of Peter toward the Lord is a revelation in itself, as surely as is the look of the Lord toward Peter.

I will not attempt to interpret that look of Jesus; but I am quite sure that it did not mean: "I told you so!" Another thing is also certain, though perhaps not quite so patent; Jesus did not by that look say to Peter, What are you doing to Me? Why are you wounding Me? Christ was too selfless to have meant that. I think He said to Peter, in His look: Peter, why are you wounding yourself? Then Peter went out and wept. Poets sometimes talk of " blinding tears." I suppose there are such, but I do not know them. I also have wept. I did not find that tears of this kind were blinding tears; they are sight-giving tears! Charles Mackay's lines are full of beauty:

" O ye tears, O ye tears! I am thankful that ye run;
    Though ye trickle in the darkness, ye shall glitter in
        the sun;
    The rainbow cannot shine if the rain refuse to fall,
    And the eyes that cannot weep, are the saddest eyes of
        all."

Peter wept; and his tears were evidences of the answer of his soul to the truth of his faith; and to the love which he had so cruelly insulted and desecrated as he denied his Lord.

Reverently in conclusion, let us look at the central picture. Here is One Who in His intelligence is victorious, though it is a dark, dark hour of apparent defeat. No debasement of intelligence is here; no insulting of intelligence. Truth declines to argue with a lie. The silence of our Lord here, and at other points during this trial, was wonderfully eloquent. The witnesses were lying. The witnesses were distorting His words. What hast Thou to say? said the high priest; and He answered him never a word. Truth is silent in the presence of a lie, because even the truth cannot contradict a lie so as to end it; and also because a lie cannot harm truth in the final issue.

But when He was challenged on oath He answered; and His answer was remarkable in the effect it produced in that court of justice. Said the high priest, "Art Thou the Christ, the Son of the Blessed?" and He said, "I am." As He said so, He swept away the refuge of lies which they were attempting to make for themselves.

Listen to the high priest, " What further need have we of witnesses?" His answer had swept that need away. The answer of Jesus compelled wickedness to act in the light. If they would slay Him, they must do so on the basis of that claim, and not for a false reason. By that one word on His part, His affirmation on oath that He was the Messiah, and the Son of the Blessed; He removed all the false witnesses, and swept away the refuge of lies. For evermore therefore, the murder of the Son of God is seen in all its ghastliness, for they rejected Him for claiming to be that which the centuries have proclaimed Him to be.

Then he added to His claim that further word: " Ye shall see the Son of man sitting at the right hand of Power, and coming with the clouds of heaven." This was a poetic declaration, borrowed from the prophet Daniel, in which prophecy the Son of man is seen coming, not to earth, but to heaven; coming to sit at the right hand of the Ancient of Days, to be the Ruler of the universe. That is what Christ told these men they should see; not His second advent, but His coming into, and sitting in the place of power.

The last note is that most of help to us. The chief glory of the light in the midst of the darkness, is that of its revelation of the deep-seated love and devotion of a disciple; and the action and grace of the Lord in giving that love and devotion their chance of recovery in spite of deflection. The very last thing in the dark betrayal night is the vision of the tears of Peter! Upon those tears the light of God's face rises; and they become radiant with rainbow glory, suggesting for evermore to hearts that believe and love, that even though in unutterable folly they deny Him, He makes a way by which His banished one may return.

XXVIII

" He saved others; Himself He cannot save."
     —MARK 15:31.

Mark 15:1–32.

THESE words were uttered by the religious rulers in
Israel, the chief priests. With them were associated the
moral rulers, the scribes. Mark distinctly tells us that
the words were spoken among themselves, but evidently
in the hearing of the assembled people. The statement
revealed the thought, at the moment, of the spiritual and
moral rulers of Israel concerning Jesus. They were
spoken, as Mark also reveals, with equal distinctness, in
mockery. They were the words of jeering contempt.

This becomes the more patent as we read the remainder
of what they said: " Let the Christ, the King of Israel,
now come down from the Cross, that we may see and
believe." Those words were saturated with the spirit of
contempt and mockery. Jesus had claimed to be the
Christ, on solemn oath before the high priest but a few
hours previously. He had claimed to be the King of
Israel, with equal solemnity before Pilate the Roman
Procurator, even more recently. Let this Christ, this
King of Israel come down from the Cross. Then mark
the last tone of satire: " That we may see and believe;"
He has always been calling us to believe, and declaring
that unless we believed we should die in our sins; let
Him now give us some proof, so that we may believe!
It was the language of jeering contempt. They were
singularly cruel and devilish words, for supposing them
to be true, in the sense in which they meant them, then
the cruelty of uttering them under such conditions is almost unthinkable and utterly appalling. Observe their

admission: "He saved others." That was a fact which even they could not deny. Everywhere, in Jerusalem, in all the towns and villages and hamlets through the countryside, were those whom He had saved. Palsied limbs were stilled with peacefulness; blind eyes were looking out with joy upon the light of day; dumb mouths were uttering forth the praises of the Lord; men long oppressed with serious disease, and women bowed down with long infirmities, were well. "He saved others." They were bound to admit the fact. There could be no contradiction. What refinement of brutality then, to taunt Him in this hour with His inability to deliver Himself! Even if they believed that His claims to Messiahship were worthless, common decency would have said, now it is over, let Him die in peace. But no! such is the human heart, in spite of all refinement, in spite of all culture. So they taunted Him in His dying, "He saved others; Himself He cannot save."

These words of the spiritual and moral rulers were singularly revealing, drawing attention to the then condition of Jesus, making us look at Him and think. They were singularly revealing also, in manifesting the ignorance of the men who uttered them. But these words, uttered in the ignorance both of contempt and hatred, were most of all remarkable in that in the uttering of them they declared, all unwittingly, the supreme and central truth concerning Him: "He saved others; Himself He cannot save."

Let us then, first look at Him as they saw Him; secondly, consider their double mistake; and finally, think of the issue of that upon which they looked, but did not understand.

In the first place we will attempt to see Him as He was seen of men that day. Two ugly words cover the whole story. They saw Him, *condemned* and *executed.* We are not dwelling in these meditations upon details. I am growingly impressed, that the only way to come to

these stories of Christ is with the self-same reticent reverence which characterized the men who wrote the story.
We have no detailed description of the actual crucifixion
in either Gospel. When these writers came to the actuality, they ever dismissed it, as it seems to me, in an almost half-whisper: "They crucified Him." I wish Art
had been as reticent, in all the centuries, and that we
had no pictures of Jesus on the Cross. I say we are not
dealing with details, but we must not forget this dark
background; He was condemned, executed; high lifted
upon the Roman gibbet; apparently one of three male-
factors, doers of evil. That is how they saw Him; condemned, found guilty by the highest religious court, of
blasphemy against God Almighty; rejected for Barabbas,
Barabbas being chosen by the priest-inspired crowd, fickle
and unstable as a crowd always is;—God pity the man
who depends upon a crowd; finally they saw Him delivered, as expedient, by political authority, that of Pon-
tius Pilate.

After He had raised Lazarus from the dead, a council
was held among these self-same chief priests and rulers,
and the subject of discussion at the council was this:
What are we doing? Everybody is going after this Man,
and unless we stop His influence, we shall—to quote the
spirit of the passage—lose our power and place with the
Roman authorities. It was then and there that Caiaphas
the high priest had said: "It is expedient for you that
one should die for the people, and that the whole nation
perish not." John interpreted the deeper meaning of
that, for he added, "This he said not of himself;" but
what Caiaphas meant was this: We must get rid of Him,
it is politically necessary to get rid of Him. That was
the ground of their appeal to Pilate, and the ground upon
which Pilate delivered Him. His condemnation was considered expedient in the interest of political necessity.

Thus we see Him upon the Cross, crucified with male-
factors; as a danger to the Roman rule, as having exer-

cised an evil influence among the people of His time, as
being the enemy of God. Therefore we look upon Him
with the eyes of these men, as done for, and done with.
The body is destroyed, the spirit is dismissed, and the
world is rid of Him. The body is destroyed; those feet
that have travelled long, long miles for three persistent
years; and those hands that have been held out in blessing, and have touched men from disease into health, from
death into life, from suffering into joy; they are fast at
last; they have nailed them to the gibbet. Those ears that
have always been open to listen to a story of sorrow, those
eyes that have flashed with the light of essential emotion
and tenderness and strength; the ears are deafening as
He hangs there, and the light of the eyes is fading. That
voice that has so often been heard, is soon to be silenced.
They have destroyed the body and they have dismissed
the spirit. The Sadducees probably denied that He had
a spirit; the Pharisees claiming that He had, now saw it
passing into Hades, the world of departed spirits. At
least they would be rid of Him. It was then that they
said, " He saved others; Himself He cannot save."

Now let us observe their double mistake; first their
literal blunder; and secondly, their spiritual blunder.

As to their literal blunder, let us for the moment forget
all that we know spiritually of the significance of these
words of our text. It is a little difficult to get away from
the ultimate spiritual interpretation, even at the beginning
of our meditation. They said, " He saved others," a
great admission—" Himself He cannot save," a strong
declaration. They were wrong, and first they were entirely wrong, even in the sense in which they meant the
thing they said. Jesus, during those four and twenty
hours, could easily have saved Himself. His being upon
the Cross was not the result of their victory over Him.
They had not caught Him, trapped Him, shut Him up,
imprisoned Him, crucified Him, and so beaten Him.
His being on the Cross was not their victory. All that

is not the deepest truth. Jesus could have escaped the Cross in three ways. He could have escaped the Cross by diplomacy with Pilate. Pilate earnestly sought some loophole of escape, wrought with strange and weird persistence to discover some way by which he could deliver Him; and a word from Jesus would have been enough. Some word of diplomacy, of policy, of arrangement; and all the priests would have been powerless to persuade Pilate to the thing he ultimately did. It was the silence, the heroic silence of Jesus that compelled Pilate to do what he finally did. If for the moment that is not convincing, then hear the words of Jesus spoken to Pilate as recorded by another evangelist: " Thou wouldest have no power against Me, except it were given thee from above." He could have escaped.

But there was another way in which He might have escaped, and in proportion as we really get into the atmosphere of this wonderful scene we shall realize it. He could have escaped by popular appeal. The cry of the crowd, presently hissed between shut teeth, " Crucify, crucify!" was but a parrot cry. They were only repeating what they had been told to say. The high priests persuaded them to it. If one catches a mob anywhere at the psychic moment, it will shout anything under God's heaven! Individually, that mob may go home to repent of what it shouted, but under the influence of excitement they will do it. The crowd was driven by the high priests because they appealed to it first. Supposing Jesus had reached them first with an appeal! The attempt of the rulers to avoid the feast time as the hour of His arrest, was based on their knowledge that this was so. They said: " Not during the feast, lest a tumult arise among the people." They knew perfectly well that He had but to stand erect for one moment, and say something to that crowd, and the whole mob would have swept the priests out of the way, and delivered Him. But He did not do it. He did not save Himself.

I cannot consider this matter without going further; for He is not wholly a man as I am. If not by diplomacy with Pilate, if not by popular appeal, then He could have escaped by Divine wrath and destruction of His enemies. Listen to Him as He said, but a little while before to one of His own disciples: " Thinkest thou that I cannot beseech My Father, and He shall even now send Me more than twelve legions of angels?" Knowing full well the danger, or at least the inadequacy of imagination, yet as I look upon that scene, being no Sadducee, believing as I do in angels as well as spirits, it seems as though the very hosts of heaven could hardly be restrained from delivering Him. One glance of His eye, one word of power, and Pilate and priests and mob would have been swept away. He could have delivered Himself. That was their literal blunder.

Involved within it, is that which is the deeper thing; their spiritual blunder. He could not save Himself! But His inability was born of His ability; His weakness was the outcome of His strength. He was strong enough not to save Himself, strong enough to decline diplomacy with the Procurator, strong enough to be silent when one word would have turned the mob into an army of His friends, strong enough to restrain His own omnipotence, and to bow, bend, stoop, submit. He could not save Himself.

Whence came that strength which manifested itself in weakness? What were the secrets of that ability which had its most eloquent expression in disability? I shall attempt to answer the question, by putting the actual facts concerning the Lord Jesus, in contrast with the ways already suggested, that were open to Him for escape.

Instead of employing diplomacy, we see Him coöperating with God; that is, acting in conformity with truth, moving along the line of the essential and the eternal; setting His face resolutely, in spite of all that such setting of His face involved, in the direction of holiness and light. Here we pass into the mists. Here we come into the presence of the mystery. Yet, through the mists, out of which the light breaks; and the mystery, through the darkness of which the revelation has proceeded, He was striving against sin, and He was resisting unto blood! Because that was the Divine pathway—why it was, is not now under discussion,—because in the Divine economy He could only slay death by dying, only end sin by being made sin in an appalling mystery, He would have no conference with any suggestion of escape from that pathway. In that coöperation with God, in conformity to the underlying and essential truth, however dark the way and mysterious the hour, He was strong enough to be weak enough to die.

Or again; the second method of escape that was certainly open to Him on the natural level was that He might have escaped by popular appeal. He did not, because He was acting in separation from man—that is by separation from sinners, uninfluenced by their advice, by their votings, by their clamour—and with God for their sakes. Perhaps we can understand this better if we allow our minds to travel away from the scene for a moment, and remember that ever and anon in human history, as those have appeared who have trod this self-same pathway—not in the same degree, but obedient to the self-same principle—over and over again the men who have fashioned the ages, and have made the conditions which have been brighter and better and purer for the world, have had to stand alone, separating themselves from humanity in the interest of humanity, travelling up new Calvaries, Calvaries for which they gathered inspiration here. So He withdrew from the crowd, He did not ask its aid. He made no appeal to them; and that for their sakes. In the interest of their condition, and in order that presently He might win from them a truer judgment, a more righteous vote, a sanctified assent, He asked nothing of them. He trod the winepress alone, separate in His heroism from humanity, for the sake of humanity.

Or again, if we really seek for the secret of His strength, it is to be found finally, fundamentally, and inclusively in that He, Who might that day have escaped the Cross by an act of Divine destruction inspired by Divine wrath, accepted the Cross in order to an act of salvation inspired by Divine love. He was still acting under the mastery of the will of His God; here also, as surely as when He declined diplomacy, and stood alone for truth, He was moving along the line of the essential and the eternal; here, He was not in conflict with God, but in coöperation with Him. He could not save Himself, because He was one with God in a double determination; the determination to smite and blast and destroy sin; and the determination to heal and lift and ennoble a sinning race. Not these things held Him; the court, and the brutality of His enemies; but His o'ermastering, and o'erwhelming love. He could not save Himself. Therefore He *can* save others.

So, finally, let us glance at the issue of what they did not understand. Yet the whole truth of that was expressed in what they themselves did say. What is the issue of that attitude of Jesus? He saved others. Perhaps it would be better to change their statement a little, not to interfere with its essential thought, but to change merely the tenses of its verbs; so that from beneath the mistake, the essential truth which they knew not may emerge. They said, "He *saved* others," and the tense was past. They were looking back. "Himself He *cannot* save," and the tense was present. They were looking at Him on the Cross. We look back at this scene, and say: Himself He *could not* save. We look around to-day, and say: He *saves* others. Though they did not understand it—even the disciples themselves did not understand, but presently light came, and ever and anon these men who wrote the records reveal in some passing phrase their past ignorance and their new illumination—the truth is this, that all those whom He had already saved, He had saved in the power of the fact that He could not, in that final way, save Himself. He had opened blind eyes, He had healed palsied limbs, He had driven fever away, He had restored physical conditions; but He always did these things upon the basis of His passion and His atonement. The writers came to know it, I repeat, and one memorable passage comes to mind, in which Matthew tells the secret of a wonderful eventide by the side of the sea. They brought unto Him from all the countryside the sick folk, and He healed them all. If Matthew had written his record that night, he would have written with wonder and amazement; but later on the publican saw things as he had never seen them; and in the light of the resurrection, when he wrote his record afterwards, this is what he said: He healed them all, " that it might be fulfilled which was spoken through Isaiah the prophet, saying, Himself took our infirmities, and bare our diseases." Behind all His physical healing, was the spiritual passion of the Lord. I reverently declare that the Man of Nazareth would never have healed a sick lad or lass, man or woman, but in the power of that hour, when they mocked Him and scorned Him.

Turning from that past, to which they looked, and considering that future toward which He was looking when He could not save Himself because He would not save Himself, let us ask what is the issue of that great fact. We will confine ourselves to the atmosphere of this very story in considering this matter; measuring the strength by the weakness; going again to the threefold door of escape that was open to Him in the natural, and considering the threefold issue in the supernatural. He might have escaped by diplomacy. He was bound by the simplicity of truth. He might have escaped by popular appeal. He was bound by a separation from popular acclaim in order to the redemption of the populace. He might have escaped by the exercise of His Divine power in wrath. He was bound by the consideration of a Divine love and mercy.

Now what has the issue been? He established authority on the basis of truth, rather than on the shifting sand of diplomacy. Jesus Christ is not ruling over men by diplomacy, by compromise. Perhaps one of the most terrific things, one of the most frightening things, and one of the most blessed things concerning Him is that He will not make a compromise with men, that He will enter into no diplomatic relationship with them by which, if they grant Him so much, He will grant them so much, He will not meet men half-way. There is no diplomacy in the government of Jesus. The day will dawn, which is not yet, but which must be, when delegated authority;—and all authority is delegated to the Christian; in his understanding of the universe, and his philosophy of the world, the final authority is God, and the powers that be are all ordained by God for beneficent purposes;—shall be based, not upon diplomacy but upon truth. I do not say that all diplomacy must be untrue, but it is in terrible danger of being untrue. I will go so far as to say that when in this country we have done with a good deal of our diplomacy, and the whole truth of foreign conditions is before the people, we shall do better than we have done; when we have simple, clear statements of the facts of the case, and not half-veiled lies that deceive. That day is coming. We are moving toward it slowly, through catastrophe and cataclysm and blood and fire and vapour of smoke; and all the way He leads, the Man Who can save others, because He would not save Himself.

Consequently, therefore, by His action He prepared for a popular vote which shall be inspired by wisdom and by love. He prepared for a people ransomed, and a people emancipated, who presently will bow to the authority of His truth, and acclaim Him Lord. To-day we may hold almost in contempt the opinion of the crowd. How

soon a man is forgotten. Let him drop out, and who
thinks or cares for him? Let a prophet be gone, and
within a decade there will be a letter in the newspaper,
drawing attention to the fact that his grave is neglected!
If a man is going to depend upon the opinion of a crowd,
God pity that man. Nevertheless, the day is coming when
all peoples and kindreds and nations and tongues and
temperaments will forget their differences, and merge in
one great song, and it will be the song that proclaims Im-
manuel, King of kings, and Lord of lords. But that day
would never have been reached but by His pathway of
loneliness.

Finally, therefore, He made possible the saving of those
very men who otherwise would have been destroyed.
What men? Those very men locally, for the universal
will best be seen here in the light of the local. The men
who were round His Cross, the soldiers who crucified
Him, the mob that clamoured against Him; the priests,
those very men could be saved because He did not save
Himself. There is a little statement of history, in the
Acts of the Apostles, full of interest: "And the word of
God increased, and the number of the disciples multiplied in Jerusalem exceedingly; and a great company of
the priests were obedient to the faith." These very men
that mocked Him, that jeered at Him, He made possible
their saving! In that is the greatness of His victory.

This, blessed be God, is the Gospel. He saves others;
Himself He could not save. Or once again, to change the
reading: To save others, He did not save Himself. He
could not save Himself, because He was determined to
save others.

If we name His name, if we wear His sign, if we
profess that we are Christ's men and Christ's women,
then we have to remember that this is not the Gospel
only; it is the law. It is the abiding principle of the
propagation of the Gospel, and must be to the end of
stress and strain and conflict. Every Christian worker

of whom it is true that he or she is saving others, cannot save himself or herself. Or again to change the method of the statement; the measure in which we are at the end of attempting to save ourselves, is the measure in which we are moving out upon the highway of being able to save others. That is true in statesmanship. That is true in all the ministry of men to the needs created by the tragedy of life. It is true of the Sunday School class; and it is true of the pulpit.

It is true of statesmanship. If statesmen are attempting to save themselves and their country, they will fail. If statesmen are seeking the larger good, and are moving along the line of giving themselves out in sacrifice in order to reach the larger goal, they will save others.

In the case of those who minister to human need, doctors and nurses, I need not argue it. It is always true of such that they are not counting their own lives dear unto them, that they may make this sacred service of ministry and sacrifice.

It is true of the Sunday School class. It is true of the pulpit. We can make no contribution toward the victory of spiritual truth save at the point of sacrifice. A young minister fresh from college, said to W. L. Watkinson, that master of satire, upon one occasion, "You know, Dr. Watkinson, preaching does not take anything out of me." "No," said Dr. Watkinson, "and therefore, it puts nothing into anyone else!" That is true, Biblically true. If we are to save others, we cannot save ourselves. The only question that we have to face is this: Are we strong enough to be weak, mighty enough to submit, able for the gracious disability out of which the forces that renew, spring for the blessing of humanity?

XXIX

"A stone against the door of the tomb."—MARK 15 : 46.

Mark 15 : 33–47.

THERE is a note of brooding melancholy about these
words. They revive some of our own most despairing
experiences. The open grave, the mortal remains laid
therein, the closing of the grave, the going back to face
the days ahead without the comradeship of the loved
one; these are the things that come crowding back upon
us as we read these words, " a stone against the door of
the tomb."

As we separate the thought suggested by the words
from the sequel of the narrative, all these feelings of the
heart are accentuated a thousandfold when we think of
the One Whose body was placed within the rock-hewn
tomb of Joseph of Arimathæa. The shadows of evening
were gathering about the garden when this thing was
done. It was the close of a stupendous day. At nine
o'clock in the morning they had crucified the prophet of
Nazareth, Who, while He saved others, could not save
Himself; and for three hours the tides of human passion
had raged around Him on His Cross. At noon supernatural darkness had settled upon the scene, and at three
of the afternoon He had breathed out His Spirit. Now,
at even, two men, Joseph of Arimathæa and Nicodemus,
are seen enswathing the body, and laying it in the tomb;
while two women, Mary of Magdala and Mary the mother
of Jesus, are watching. These acts of love being completed, Joseph rolled the stone to the entrance of the already prepared tomb: "A stone against the door of the
tomb."

Here we pause. This is death's victory. The world is
without Christ. What lay buried in that grave? Our

meditation is an attempt to answer that enquiry; that we
may consider together the beauty of that which was dead,
and the ugliness of the fact of death.

First we see the death of things of beauty. " A stone
against the door of the tomb." When referring to the
beauty of that which was dead, I am thinking not so
much of the personal and sentimental, as of the universal
and essential. To the disciples at the moment, the former
things were of course the most real, and supreme; the
personal loss, the sense of loss, the sentimental consciousness. It is at this point that we feel the most acute human sympathy with them, realizing that in that scene
and those circumstances, there are elements with which
we are appallingly and tragically familiar to-day; not
with a familiarity that breeds contempt, for no man who
loves life loves death, or pretends to admire it. It is
ghastly, horrible, devilish, wherever it appears. Yet
larger things were involved in the disciples' sense than
those which were personal and sentimental; and our
thought is not so much of them in that personal and sentimental sense, as of the world, of the ages, of life in its
entirety. In that grave wherein lay the body of the dead
Jesus, life was challenged, insulted, and spit upon, as it
never had been before, and as it never has been since.
Whatever we may feel about the tragedy of death, here
it is in its most ghastly form; for here, central to human
history, is a death by the side of which none other seems
to be able to compare.

I enquire what then lay within that tomb? I propose
to answer the enquiry by referring to four things that
for those three days and nights the world had lost, and
which the world had lost for ever if this had been the
end of Jesus. The things of beauty which we have been
looking upon as we have studied this Gospel; which our
eyes have seen, and we have beheld, which we have heard
as we have caught the accents of the voice of the dead
Man, which we have spiritually touched and handled as

we have grown familiar with Him, walking the ways of men; these things of beauty have been slain, and now lie dead in that rock-hewn tomb.

In that tomb there is first a dead conception of God. There is moreover, a dead ideal of humanity. There is beyond that, a dead passion to redeem. Consequently and finally, there is a dead religion.

A dead conception of God. Not long before His Cross, when one of His enquiring disciples, Philip, had in his agony cried out amid the shadows of the upper room, "Show us the Father, and it sufficeth us," Jesus had said, "He that hath seen Me hath seen the Father." In order to be true to the line of our meditation, without arguing the truth of that declaration of Jesus, but accepting it as from Himself, we now enquire what conception of God had been presented in Him? What was His idea of God? Not the idea of His teaching, for His claim was not that men who had heard Him had discovered the truth about God; but that "He that hath *seen Me* hath seen the Father." In the uttering of that word, on the purely human level, our Lord was proclaiming a truth that is of universal application. Every man reveals his god by what he is in himself. Every man has a god, however much he may deny the existence of the God in Whom we believe, however much he may declare that he bends the knee to none in worship, and recognizes no authority over him other than that of his own will. The god of a man is that to which he yields the devotion of his life, in thought and energy. It may be gold, pleasure, fame; but seated at the centre of every human life is some master idea, passion, desire, enterprise; and that is the god of the man. Sooner or later that god will manifest itself in the man's life. There is a sense therefore, in which every man may say, He that hath seen me hath seen my god; for a man becomes like his god.

Now when Jesus said: "He that hath seen Me hath seen the Father," I am aware that there were profounder

significances in the word than this particular one, but we
may begin here. What have we seen in Him as we have
walked with Him during this time of our meditation upon
this one brief Gospel? We have seen in Him grace and
truth; mercy and justice; peace and righteousness. The
wonder of the revelation, however, does not consist so
much in these particular qualities as they have been represented in Jesus, but in the fact of their union in Him.
This union was a new revelation in man, and therefore a
new revelation of God. Man had known something of
God in the past, as to His truth, His justice, and His
righteousness; and it is equally true—and no man can
have been a diligent student of the old Hebrew prophecies
without admitting it—they had known very much of His
grace, mercy, and peace. But in Him these things were
united, without doing violence to the distinctive value of
either. The wonder and the marvel of the conception of
God that had been given to these men who surrounded
Jesus, was that in Him these things thus met. John declared, " We beheld His glory, glory as of the only begotten from the Father "—and then he described what he
meant in a phrase—" full of grace and truth." Grace,
compassion, mercy; truth, the right, devotion to the essential; and yet the two things always merged in Him;
grace and truth, mercy and justice, peace and righteousness. In the few brief years of His public ministry, His
conception of God, not in His teaching alone, but in all
that He was in Himself, had been given to a little group
of men. It was a thing of ineffable beauty, a thing of
surpassing wonder, a thing that we are compelled to admit, that after two millenniums have gone the Church
has not been able finally to express the beauty of, with all
its thinking, and all its devotion. Now that conception of
God lies dead in a grave; and the stone is rolled against
the door of the tomb.

In the second place there lay dead in that grave an
ideal of humanity. Once again to quote the words of

Jesus Himself, He had said to men, "He that followeth
Me shall not walk in the darkness, but shall have the light
of life"; His meaning being that if a man would follow
Him, that man would in Him see the light and glory of
his own being. He claimed to have fulfilled in His own
living the real meaning of the secret of the possibility of
every human life. Looking back at Jesus from the standpoint of our common humanity, what then have we seen
in Him? We have seen a Being, spiritual, but very definitely material. We have seen One Who in all His thinking and all His speaking and all His acting was perpetually conscious of the supernatural, the vastness that lies
beyond; but equally and patently conscious of all the
temporal and near, the things His hands touched, and
upon which His feet trod. We have seen One characterized by an awful dignity, even in His humanity; a
majesty so pronounced and so profound, that I make
one brief statement with which all will agree, no one ever
dared to take a liberty with Him. There was an aloofness about Jesus that held men away from Him. Yet
there was a meekness which brought all men into the
closest touch with Him; and publicans and sinners dared
to draw nigh to Him for to hear Him.

Here again, the ideal of humanity revealed in the Person of Jesus is not so much that of these separate qualities, for we have also seen men who have been spiritual;
we have come into contact with people supremely, conscious of the supernatural things; individuals who were
characterized by a dignified majesty that prevented our
taking liberties with them. On the other hand we have
found in the common crowd of people, men and women
living within the temporal; and also people who were
meek and merciful and generous. But the ideal of humanity in Jesus was the merging of these things in Him;
for to Him the sacred and the secular were not two
realms for ever to be kept apart. To Him all secular
things were sacred; all sacred things were secular. The

things of the vast eternities to Him were the things with which men were to deal every day and every hour in every circumstance, and every condition. All the little things of life were to be dealt with as related to the eternal things. With Him His majesty expressed itself in meekness. With Him His meekness was powerful in its majesty. These men had lived in close companionship for three years with a Man Who towered above them —apart from His Deity, and His claims to Deity—in His humanity. He was surpassingly wonderful, at once awe-inspiring and beautiful, in His revelation of the possibility of human life. Now that One lay dead, and they had rolled a stone to the door of His tomb.

Yet once more; and because of our own condition of heart and soul and life and experience, this thing is more wonderful than all. These men had seen in these three years, a human Being mastered by one passion, that of redeeming lost things. This was the story of His life: "The Son of man came to seek and to save that which was lost." That was new; that was something even the Hebrew religion, divine as it was in its origin, had never understood, never preached; that was something that Greek philosophy had never dreamed of, and would have laughed out of court as being unutterable foolishness. Men had known high inspirations before the coming of Jesus; they had desired to create the new, and that passionate desire was the inspiration of all artistic effort; they had craved to know the truth, and that craving was the inspiration of all philosophy; they had endeavoured to preserve the good, and that endeavour however much they had failed, had been the underlying reason of every attempt at government.

But in Jesus there appeared,—in the midst of the millenniums, centuries, cycles; in the midst of the artistic aspirations, the philosophic endeavours, and the efforts at government;—One Who said: My master-purpose in the world is not to create the new, is not to know the truth, is not to preserve the good; but to get hold of the effete, and make it new; to touch the false, and transmute it into the true; to reach the bad, and make it good. "The Son of man came to seek and to save that which was lost." In proportion as we have the great human experience, in proportion as we are able to escape from ourselves individually, and to think in the terms of humanity as a whole, humanity as we know it, with all its sorrows and sighings, and wounds, with all its weariness, agonies, and heartbreaks, we shall realize that this is what we need supremely; some One Who can lay His hand upon the dead, withered flower, and make it live and blossom with new beauty; Who can lay His hand upon poor, withered, unworthy life, and make it beautiful again; a heart that beats with all the movements of compassionate Deity. That was the passion of Jesus. Where is He? Dead! They have rolled a stone to the door of His tomb!

Ultimately therefore I see dead in that grave, not merely a conception of God, an ideal of humanity, a passion to redeem; but resultantly, a religion; in all the broadest, widest, and most inclusive sense of that great and gracious word. A religion having foundations, having structural processes, having a finality in view; a religion that fundamentally was faith in God and in man; a religion that structurally was love working toward the satisfaction of the Divine heart, and the well-being of human conditions; a religion which in its finality was hope, rejoicing in hope of the glory of God, and consequently rejoicing in hope of the glory of man.

Speaking of Jesus of Nazareth again, as within the strict limitations of His humanity, and the fact of His manhood; that was His religion. It was based on faith in God and faith in man. The first need not be argued. The Christian religion, however, is not merely a religion of faith in God; it is also a religion of faith in man. If we profess to believe in God, and do not believe in man,

[333]

we are not Christians. The man who is for evermore
declaring that humanity is an evil thing in itself, and that
it must perish, is thinking without regard to the Christian
religion. The word hopeless, with regard to man, must
be cancelled from the vocabulary of all truly Christian
souls. Jesus knew no hopeless cases. Individually, or
socially, He believed in men. He so believed in them
that He was willing to die to realize their latent, paralyzed, possibilities. That was the fundamental fact in
His religion; belief in God, and belief in man.

How was His purpose to be realized? By loving God
and by loving man. Here no argument is necessary.
When He was asked which was the greatest commandment, His own word covers the whole ground: " Thou
shalt love the Lord thy God with all thy heart, and with
all thy soul, and with all thy mind "; and, " Thou shalt
love thy neighbour as thyself." His faith in God and
His faith in man was the inspiration of activity, growing
out of His love. The Man Who thus had stood among
His compatriots, and consequently at the centre of human
history, giving to men this conception of God, giving to
men this ideal of humanity, suggesting to men this new
inspiration of life, and thus creating for men a religion;
where is He, and what has become of Him? They have
murdered Him; and now lies He there, and none so poor
as do Him reverence. They have rolled a stone to the
door of the tomb.

That we may be led a little further along what is necessarily a melancholy meditation, I want to speak of the
ugliness of the death of these things of beauty. His conception of God was denied. In His death there was
neither grace nor truth. In the activity that produced
His death there was neither mercy nor justice. In His
dying there was neither peace granted to Him, nor righteousness. All the things opposed to the things of God,
joined to slay Him. Consequently His conception of God
was destroyed in the hour of His dying. They put Him

[334]

on the Cross. By their own action He was slain, and
God was withdrawn from human life by the volition of
humanity. This God of Jesus, the God of His thinking,
His conception of God was absolutely refused.

His ideal of humanity lay dead. His ideal of humanity was proved impossible by His dying. Men mocked it,
men trampled on it, men slew it, and would have none of
it. Consequently the ideal must be abandoned. When
they nailed Him to His Cross, and took the dead body
down from the Cross and laid it in the grave, they said in
effect: No, we will not have that. That is not the ideal
of humanity to which we are willing to bow. They said,
as He had indicated in one of His parables, " We will not
have this *Man* to reign over us." That is not the ideal of
humanity that we will accept!

More tragic still in a contemplation like this, producing
more poignant grief in the heart than either of the other
two; more terrible than the loss of the conception of God,
than the loss of the ideal of humanity, is the fact that
there lay dead a passion to redeem. It was refused. It
was thus declared not worth while to try and redeem
men. This was the conviction of the philosophy and
wisdom of the age. Moreover it was impossible, and
therefore it was foolish. Fling it out. We will not have
it. Worthless things are not worth redeeming. There is
no wealth in waste. And they were right, apart from
Him. It is not worth while, because it cannot be done.
That master-passion of the love that goes after lost things
was dead, and in its tomb.

Consequently religion was dead. The foundation was
destroyed, for He died, and was buried! We cannot believe either in God or man, if this be the end. Many are
now reading Russian literature. So far as I have read,
and am able to express any opinion, I do not know anything more wonderful in any literature than the writing
of Dostoievsky. In his novel *The Idiot*, he describes two
men, looking at Holbein's picture of Jesus being taken

[335]

from the Cross. It is a terrible picture. One of the Russians, looking at the Cross, says: "I like looking at that picture." "That picture! that picture!" said his companion. "Why, some people's faith is ruined by looking at that picture!" That is an illustrative story. That picture must ruin my faith if there be nothing to come after it. They have put that dead body in the tomb, and rolled against the door a stone. I have seen it, and cannot believe in the goodness of God, nor in the possibility of humanity.

Consequently the structural motive of religion is withered at its root, for if I cannot believe in God I cannot love Him. And if I do not believe in humanity I cannot love it.

Finally therefore, and necessarily, the inspiration of religion is quenched; for if I cannot believe in God and love Him, nor in man and love him, I have no hope about to-morrow. A stone is against the door of the tomb!

What did that tomb contain? In the story in Mark there is something which is more significant than perhaps appears upon the surface. Joseph asked for "the body of Jesus." Pilate gave him "the corpse." There is a great difference in the two words. They are entirely different. Joseph begged for the *body* of Jesus, the σῶμα; Pilate gave him the *corpse*, the πτῶμα. Joseph begged for the *body* of Jesus. The Greek word there referred to a body, as sound, and complete. I think when Mark wrote this Gospel, probably under the direction of Peter, he used these words carefully. This Greek word here used for a body, Homer always employed for a dead body, but from Hesiod onward in Greek writings, it was used of a living body. When Joseph asked for the body, he asked in the respectful term that referred to the body in its entirety and its beauty. It was the word that a lover would use. Pilate said He could not be dead already, and sent for the centurion; and as soon as the centurion showed that Jesus was dead, he gave to Joseph the *corpse*. What is the significance of that word? The ruin! That is what Pilate granted to Joseph. That is what they put in the grave.

Is that the end? If so, these are the things that we have lost; a conception of God, an ideal of humanity, a new master-passion in life to redeem, and therefore a religion. If that be the end then I declare that every succeeding grave is the continuity of ghastly despair, including the latest graves. If that be the end, then tombs forever accentuate the ghastly failure.

This melancholy consideration is necessary lest we fail to appreciate the transcendent wonder of the sequel. I dare not, however, end a meditation thus. So, while our meditation has been around certain words, we may be led to the sequel in Biblical words, where the same terms are employed, and so our present meditation may be complete. What have we seen? "A stone against the door of the tomb." Let us read again: "And very early on the first day of the week, Mary Magdalene, and Mary the mother of James, and Salome come to the tomb when the sun was risen. And they were saying among themselves, Who shall roll us away the stone from the door of the tomb? And looking up, they see that the stone is rolled back!"

In the ineffable glory of the light that breaks, we say, That conception of God is not dead, that ideal of humanity continues, that passion to save will still inspire, and our religion abides,—faith, love, and hope. Therefore all our graves are prophecies of God's great final victory.

XXX

"And looking up they see that the stone is rolled back."
—MARK 16: 4.

Mark 16.

IN the first eight verses of this chapter we have a vivid
picture of events in the earliest hours of the first day of
the week, following that in which our Lord was crucified
and buried. First, three women are seen on Saturday
evening (that is, after six o'clock, when the Sabbath
ended, and the first day began), buying spices for the
anointing of the body of Jesus, which two of their number had seen laid in the tomb. The three who bought the
spices were Mary of Magdala, Mary the mother of James
and Joses, and Salome; and it is interesting to observe
that these three were the women named as having
watched the crucifixion from afar. After the passing of
some hours—" when the sun was risen "—they came to
the tomb, and the " they " here of Mark's record would
seem to refer to the second Mary and Salome only, for
John explicitly declares that Mary of Magdala had arrived earlier—" while it was yet dark." She had come to
the sepulchre first; and the other two came a little later.
She came " while it was yet dark "; they came " when
the sun was risen." She also saw the stone taken away,
but instead of waiting, and going into the grave, she ran
on to bear the news to Peter and John, who evidently
were living in separation from the other disciples, declaring that they had taken away the Lord out of the tomb.

Be all that as it may, the story is in no way invalidated,
the whole emphasis being on what these people expected
to find, what they found, and the results which followed.
As they came then, they remembered the great stone
which they had seen rolled against the door of the tomb,

and "were saying among themselves, Who shall roll us away the stone from the door of the tomb?" They knew their physical weakness, and that it was a great stone— "exceeding great," and so they knew that they could not move it. Then they looked up, and as Mark says "they see that the stone is rolled back." These two women were evidently not of Mary Magdalene's temperament, for they did not jump to the conclusion that His body had been removed. Probably surprised, and certainly glad, they entered in with the spices to anoint the dead body of Jesus.

Then came the supreme astonishment. Instead of the dead body of their Master they saw "a young man arrayed in a white robe." They were amazed, and immediately the heavenly watcher addressed them: "Be not amazed; ye seek Jesus the Nazarene, Who hath been crucified; He is risen, He is not here: behold, the place where they laid Him! But go, tell His disciples and Peter, He goeth before you into Galilee: there ye shall see Him, as He said unto you." Then, in a sentence or two, Mark gives a most graphic picture. These women left the tomb, and fled. Seized with trembling, and astonishment;—the actual Greek word there is "ecstasy," —seized with trembling and ecstasy, filled with fear; so they fled.

In the next eleven verses we have massed together some of the principal events of the next forty days, up to and including the ascension of the Lord. The last verse declares in yet briefer form, but with remarkable inclusiveness, the story of the days following His ascension. They went everywhere preaching; the Lord accompanying them, working with them, and confirming the Word by the signs that followed.

These last twelve verses constitute a battleground of textual criticism, and by many are rejected as not genuine. I do not propose to stay for a moment to discuss the matter. Suffice it for me to say that while recognizing the difficulties giving rise to the contention, I most strongly hold that they are certainly genuine, the weight of evidence both external and internal, compelling me to that conclusion.

To return to the text itself, " the stone is rolled back." That declaration, as it introduces us to the fact which it indicated, constitutes the answer to all the forebodings to which " the stone against the door of the tomb " gave rise. Let us then consider the fact indicated by that stone rolled back from the tomb; and note some of the results following thereupon.

The fact indicated! The stone rolled back was not the supreme fact, but rather an indication of the fact, something which was intended to draw attention to the fact itself. The rolling back of the stone happened after the resurrection. It was not rolled back from the tomb in order that Jesus might pass out of the tomb. He had left the tomb before the stone was rolled back. Matthew gives a fuller account of the event, and says that there was a great earthquake, that an angel descended, whose appearance was as lightning, and his raiment white as the snow, and the keepers—the soldiers who had been obtained from Pilate to keep watch over the tomb—did quake and became as dead men. The coming of the angel was for the rolling back of the stone; not that Jesus might pass out of the grave; but to show that He had gone.

When the stone was rolled back, what was there to be seen? An empty tomb, and undisturbed grave-clothes. These grave-clothes were lying in the very folds that they had been in, around the body of the dead Christ; and the napkin that had been on the head, was laid separately— as John is particular to say—that is, as it would be separated from the other wrappings, as they were round the dead body of Jesus. Familiarity with Eastern customs will help us here. The wrappings around the dead were voluminous. They were enswathed in these bandages in

the most careful and systematic and even scientific manner. What Peter and John saw when they looked into
the grave was those grave-clothes lying exactly as they
had been wrapped around His body; but His body was
not there! It was that vision of the grave-clothes undisturbed, that convinced Peter and John that He was
risen. If the grave-clothes had been disturbed, and carefully folded up, then they might have imagined that
somebody had unwrapped them, and that the body of
Jesus had been stolen, as certain people said it had; but
the undisturbed wrappings in the tomb demonstrated to
these men that He was risen. This then, was what they
saw when the stone was rolled back—an empty tomb, and
undisturbed grave-clothes. Of these signs angels became guardians, until they had borne testimony to the
disciples, which would settle forever the question whether
our Lord was truly risen from the dead.

What then is the fact that was thus indicated? The
very fact which the angel announced: " Ye seek Jesus the
Nazarene. . . . He is risen: He is not here." Jesus
of Nazareth had been raised from the dead; had emerged
from all its material bondage and bandages; had passed
into a new life, the same but entirely different; had
proved Himself Victor over death, and Conqueror of the
grave. That is the central fact of Christianity through
all the centuries. If that is not true, Christianity is
doomed.

It is the central fact of Christianity. It is the fact that
cannot be explained save by revelation, and revelation has
never explained the process of the resurrection. It has
explained it in so far that it has declared that God raised
Him from the dead. Whether that declaration be believed may depend upon our conception of God. If God
be a prisoner in His own universe, having created an
order in the midst of which He dwells imprisoned, so
that He cannot move out of what we call the ordinary,
then perhaps that never happened. Even then, before we

can be reasonable in unbelief we must be sure we know all the ordinary! But if God is greater than His universe; if in brief, He is the God of the Bible, Who spake and it was done, Who commanded and it stood firm, Who upholds all things by the word of His power, and is able out of apparent nothing to bring cosmos and beauty into being, and to deal with chaos and disorder, and destroy them; if this be our God, then though we never have an explanation of the process of resurrection, we have a fact upon which we can rest. God raised Him from the dead.

I will go further, and declare that the resurrection is a fact that cannot be proved, except to the faith of the heart. The resurrection cannot be proved mechanically, mathematically, by the demonstration of our small clevernesses. It will always evade us. It never has been so proved; it never can be done. Man cannot prove God by these self-same processes. God is not to be demonstrated mathematically, mechanically; not even philosophically, unless our philosophy be the philosophy of revelation. We cannot prove the resurrection by reason. Therefore the apostle wrote at one time, " If thou shalt confess with thy mouth Jesus as Lord, and shalt believe in thy heart that God raised Him from the dead, thou shalt be saved: for with the heart man believeth unto righteousness." Belief with the intellect never produces moral and spiritual results. Belief with the heart does; that belief that rises out of a great agony, and a great sorrow, and a great shame, and fastens upon a declaration, and rises healed and helped—that faith is the faith that demonstrates the resurrection. Apart from such faith we cannot prove it. No man knows Jesus rose from the dead, save the man who in helplessness of soul has trusted Him, and has received that spiritual, mystic, inner witness, that knows no denial, and laughs at criticism. That man knows that He Who died, and was buried, rose again, and ever lives to make intercession.

Not only is it a fact that cannot be explained; not only

is it a fact that cannot be proved; it is also a fact that
cannot be denied save by ignorance. I use that word
sympathetically. If there is a man who does deny it, then
he does so in ignorance. The word "ignorance" is derived from the Latin. We may use the Greek equivalent
and say, It cannot be denied, save by agnosticism. The
Greek word "agnostic" sounds more poetical than the
Latin equivalent "ignoramus," but they mean the same
thing; the man who does not know. We can respect such
a person, and respect his honest agnosticism about this
very fact; only it should be understood that the moment
when agnosticism becomes an impertinence, is the moment when a man makes it a resting-place for his soul.
When a man makes it a harbour of refuge, then he is
really a prisoner in his own agnosticism. No intellectual
soul finds its last resting-place in ignorance. The resurrection cannot be disproved by agnosticism. Such treatment can never disprove it. The resurrection cannot be
disproved by denying it. Nor can His appearances after
the resurrection be disproved.

Some one may say: Yes, but do you thus escape your
problem? You say the fact is proved by other facts. But
the other facts are disputed as much as the fact which
you make them prove. But, I inquire on what ground
these subsequent facts are disputed. The appearances
of Jesus of Nazareth, alive from the dead, after He had
been most certainly crucified, are as well authenticated
as any facts of history which we do not hesitate to believe
to-day. When you deny them, by that denial you declare
that all history is invalid. You may be right! Perhaps
those things did not happen under Julius Cæsar, which
were said to happen in this little island of ours! Perhaps there is no history!

The final, and conclusive fact, however, is that the
whole Christian propaganda is the last proof that He rose
from the dead; for the whole of it has been based upon
this belief, and inspired by this fact. Had there been no

resurrection, what then? There had been no Christian Church, no Christian propaganda, no Christian influence. Everything for which the lonely Nazarene stood, lay murdered, dead, in the tomb when they rolled against it a great stone. His disciples had been scattered like chaff before the wind, and the whole movement had been stamped out. How did it live again? It lived again, and it lives, because He lived again, and lives!

Let us then pass on to consider some of the values resulting from the fact of the rolling back of this stone. Here I can only deal with certain aspects of the one inclusive result, which is Christianity. I want to name three aspects of that one result, which also have been continuous.

The result of the empty tomb, and the fact of the risen Christ which it indicated, was first, the transfiguration of the Cross for His disciples; secondly therefore, it was the vindication of His teaching for His disciples and all such as consider that teaching; and finally, it was for His disciples and for all time an interpretation of His Person.

These men, gathered round about Jesus—His disciples, His apostles, and subsequently other disciples,—these people first came into contact with His Person. It was the personality of Jesus which made an appeal to these men in the earliest days. Then as they walked and talked with Him, they came to know His teaching. At last they knew His Cross. The resurrection transfigured the Cross, vindicated His teaching, and interpreted His personality. Their experience had been that of contact with His Person, attention to His teaching, and shame and shuddering in the presence of His Cross. Now, interpreted by the resurrection, they saw the transfiguration of the Cross; they knew the vindication of His teaching; and they received the amazing revelation of the deepest and profoundest fact concerning His Person.

The resurrection meant the transfiguration of His Cross. Remember once more how these apostles had

feared the Cross. They feared it for Him. They feared
it for themselves. Their fear was by no means low and
mean. I used to criticize these disciples for fearing the
Cross, but I have given up doing so. I used to deduce a
good many lessons therefrom about our own fears of the
Cross. I think those lessons are needed still, but I think
the illustration was false. The more I study these Gospels, and follow these men, the more I sympathize with
them in their shunning of the Cross. I do not think that
it was selfishness made Peter say, "That be far from
Thee, Lord." It was pure affection for his Lord. He
feared the Cross. To him it was intolerable to think that
Jesus could be mauled to death by brutal men. I think
they feared for themselves also, but on no selfish level.
If He were going to die, where were all their high hopes?
He had talked of a Kingdom. All that must come to an
end if He died. They did fear the Cross. From the moment when He began explicitly to declare it to them, they
could hardly bear to walk and talk with Him. That is
manifest in all the accounts of His last months with
these men. They only saw the wrong of the Cross. They
were right in so far as they saw. There is nothing so
shameful in all human history as the Cross of Jesus.
There is nothing that reflects in such unmistakable and
deadly manner upon the human heart as the Cross of
Jesus. Oh, the vulgarity of it! the utter devilishness of
it! If we lose that early sense of the horror of it, then
we are losing a good deal more than we realize. It was a
terrible thing! When the disciples saw that it really happened; that brutal men caught Him, mauled Him, bruised
Him, murdered Him; they felt that it was all over, and
they fled.

Now observe in the second place how these men came
to glory in it. "God forbid that I should glory, save in
the Cross of Jesus Christ my Lord." That was the writing of the apostle, born out of due time, who nevertheless
was not a whit behind the chiefest apostle. He was

thinking for the whole of them. The apostles gloried in it for Him, and gloried in it for themselves. They counted it all joy that they were considered worthy to suffer shame for the name. What had happened? The resurrection made them look back, and look again, and yet again; and the rough, brutal, devilish Roman gibbet, began to bloom and blossom and flame and flash, with the love of God. If there had been no resurrection, there would have been nothing but the black tragedy of a murder. The resurrection revealed to these men, and has revealed to us for all time, that in that dark hour, God wrought in the darkness for light, through death unto life, in bondage for the creation of liberty. Come, "behold, the place where they laid Him! He is risen: He is not here." "The stone is rolled back." We go again to Golgotha, to Calvary, to the green hill, and there lay our intellectual clevernesses in the dust, and worship:

> "For God comes down our souls to greet,
> And glory crowns the mercy-seat."

But again, that resurrection was the vindication of His teaching. We may mass the teaching of Jesus in certain regards, His teaching concerning relative values, His teaching concerning moral standards, His teaching concerning redeeming motives. Along these lines His teaching proceeded through all the three years; line upon line, precept upon precept, here a little and there a little, He had been dealing with these things.

Concerning relative values He perpetually insisted upon the supremacy of the spiritual over the physical; calling men always into that attitude where they sought first the Kingdom of God, remembering that all the things of material necessity should be added to them; calling men to know no fear of men that only kill the body, and after that have no more that they can do; persistently declaring to men that the spiritual is supreme over the physical,

and as insistently claiming the sacredness of the material.
There was nothing in the teaching of Jesus approaching
the Gnostic heresy that declared that the flesh is in-
herently evil. Plato could only get rid of sin by getting
rid of the body. Jesus retains the body; and declares
that God feeds the body·as well as the soul, that the body
is as sacred a thing as the soul, since the soul makes it
its sanctuary. He never castigated His body, He never
inflicted flagellations upon His flesh. That foolish practice was reserved for a decadent Christianity to discover.
He lived a life that was natural and beautiful in the
physical and the material. They had taken that fair and
beauteous body, and brutally murdered it, and put it in
the grave. But said the angel, "He is not here: He is
risen"; and in that rising His teaching was vindicated.
He did not fear those who should kill the body. He
knew well that they could do no more. His victory over
death was His vindication of the supremacy of the spiritual. It was also a vindication of His conception of the
sacredness of the material. If the body were an evil
thing, when He emerged into the spiritual life, after the
resurrection, He would have left the body; but He took
the body also; and from that moment unto this, all human
bodies are what the Church has called them, "sacred
dust." When He came back—and here is where intel-
lectuality will break down—He came in a risen body to
eat broiled fish with His disciples; to be up in the morning when men are fishing, to light a fire and prepare a
breakfast! Do not cut out those last chapters of John, I
charge you again. Keep them where they are; for they
are necessary. The supremacy of the spiritual, and the
sacredness of the material were both vindicated by the
fact of His resurrection.

Again, concerning moral standards, He had taught the
glory of holiness; but He had also claimed the power to
forgive sins. He stood among the sons of men the most
insistent Demander of purity; yet to sinning men and

women He had said, "Thy sins are forgiven thee"; "Hath no man condemned thee? Neither do I condemn thee: go thy way; from henceforth sin no more." He had taught two things apparently contradictory; the necessity for absolute purity, and yet the possibility of so forgiving the sins that out of the sense of forgiveness there should spring a new moral incentive. By the resurrection that teaching was vindicated. By the resurrection the glory of holiness was revealed. Said Peter on the day of Pentecost, "It was impossible that He should be holden of death." Why? Because in Him is no sin, and by His resurrection sin was destroyed. Yet more than that—and this is the supreme thing to every human heart. By that resurrection the possibility of forgiveness was vindicated, for the resurrection is the sign and symbol to men everywhere that God has accepted that mystery of atoning work for the redemption of humanity. The actual experimental fact of forgiveness is a new moral incentive. A man says, I am forgiven, and goes on sinning, and we know that the truth is not in him. A man says, I am forgiven, and I hate sin and will turn myself from it; I may flounder and fall, but so help me God, I am against it myself; that man is telling the truth; and out of his sense of forgiveness a moral inspiration has sprung up. All that was vindicated by the resurrection.

And once again: His teaching concerning redeeming motives was vindicated. He had taught the beauty of sacrifice; and no one had believed Him. He had declared the strength of love; and they had murdered Him, and found Him weak enough to die, as they said in unutterable contempt. Now behold Him, alive from the dead! In the resurrection is the vindication of the beauty of sacrifice, the vindication of the ultimate triumph of the sacrificial life. In the resurrection is the wonder of eternal love. Love is stronger than death, and mightier than the grave. That motive of compassion which we referred to as one of the lost things if He were dead, flamed again, in light and power and beauty, by the way of the resurrection.

Finally we come to that which in some senses is supreme, but which may now be dismissed briefly; by the resurrection these men came to a new interpretation of His person. How far had they gone before His Cross? They had travelled a long way. They knew the Man Jesus, they honoured Him, and they loved Him. They knew that the Man Jesus was the Christ. They had accepted His Messiahship, they had followed Him as Messiah, and obeyed Him as such. They had gained an intellectual conviction that He was the Son of God, as Peter himself declared at Cæsarea Philippi, "Thou art the Son of God." But an intellectual conviction is never a spiritual and moral dynamic, unless it have with it something else, mightier than intellect.

What now happened? I go again to the writings of Paul. Speaking of Jesus in the beginning of his great Roman letter he says that after the flesh He was of the seed of David, but that He "was declared the Son of God with power by the resurrection from the dead." I like to take that Greek word for "declared," and Anglicize it. This is what he said, "He was *horizoned* the Son of God with power." He was placed upon the horizon in a new light, so that men saw clearly, as they see the sun in its rising, Who He was. By that resurrection they discovered this deepest truth concerning His personality. Presently eight days afterwards in the upper room, a magnificent man, an agnostic, but honest withal, and broken-hearted withal, did say in the presence of that fact that Jesus was alive, "My Lord and my God." They all came for ever after to speak of Him with reverence as "the Lord Jesus Christ."

So "the stone is rolled back." Therefore all our fear, as we saw "a stone against the door of the tomb" was groundless. The conception of God abides. The ideal of humanity not only remains, but is attainable. The passion to redeem is operative, and has been through all the centuries. The religion of Jesus triumphs; faith as its foundation, love as its structural power, hope as its finality. Because these things are so, all gravestones are temporary things, for they must all be rolled away.

Thus ends our study of Mark. In the first sermon I preached on this Gospel, dealing with Mark's own description of his writing as " The beginning of the Gospel of Jesus Christ the Son of God," I quoted as applicable to the whole Gospel, some very striking words of Mazzini. Let me close with them, as summarizing the whole story, as we have tried to consider it.

" He came. The soul the most full of love, the most sacredly virtuous, the most deeply inspired by God and the future, that men have yet seen on earth—Jesus. He bent over the corpse of the dead world, and whispered a word of faith. Over the clay that had lost all of man, but the movement and the form, He uttered words until then unknown; Love, Sacrifice, a heavenly origin. And the dead arose, a new life circulated through the clay, which philosophy had tried in vain to reanimate. From that corpse arose the Christian world, the world of liberty and equality. From the clay arose the true Man, the Image of God, the precursor of humanity."

Printed in the United States of America